PIMLICO

280

PAUL

A. N. Wilson is an award-winning novelist and biographer. He is the author of the bestselling *Jesus*, which caused a sensation when it was published in 1992. Equally controversial, *Paul* is stimulating, scholarly and highly readable.

A. N. Wilson's novels include *The Healing Art* (Somerset Maugham Award), *Wise Virgin* (W. H. Smith Award) and the five books in *The Lampitt Chronicles*. His biographies include studies of Sir Walter Scott (John Llewellyn Rhys Prize) and John Milton, as well as of Tolstoy (Whitbread Award for Biography), C. S. Lewis and Hilaire Belloc.

He lives in north London.

PAUL

The Mind of the Apostle

A.N. WILSON

PIMLICO

Published by Pimlico 1998

10 9

Copyright © A. N. Wilson 1997

A. N. Wilson has asserted his right under the Copyright, Designs
and Patents Act 1988 to be identified as the author of this work

First published by
Sinclair-Stevenson in 1997

Pimlico
Random House, 20 Vauxhall Bridge Road,
London SW1V 2SA

www.rbooks.co.uk

Addresses for companies within
The Random House Group Limited can be found at:
www.randomhouse.co.uk/offices.htm

The Random House Group Limited Reg. No. 954009

A CIP catalogue record for this book
is available from the British Library

The Random House Group Limited supports The Forest Stewardship Council (FSC),
the leading international forest certification organisation. All our titles that are printed
on Greenpeace approved FSC certified paper carry the FSC logo.
Our paper procurement policy can be found at
www.rbooks.co.uk/environment

ISBN 9780712666633

Printed and bound in England by
CPI Antony Rowe, Chippenham, Wiltshire

CONTENTS

AUTHOR'S NOTE

The version of the Scriptures used in this book is the *New Revised Standard Version* edited by Bruce M. Metzger and Roland E. Murphy (New York, 1991). My ideas about Paul have evolved over many years, and it is impossible to calculate or express the debts owed to the books and thoughts of others. A recent seminar with Hyam Maccoby and Michael Goulder was especially stimulating, as was the conversation of James Carleton Paget, who was kind enough to read the typescript. My brother Stephen Wilson helped with the puzzle of Paul's name.

ABBREVIATIONS

Ant	*Antiquities* (Josephus)
AV	Authorised Version of the Bible (The 'King James' Version)
BC	*The Beginnings of Christianity*, ed. F. J. Foakes Jackson and K. Lake (1920–33)
BJ	*De Bello Iudaico (Jewish War)* (Josephus)
BJRL	*Bulletin of the John Rylands Library*
Bruce	F. F. Bruce, *Paul: Apostle of the Free Spirit* (revised 1995)
Bruce Acts	F. F. Bruce, *The Acts of the Apostles*, The Greek text with Introduction and Commentary (1951)
ET	English Translation
HGB	Hastings' Dictionary of the Bible
HJP	*History of the Jewish People in the Age of Jesus Christ*, E. T. (E. Schürer)
HN	Pliny's Natural History
JBL	*Journal of Biblical Literature*
JRS	*Journal of Roman Studies*
JTS	*Journal of Theological Studies*
LXX	Septuagint (Pre-Christian Greek Version of the Jewish Scriptures)
NEB	New English Bible
RSV	Revised Standard Version
WWW	*The Acts of the Apostles: A Companion*, by Richard Wallace and Wynne Williams, Bristol Classical Press, 1993

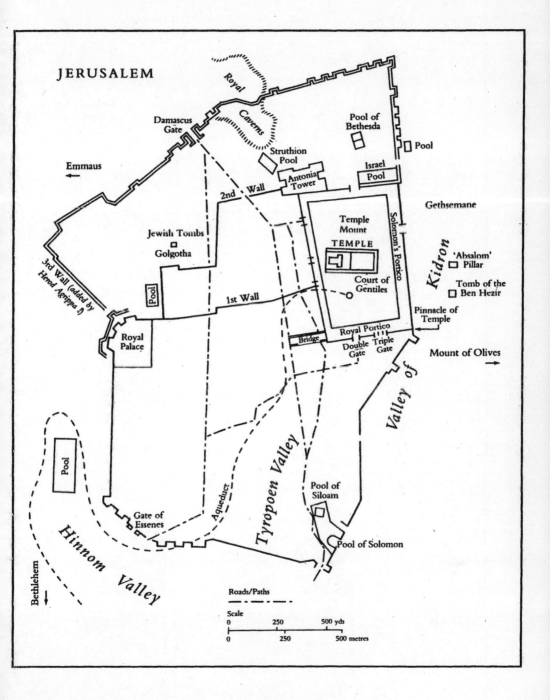

JERUSALEM

Royal Caverns

Damascus Gate

Emmaus

3rd Wall (added by Herod Agrippa I)

2nd Wall

Jewish Tombs

Golgotha

Pool

1st Wall

Royal Palace

Gate of Essenes

Aqueduct

Hinnom Valley

Bethlehem

Pool

Struthion Pool

Antonia Tower

Pool of Bethesda

Pool

Israel Pool

Temple Mount

TEMPLE

Court of Gentiles

Solomon's Portico

Gethsemane

Kidron

'Absalom' Pillar

Tomb of the Ben Hezir

Pinnacle of Temple

Bridge

Royal Portico

Double Gate

Triple Gate

Mount of Olives

Tyropoen Valley

Valley of

Pool of Siloam

Pool of Solomon

Roads/Paths

Scale

0   250   500 yds

0   250   500 metres

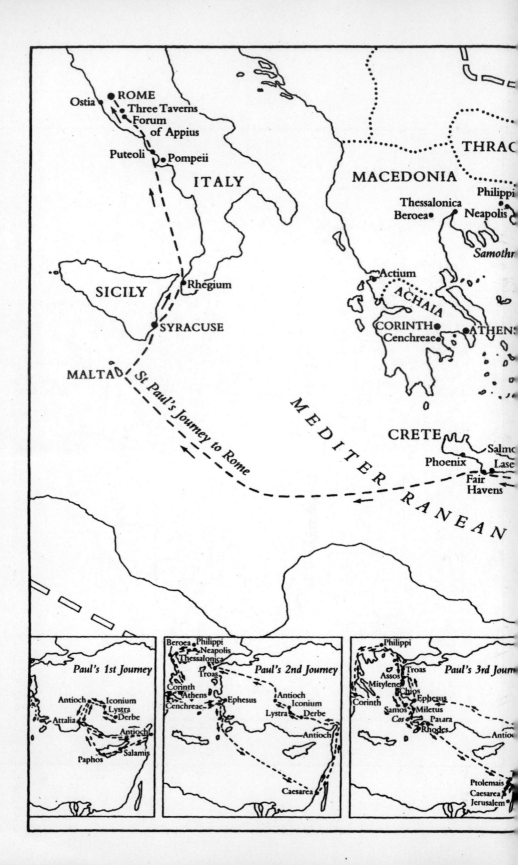

BLACK SEA

BITHYNIA

MYSIA

GALATIA

Troas

Lesbos

ASIA

PERGAMUM
Thyatira
SARDIS
Philadelphia
SMYRNA
Hierapolis
Laodicea
EPHESUS
Colossae
MILETUS

PISIDIA

Cos

Cnidus

Perga

Patara
Attalia
Myra

Rhodes

CAPPADOCIA

Antioch

Iconium
Lystra

Derbe

Tarsus

Cilicea
Trachea

CILICIA

ANTIOCH
and SYRIA

CYPRUS

Salamis

Paphos

Palmyra

SEA

Berytus
Sidon
DAMASCUS
Tyre

Caesarea
Samaria
Joppa
JUDAEA
Gaza
JERUSALEM

ALEXANDRIA

NABATEA

Cairo

Miles 0   100   200

Km   0   100   200

□ ─ □   Boundary of
        Roman Empire c. AD 65

· · · · · ·   Provincial Boundaries
              c. AD 65

RED SEA

I

THE EMPEROR NERO'S LEGACY TO THE CHRISTIAN CHURCH

ON 19 JULY in the year AD 64, a fire broke out among the squalid, timber-built little shops which clustered around the Circus Maximus, the great sports stadium in Rome. It raged for six days, spreading across the base of the Palatine and the Caelian Hills, and by the end of a week it had destroyed many of the best-loved buildings and landmarks of the Imperial capital – Luna's temple on the Aventine, Numa's palace, the shrine of Vesta near the Forum (though the great Forum itself remained unscathed). After six days, the fire-fighters seemed to have brought the conflagration under control but it was reignited, either by accident or design, on the Capitoline Hill and by the end of the month three of the fourteen *quartiers* into which the Emperor Nero had divided the city were in ruins. Nero's own magnificent apartments on the Palatine and Oppian Hills were gutted, though the flames did not touch his stupendous Golden House (*Domus Aurea*), which was still being embellished and redesigned at the time of his death four years later.

Nero himself was thirty-five miles away from Rome, at his favourite seaside resort of Antium, at the time of the fire's outbreak, but he was a sufficiently shrewd politician to hasten back in order to be with his people. It was the plebs, housed in ramshackle houses of wooden construction, who would be most sorely affected by the fire. Having wooed them with 'bread and circuses' – and what circuses! – he was to do his best to stand beside them in what was the worst calamity of the city's history. He personally took part in the fire-fighting and he threw open all the public buildings on the Campus Martius, along the riverside, to house the homeless. He sent to Ostia for food supplies, fixing the price of grain at half the going market rate.

But Nero, who at twenty-six had already been emperor for a decade, had had time to accumulate many enemies. The first five years of his reign, the *quinquennium* which all Romans were inclined to view as a Golden Age, had gone sour. Nero's capricious cruelty and his effete philhellenism had won him some powerful rivals for power in the Senate and in the army. His sincere devotion to the arts and his wish to beautify the city made some people suppose that he had deliberately started the fire himself so as to clear the space for more grandiose building projects. His wish to be taken seriously as a poet was an allowable fancy in a soft-faced double-chinned lad, but the aristocrats of the Senate had viewed with dismay his willingness to show off in public by performing as a charioteer, an actor, a singer.

It was typical that the flames of his beloved city should remind the Homer-loving young man of the fires which destroyed the sacred city of Troy. The rumour went about that while the flames were at their height, Nero had been seen on the Maecenas Tower on the Equiline, dressed in the stage costume with which he had sung his public arias, gazing at the Inferno beneath and declaiming or singing. That this is probably a fiction has not prevented this image of Nero, fiddling while Rome burns, fixing itself for ever in the human consciousness as an emblem of irresponsible government.

In fact, there were many aspects of Nero's government which explained and justified his popularity with the Roman people. He was not popular just because he arranged lurid spectacles in the circuses and theatres, nor only because he took delight in judicious and selective murder of members of the upper class – including his first wife, his two childhood tutors and his own highly dislikeable mother, Agrippina. He was popular because he brought stability, and it did not much matter whether it was his own wisdom or that of his mentor Seneca which brought such comparative peace to the first five years of his reign. Ever since the death of Augustus in 14, the Romans had waited to see whether the Imperial experiment could outlast the lifetime of the first great dictator, or whether it had been Augustus's own personal strength and ruthlessness which had held the peace. There were many who hankered after a return to the Republic, which had still (technically at least) been in existence at the beginning of Augustus's reign as Princeps. The reigns of Tiberius, Caligula and Claudius were not obvious object lessons in the desirability of personal despotism. But with the arrival of young Nero, under the guidance of his Stoic tutor Seneca and assisted by Afranius Burrus, there had been a genuine hope that the Empire was at last in the hands of a philosopher-king.

Throughout his reign, Nero managed to avoid the horror of a civil war. There was no unemployment in Nero's Rome, and, though there was inflation, it was most marked in the price of real estate.[1] Governments are always popular at times of inflationary real-estate prices.

He was particularly wise in the field of foreign policy. There was no inherent virtue, in Nero's eyes, in expanding the territory for its own sake, and he had adopted a cautious approach to the wilder borders of the Empire. The Germanic tribes in present-day Belgium and Germany made perpetual trouble for the legions throughout the reign. A smouldering Balkan war was in continuous progress. Nero had negotiated a rocky, but just about durable, peace with the Scythians. He had been highly sceptical about his uncle Claudius's wish to conquer the barbaric British – a scepticism in some ways justified by the terrible losses of the legions in the British wars of 60 – and he had been canny in his dealing with that hotbed of trouble for the Romans, Palestine.

By 64, however, even without the fire, Nero was in a vulnerable position as emperor. Rome was a vastly over-crowded city of two million inhabitants, a million of whom were slaves. There was no logical reason for supposing that the great fire was the result of arson, though criminals and gangsters frequently did set fire to the dwellings of their enemies. Juvenal speaks of 'treacherous hired assassins starting fire with sulphur',[2] and, in another of his satires, he speaks of the Roman citizen's constant dread of being burnt to death. ('Is there a solitude so hopeless that it would not be preferable to the fires and to the constant falling in of houses to the thousand perils of dangerous Rome?'[3] From the moment night fell, rich and poor trembled with fear.) One of Nero's first political acts, aged fourteen, was to petition the Senate – in an eloquent speech written for him by Seneca – for ten million sesterces to rebuild the city of Bononia (Bologna) which had been accidentally rased by fire.

The public alarm at the time of the Great Fire of Rome created the greater danger of political anarchy, and, with the development of rumours that Nero himself had been responsible for the conflagration, it was expedient to find scapegoats which would satisfy the mob. With

[1] Bernard W. Henderson, *The Life and Principate of the Emperor Nero*, p. 282. See also Gerard Walter, *Nero*. For newer perspectives on Nero see the richly entertaining *Reflections of Nero*, edited by Jaś Elsner and Jamie Masters.
[2] *Satires*, XIII, 144–6.
[3] *Satires*, III, 6–8.

his customary combination of political shrewdness and theatrical panache, Nero announced that the disaster was the responsibility of an almost unheard-of Jewish sect known as the Christians.

Tacitus, who exonerates the Christians of all blame, does not seem to have known much about them, nor to have held them in very high esteem.[4] ('All degraded and shameful practices eventually collect and flourish in Rome,' he says in a languid aside.) The historian, who was nine years old when the fire happened, wrote his *Annales* of Imperial Rome from the political viewpoint of a republican who regarded the emperors as a succession of semi-criminal thugs. His hatred of Nero would not allow him to suppose that there was the smallest ground for believing that the Christians had, in fact, been responsible for the burning of Rome.[5]

While it would be ridiculous to believe Nero's own propaganda, and difficult to find any Christian motive for destroying the houses of thousands of poor people, it would seem equally rash to dismiss the idea that the Christians were innocently responsible. We do not know the whereabouts of the first generation of Roman Christians, but we can discern from the pages of early Christian writings that the earliest converts, arriving in Rome from Asia Minor and the Levant, would have been just the class of people who might have tried to earn a living as small shopkeepers. While the chariot races and gladiatorial combats on view in the Circus Maximus[6] might not have been to their austere taste, there is no reason to suppose that, with a living to earn, they would not have opened small wooden shops in such regions, where crowds congregated regularly. Who knows? An accidental fire might well have started in the hutment of some early Christian zealot baking bread or sizzling kebabs. The rumour passes from mouth to mouth. 'It was in that Greek's shop, the fire started – or that Cilician's – or that Jew's.'

Nero would not be the last demagogue to see the political value of blaming a group of foreigners for a public disaster. Why not have done with it and simply blame the Jews? If Horace and Juvenal are to

[4] *Annales*, XV, 43.
[5] 'Tacitus' Nero is a literary figure, rather than the casual result of impartial historical reconstruction.' Joan-Pau Rubiés, 'Nero in Tacitus and Nero in Tacitism', in Elsner and Masters, *op. cit.*, p. 40.
[6] The Colosseum, associated in folk memory with Christian persecutions of a later date, was not completed until after the siege of Jerusalem in AD 70, when the emperor Titus brought Jewish slaves to Rome for the purpose.

be believed, the Jews were detested by the majority of Romans. Nero's uncle Claudius had expelled them briefly from the city; and one might have supposed that Nero would lose no popularity with the plebs if he had fixed the blame for the fire on the numerous Jewish population of Rome.

But the truth is that Horace and Juvenal are not, completely, to be believed. The Jews had their enemies in Rome, but they were also enormously popular. Nero's beautiful wife Poppaea – Tacitus says she had every asset except goodness – was said to belong to that large group of Gentiles known as the 'god-fearers,' who, while not being Jews themselves, were attracted to the simplicities of monotheism.[7] There was a 'craze' for Judaism in Nero's Rome and it would have been politically insane to upset possibly thousands of Roman citizens by attributing the fire to a Jewish plot. Besides – and this is the most important political fact underlying all the pages which follow – there was a desperately dangerous situation developing in Palestine: the possibility of a war between the Jews and the Romans. Having lost two legions in Britain, Nero did not wish to risk inflaming the situation in Judaea.

The territories which today comprise Israel, the 'occupied' Palestinian regions, Lebanon, Jordan and Syria were no more stable in the year 64 than they have been in the second half of the twentieth century.[8] In the three centuries before Christ, the region had been ruled first as part of the Persian Empire and then, when that collapsed, not so much by the Greeks who conquered it, as by the Hellenised Seleucid dynasty of the Syrians. (It was against this Hellenising rule that the Maccabees fought so jealously to guard the purity of the Jewish faith.) As the power of Rome grew, both the Seleucids and the families of Jewish high priests in Jerusalem had endeavoured to get on good terms with the Republic. It was Pompey, in 63 BC, who had actually besieged Jerusalem and divided up the area, redefining the borders of its various kingdoms and principalities as they had grown up during the previous century of conflict. Guided by a policy of 'divide and rule' he allowed each of the various principalities and kingdoms some autonomy, but kept them under the over-all control of Rome. It was a system in many ways comparable to the British

---

[7] She is described as 'a god-fearer' by Josephus, *Ant*, XX.
[8] The reader is referred to the magisterial study by Fergus Millar, *The Roman Near East, 31 BC–AD 337*.

government of India in the nineteenth century. It was Pompey, for example, who deprived the puppet king John Hyrcanus of any but religious powers, dividing up his kingdom into five circumscriptions, run by five councils centred upon Jericho in Judaea, Sepphoris in Galilee, Gadara and Amathus in the Piraea and Jerusalem.

This arrangement continued, causing more or less disgruntlement among the local population, until the civil war in the Roman Empire and the murder of Caesar in the spring of 44 BC. The Jews of Alexandria and North Africa had sided with Caesar, winning for themselves many privileges to which they would cling for the next hundred years – among them, exemption from military service. In exchange for the support of the dynamic Idumaean king Herod, Cassius, the Roman general fighting Caesar, made this brilliant Arab Herod king of the Jews. When Cassius fell to the victorious Mark Antony in 42 BC at Philippi, Herod was clever enough to hold on to his position, though with some modifications, rather than allowing the region to fall under the dominion of Antony's lover and ally Cleopatra, queen of Egypt. It was the Herodian dynasty who continued to dominate the region for the next 110 years until the Romans laid siege to Jerusalem in AD 70 and levelled it to the ground; though after the death of Herod the Great in 4 BC, the territory was again divided into quarter-kingdoms or tetrarchies, each with differing degrees of autonomy, but all answerable to a Roman governor.

The Jews resident in Palestine were themselves divided about the Roman question. The vast majority of them resented the Roman presence in their country. Few actually belonged for any length of time (though they might dabble with them in their youth) to any of the semi-formalized sects or groups within Judaism, such as the Zealots or the Essenes, who were violently opposed to the blasphemous Roman presence in the holy city of Jerusalem. But there were other Jews, particularly those of the Dispersion or Diaspora, who accepted the Roman Empire as a fact of life, prepared, many of them, to absorb the Roman *realpolitik* as they were prepared to adapt their religious views to the prevailing Panhellenism. There was no single monolithic entity at this period which one could label 'Judaism'; but there were millions of Jews. While all subscribed to the notion that the God of Israel and the First Cause were one and the same being and that His laws had been dispensed to Moses on Mount Sinai and were inscribed in the Scriptures, there were many variations of practice and belief among those who followed the Jewish faith. Perhaps one tenth of the entire population of the Empire were Jewish. In today's world, the proportion of Jews to the rest of the population is tiny. In Nero's world it was considerable, and no political leader who wished to keep the peace would have gone out of his way to antagonise the Jewish race.

There was, however, this tiny sect which had begun to be known as the Christians. Nero might well have heard about them from Poppaea. ('Unable to distinguish between husbands and adulterers,' according to Tacitus, Poppaea did not long outlast the Christians who died in the fire. Nero kicked her to death while pregnant in the following year. She was not cremated after the Roman fashion but stuffed with spices and her funeral took place in clouds of incense. She was then publicly proclaimed to be divine.)

Tacitus tells us that the originator of the Christians, Christ, had been executed during the reign of Tiberius by the governor of Judaea, Pontius Pilate. Probably this event had occurred in AD 30. The fact that 'Christ' had been killed by the Roman governor – that he had, as the Jewish historian Josephus relates, suffered the standard Roman execution, crucifixion – tells us that the Romans had viewed him as a political danger. As soon as we translate the Greek word 'Christ' back into Hebrew we know why.

Christ is not a name it is a title. It means Messiah, 'the anointed one'. In the incendiary political climate of AD 33–64, there were many Messiahs and messianic movements within Judaism. Many of the more politico-religious Jews, who sought the deliverance of Jerusalem from Roman occupation, believed that the Lord's Anointed would bring this deliverance to pass. If the prophetic books of the Scriptures are to be believed, he will not necessarily do it peacefully. Such a belief was incompatible, really, with acceptance of the Roman Empire as an idea; it would certainly have been incompatible with Roman citizenship, the willingness to swear allegiance to the Divine Emperor. There were Jews of the Diaspora who were Roman citizens, and, for various historical reasons, they had been granted a dispensation on religious grounds from doing anything which would compromise their faith. But for the extremists, who looked for a Messiah to lead a Jewish war against the legions, such compromise would have stuck in the throat.

Searching the prophetic books of their Scriptures, these Jews would find plenty of material on which to nourish and feed their messianic hopes. The Messiah would come down from the clouds in the likeness of the Son of Man in the Book of Daniel; he would establish a kingdom which was an everlasting kingdom, having first crushed his enemies under his feet; the old temple of Solomon would be restored in Jerusalem; the Gentiles would worship the God of Israel. Many, such as the Pharisees,[9] must have felt that the widespread growth of 'god-fearers' among the Gentile population of the Empire, pointed to the imminent advent of such a day.

The 'Christians' were not, as it happens, a unified group, any more than any of the other quarrelsome sects of Judaism were unified. We know from their surviving writings (which must be only a proportion of what was written at the time) that there were a variety of 'Christianities' in existence. Violent outbursts had already taken place within the sect, requiring the arrest and execution of some of their number. One of the 'Christians', himself a Roman citizen by the name of Paul, had needed the protection of an entire regiment to escort him from Jerusalem to Caesarea, where he had appealed for trial in Rome itself.

The deftness, from a political point of view, of blaming the Roman fire on the Christians, lay in the fact that this sect – presumably unknown to most Gentiles – was detested by the generality of Jews, so that there would be no danger of offending any but the tender-hearted (not many of them in Nero's Rome) by arresting them as

[9] The name derives from a Hebrew word meaning 'separated ones'. Josephus (*Ant*, XIII, v, 9) records their existence as a separate group as early as 135 BC but many modern scholars think that they emerged slightly later. After the fall of Jerusalem in AD 70, they disappear from history. Much of what we know about the Pharisees, therefore, is based on mere speculation. It is generally agreed, however, that they were a group who believed in education, and missionary activities. It would seem that their distinctive contribution to Judaism was to apply, through rigorous Scriptural study, the teachings of the Torah to the situations of everyday life. They were, in a sense, less 'conservative' than the Sadducees and allowed for the development of doctrine – for example, believing in life after death. They were popular among the common people largely because of their opposition to the Roman occupation of Palestine and for the homeliness and practicality of their teachings. They would seem to have had much in common, in this respect, with Jesus, and there are those who believe that Jesus was a Pharisee. Many Jews see them as the spiritual forerunners of the Rabbinic tradition which gave birth to the Mishnah, that encyclopedic attempt to search out and define the practical obligations of Jews living in the world under obedience to God. They evidently (see below) disagreed with Paul's willingness to admit Gentiles to the community of faith without the requirement of circumcision. These quarrels, of which Paul's letters provide abundant and furious evidence, led to the eventual separation of Christians and Jews, dramatised in the literature of a generation after Jesus as Gospel stories about Jesus himself quarrelling with the Pharisees. Since there is no evidence that Jesus relaxed the requirement for circumcision, or indeed that he had a mission to Gentiles at all, it would seem unlikely that he himself demonised the Pharisees in the way that the Gospel writers were to do.

arsonists and making them into a public display. There was a death penalty for arson in Roman law. Even those who had started fires accidentally in Italian cities were bastinadoed. But for the band of scapegoats whom the theatrically-minded princeps had decided to stigmatise, only the most spectacular of punishments would suffice.

Variety, for the sadist, is the spice of a public spectacle. Some of the Christians were crucified, as their Master had been thirty years before in Palestine. Others were dressed in the skins of wild beasts and put into an arena with wild, hungry dogs, who tore their human prey to pieces with their teeth. Others were forced into leather jerkins, liberally daubed with pitch, set alight, and used as illuminations in Nero's gardens in the Vatican.

It is worth emphasising the obvious point that, in making this grotesquely vicious public example, Nero had no religious interest whatsoever. He did not care, any more than did any Roman magistrate, what strange spiritual fancies passed through the brains of his subjects. The Roman Empire, like the Ottoman Empire after it, survived in large measure because of its cynical and tolerant attitude towards the different religious persuasions of its inhabitants. It was the first totalitarian state in history and its imposition of state-sponsored emperor worship was an innovation; but if local religions did nothing to upset the harmony of the state then the emperors and their legions did nothing to interfere with them. Widespread persecution of Christianity belongs to a period long after the lifetime of Nero's victims. It did not really happen on any appreciable scale until the middle of the third century, ending in Diocletian's persecutions of 303, when, as Gibbon reminds us, 'fraud, envy and malice, prevailed in every congregation'.[10] Even these, in terms of numbers, were modest atrocities compared with the persecution of heretics by the Christian Church once it had become the official religion of the Empire in the reign of Constantine (who died in 337). The anathematising of religious opponents, the punishments, for religious heresy, of exile, imprisonment, torture and death were unknown to the polytheistic mind-set of the 'pagans'; no Roman emperor, however brutal, was to launch a Crusade to match that of Innocent III against the Albigenses when, in the massacres of Bezier (1209) and the battle of Muret (1213), thousands of innocent cranks were put to the sword.

Nero's cruelty to the Christians in the gardens of the Vatican at the

[10] *Decline and Fall of the Roman Empire*, C, xvi.

dawn of the gentle age of Christendom has been seen ever afterwards in Christian tradition as the beginning of a religious persecution. It was nothing of the kind. The advantage of singling out the Christians for special blame after the fire consisted in their tiny numbers, in the fact that, as a sect, they were quite obscure. Few would feel aggrieved at their demise. Christian folk-legend has not been slow, in the intervening centuries, to build up Nero as a religious persecutor; nor is it any accident that the Bishops of Rome should have chosen to take up their residence on the supposed site of this hideous torture. But if a martyr is someone who dies for their faith then the victims of the Neronian persecution were not martyrs. Jesus was in all likelihood a martyr – a man who died for his own particular vision of what it meant to be Jewish, and who was arraigned by the Roman governor as a troublemaker: 'the King of the Jews'. The human torches screaming in Nero's gardens were not martyrs in this sense.

But Nero had given the Christian movement two vitally important privileges: a public name and a number of dead, who could be seen instantaneously as martyrs. Any obscure group poised to play an important part on the world stage must thank, in retrospect, the ruling power that first bans, or drives into exile, or murders, some member of the sect. The magistrate who decreed that Lenin's brother should be hanged can have had no more idea that he was going to have an influence over world history. Similarly, Nero, with a theatricality of which only he would be capable, provided the Christians with a 'send-off' into the history books. Tacitus, ever eager for florid examples of cruelty in Nero's character, immortalised the scene for us, but this was caviar to the general; and it is only by the merest of accidents that Tacitus survives in the world at all.[11] The Christian literature, by contrast, flourished from the beginning, and this is one of the most remarkable phenomena in the story. The fact, for example, that Nero had no religious motive whatsoever in wishing to make human torches out of the Christians in his garden pyrotechnics did not prevent their instant canonisation in the eyes of their coreligionists.

One of their number, a Jew named John, who fled the city of Rome just in time, took this terrible calamity as a token or sign that the end of days was at hand. For thirty years, since his death, Jesus the

[11] One manuscript alone survives the ravages of the Dark Ages. See C. D. Fisher (ed.), *Cornelii Taciti Annalium* (Oxford, 1906), p. v.

Messiah had mysteriously failed to return to earth, though he was expected to come imminently on the clouds. 'Every eye will see him, even those who pierced him [i.e. the Romans and not, as in Christian hymns, the Jews – for it was the Romans who killed Jesus]; and on his account all the tribes of the earth will wail.'[12] Seer John's people, Jesus's people, the Jews, remained unvindicated. But now that the Beast, the dreaded Whore of Babylon, Rome, had begun to persecute the Holy Ones of God, it was surely a sign that they would be swiftly avenged. Taking refuge on the Greek island of Patmos, this visionary was granted a series of revelations of the Almighty's purpose in History. The meanings of these unforgettable and potent images – the Four Apocalyptic Horsemen, the Lamb Triumphant on his Throne, the chorus of praise uplifted by the Redeemed, the torment of those, Jewish and Roman, who have not recognised Jesus as Lord – are matters which have provided a rich source of study, for theologians, literary historians and psychiatrists. The historian who tries to date and place John's Revelation is guided by the author to a quite specific time span. The words of the revelation are written down four years after the Roman fire, and shortly after Nero's own death. We know that they were written before the ultimate calamity of the Sack of Jerusalem by the Romans in AD 70, since the worst fate our seer can imagine befalling the Jewish capital is that a tenth of the sacred city will be destroyed.[13] He writes of the earthly temple as still in existence.[14] No one who knew of the total devastation and ruin of Jerusalem could have prophesied so comparatively mild a fate for it. Moreover, we are told that the great whore, who is 'Babylon the great, mother of whores and of earth's abominations',[15] represents Rome. She is seen in the vision rutting with a beast which has seven heads, and these heads, our author explains, are the seven kings (or emperors, *basileus* in Greek). 'Five have fallen, one is living, and the other has not yet come; and when he comes he must remain only a little while.'[16] All this, as a piece of historical writing, places Revelation firmly in the short-lived reign of Galba. Five emperors have fallen – Augustus, Tiberius, Gaius, Claudius and Nero. The sixth, Galba, will be replaced by Otho, who also will not last long. Accurate as far as it goes. What makes the

[12] Revelation 1:7.
[13] Revelation 11:13.
[14] Revelation 11 *passim*.
[15] Revelation 17:5.
[16] Revelation 17:10.

Revelation of John painful reading for the Jewish historian is the wild inaccuracy of its prophecies in general. John foretells the establishment of an everlasting earthly Jerusalem, while Babylon, that is Rome, is completely destroyed. Within two years of the Revelation being written down and sent to his fellow believers in seven towns of Asia Minor (western Turkey) Jerusalem had been devastated. As Jesus may or may not have predicted, not one stone of it remained upon the other.[17]

The fate of the Jews, their temple and their city is of absolutely vital relevance to everything which we have to consider in the pages which follow. If the Christians really entertained thoughts about Rome and its divine emperors of the kind which are reproduced in John's Revelation, it is small wonder that they should have been persecuted. Tacitus tells us that the Christians arrested in Rome after the fire were condemned, not so much for incendiarism as for their obvious hatred of the human race.[18] John the Seer – whoever he was – exudes a powerful hatred of the human race and an exultant hope that the greater number of human beings will imminently perish in a lake of fire.

While it might have seemed true that Christianity, the religion which invented the idea of Hell and Eternal Torment, was founded on a set of anti-humanist principles, was it true that it was inherently anti-Roman?

Just as within Judaism – as we read in the pages of Josephus[19] – there was a debate raging about the allowability, or otherwise, of compromise between being a Jew and being a part of the Roman

---

[17] Mark 13:2. An exaggeration, as any visitor knows who has inspected the remains of the Western Wall of the Herodian Temple and the huge steps leading up to what had been the southern wall. Nevertheless, when we recall that the Romans obliterated the very name of Jerusalem from the map and built their own city of Aelia Capitolina on the ruins, the prophecy of Jesus seems much closer to the truth than the prophecy of Seer John. One reason for this, of course, could be that the words were inserted into Jesus's mouth by a devout author who wrote after the destruction of Jerusalem. For the likelihood of this, see the Appendix, on the dating of the New Testament documents.

[18] 'Indicio eorum multitudo ingens haud proinde in crimine incendii quam odio humani generis conuicti sunt.' *Annales*, XV, 44.

[19] Flavius Josephus (*c.* 37–*c.* 100) is the great historian of the Jews in the first century. Of a priestly family, he was directly involved in the dramatic events of 66–70, first fighting for his fellow-countrymen and then defecting to the Roman side. He was a protégé of Nero's wife Poppaea. During the siege of Jerusalem, he acted as an interpreter to Titus, who destroyed the city. He was rewarded with a villa in Rome where he wrote his history of the Jewish war (*De Bello Iudaico* [*BJ*] and his *Antiquities* [*Ant*], a history of the Jewish people, both invaluable source books for our period.

Empire, so within that small Jewish sect or heresy called Christianity there was a discernible rift on this central question.

Evidently, the Christianity of the Revelation, with its powerfully anti-Roman bias, was not the only sort of Christianity in existence during the period when the New Testament books were being compiled. Only a decade or so previous, a very different sort of Christian had written in these terms to his fellow-believers in Rome: 'Let every person be subject to the governing authorities; for there is no authority except from God, and those authorities that exist have been instituted by God. Therefore whoever resists authority resists what God has appointed, and those who resist will incur judgement.'[20]

When we read the words just quoted (but taken out of context) – their assertion that the power of the emperor Nero was divinely-given; that what should be, was, what was, should be; that any rebellion against the Roman authority deserved his punishment – we should not immediately guess that their author 'gloried' in the name of one who had been executed by a Roman procurator in Judaea in the early 30s. The author is Paul, a figure who dominates the pages of the New Testament and who made an indelible effect on the future of the Christian religion. As such, he could be described as one of the most important and influential figures who ever lived. The tensions within the Christian movement – Jewish or non-Jewish? Roman or anti-Roman? Apocalyptic or practical? – are tensions which we can reasonably find within the writings, and perhaps within the personality, of Paul himself. We cannot write a biography of Paul in the way that Tacitus or Suetonius has supplied us with colourful, not to say sensational, lives of Nero. But we can rediscover Paul's world – and Nero's world – and hope, in so doing, to understand something about the origins of Christianity and hence the origins of our own world.

At the time of the fire in AD 64, very few people had heard of Christianity, and there would have been even fewer who could have defined what it was. Nero was the divine emperor, the strongest and most powerful person in the world. Christianity was destined, hundreds of years later, to become the dominant influence in Western civilisation, prefiguring a time when, as was whimsically observed by an early twentieth-century scholar, people called their dogs Nero and their sons Paul.

[20] Romans 13:1–2.

The fact that the Gentile world adopted Christianity is owing almost solely to one man: Paul of Tarsus. Without Paul, it is highly unlikely that Christianity would ever have broken away from Judaism. Only a moment's reflexion tells us what a different world it would have been. The whole Jewish inheritance, which is woven inseparably into the Christian religion, would never have been available to the Gentile imagination. The stories which, until our generation, were told to almost every child in the Western world, would have been the exclusive preserve of the Jews: Adam and Eve, Noah's Ark, Daniel in the Lions' Den. The concept of moral law as a divinely-given set of precepts, spoken by the Almighty to Moses on Sinai, underpinned, at least until the eighteenth century, the ethical, political and social fabric of Western statecraft. God himself is, for Western Man, the God of Israel. If metaphysicians for the first two millennia after Christ have drawn on non-Jewish traditions – above all on those of Plato and Aristotle – for talking about God, it is nonetheless to the Hebraic tradition, of a God who created the world of matter and who is involved with his creation, that Western philosophers have always returned. And this is the inheritance which Paul opened up to the Gentile world.

This is something so extraordinary that many people do not notice it. It is one of those huge facts which is so obvious, like the fact that most people in America speak English, that we do not often pause to ask how it happened. This is to some extent because of the misconceptions which exist about Paul in the popular mind; misconceptions which come about partly because Paul is widely regarded as someone who distorted the original message of Christianity. Jesus, it is thought, preached a simple message of love. Paul came along in a later generation and complicated it with a lot of difficult 'theology'. Paul, it is supposed, was a bigoted Jew who, as a result of his conversion on the road to Damascus, became a bigoted Christian. He is widely regarded as a misogynist, the father of that strand in Christianity which sees the female sex as inferior to the male. Notoriously, he condemned homosexuality.

Those who read further in this book will perhaps change their preconceived view of Paul as a stiff-necked reactionary who wanted the free-and-easy Jesus-religion to become a church with a set of restrictive rules and regulations. They will perhaps come to see him as a prophet of liberty, whose visionary sense of the importance of the inner life anticipates the Romantic poets more than the rule-books of the Inquisition. But such a view is only possible if Christianity itself is understood as an institutionalised distortion of Paul's thought, the inevitable consequence of the world having lasted (at the time of writing) more than nineteen hundred years longer than he predicted. Paul did not imagine that there would be such a thing as Christianity, or Christian civilisation, any more than Jesus did.

Part of the confusion stems from what Christians have traditionally told themselves about Paul's life. In the Acts of the Apostles, a book which reached its final form in perhaps the year 80, fifteen or twenty years after Paul's death, there are several accounts of Paul's 'conversion'. Already the author writes as if it is perfectly clear that Jesus had started a new movement (called by the author the Way) which was destined by divine providence to become available to Gentiles. As we shall see, this idea of things betrays the bias on the part of the author rather than giving an accurate account of the historical facts. The truth of what happened in the very early days – in the lifetime of Jesus and in the days following his death – is historically irrecoverable.

The author of Acts does not conceal from us the fact that the Way was a Jewish movement, whose followers regularly worshipped in the temple at Jerusalem. They believed that the Jewish prophecies had been fulfilled in Jesus and that, as a token of divine approval, God had raised up Jesus from death. We are told that one of their number, a man named Stephen, was particularly eloquent in his denunciation of the Jewish authorities – the high priest and his entourage who were responsible for handing Jesus over to the Romans for execution. His claim to see a vision of Jesus standing at the right hand of God enrages them, and a mob drag Stephen outside the city walls and stone him.

The rabble who attack Stephen in this episode could have been a mere lynch mob, or it could be a garbled account of the death-penalty for blasphemy – for Jews who blasphemed could, according to their law, be killed by stoning. If Stephen committed a blasphemy, it is difficult to know what it was, since he did not appear to believe – what was later to become a Christian doctrine – that Jesus was Divine, or the Son of God, or the Second Person of the Trinity. Such concepts were not in currency in the early Jerusalem church described in the book of Acts.

The author of the book was probably working from several sources. It is perhaps at this point that, having relied on sources which remembered Stephen's eloquent speech, he suddenly turns to a completely different story; for, without warning, he introduces into his narrative a 'young man named Saul'. So far in the story nothing has been said about this Saul, though in later passages of Acts we learn that he was a Roman citizen, born in what is today eastern Turkey, but educated in the Jewish Law in Jerusalem. It is not explained why this Saul should feel such murderous anger against the followers of the Way, but, armed with letters from the high priest, he sets out to Damascus 'so that if he found any who belonged to the Way, men or women, he might bring them bound to Jerusalem'. We can deduce from other evidence that this event took place, if it took place at all, in or around the year AD 32.

It was on the Damascus road, according to this account, that a light from heaven suddenly flashed around Saul and he fell to the ground. He heard a voice saying, 'Saul, Saul, why do you persecute me?' And when Saul asks who it is who addresses him, the reply comes, 'I am Jesus, whom you are persecuting.' The men who were with Saul heard the voice, but they did not see the vision. When the heavenly light has faded, Saul is found to be blind and he is led into the city. For three days he neither ate nor drank.

One of Jesus's followers in Damascus, a certain Ananias, is told in a vision to go to the street called Straight and to lay his hands on Saul. When Ananias remonstrates and says that Saul has been a persecutor of the Way, the Lord replies, 'Go, for he is an instrument whom I have chosen to bring my name to the Gentiles and kings.' So Ananias did as he was told, and he went and laid hands on Saul, and the blindness departed – 'something like scales fell from his eyes'. By this account, Saul immediately began to proclaim Jesus in the synagogues, saying, 'He is the Son of God.' After a few days, 'the Jews' were plotting to kill him, and he was obliged to slip away from the city by being lowered from the wall in a basket.

That is how the story of Saul, subsequently known as Paul, was first written down in the Acts of the Apostles. Already, we have the picture of Christianity as a religion that is separate, or destined to be separate, from Judaism; and what happened to Paul on the road to Damascus is read by later generations of Christians as the story of how Saul the Jew was 'converted to Christianity'. What makes us think that there was such a thing as Christianity to which Saul/Paul could be converted? Merely to say that Paul was converted to Christianity begs more questions than it answers.

Nero's great achievement as an unconscious propagandist for Christianity was to make it seem as though this chaotic collection of Jewish heresies had an 'originator', or that the various small groups of Christians scattered, by 64, throughout the Empire, from Jerusalem to Rome itself, all represented the same point of view. Once again, in retrospect, it must have seemed obvious to anyone that this was so. The 'early Christians' were our spiritual ancestors. They might not have shared all the customs and practices of a modern Lutheran or Roman Catholic but *basically* they all believed in – well, in Christianity. And surely it is obvious what Christianity is?

As the second millennium of Christian history comes to an end we might consider this a foolish question which barely requires an answer. Surely, Christianity is the system of beliefs which most of the main Christian denominations hold in common: it is the belief that God fulfilled the promises first made to the Jewish race in the person of Jesus Christ; that the birth, ministry, passion, death and resurrection of Jesus brought redemption to the human race; that through him, all people, Jews and Gentiles, could be restored to that relationship which had obtained between humanity and the Godhead before the Fall. That, surely, is Christianity? And the belief that Jesus, before he died, established an everlasting covenant with his people, the token of which was the Eucharist, the sacrificial meal by which, offering bread and wine to God, Christians receive the Body and Blood of Christ? In other words, Christianity is one of the world religions, founded by Jesus, in a manner comparable to the establishment of Islam by the Holy Prophet or Buddhism by the Lord Gautama.

The historian has to interrupt this series of assumptions. Deeply ingrained as they may be in the Gentile consciousness, they can not be substantiated. When we have looked at the evidence, it will seem at the very least highly unlikely that Jesus, a Galilean exorcist executed in *circa* the year 30, probably for sedition, had any ambitions to found a world religion. All the indications are that this charismatic healer and preacher limited his sphere of activities to rural and exclusively Jewish regions. For example, though he was probably born, and certainly operated, near the great Hellenistic city of Sepphoris in Galilee, we hear no mention of this city in the Gospels. We read only of a Jesus who chose to move about among the fishing-towns and agricultural communities of Galilee – hotbeds of political dissent against Rome, according to Josephus. The Gospels were written to make us suppose that Jesus did indeed reach out to all mankind as some Saviour-figure who would embrace Gentiles as well as Jews, so it is all the more remarkable that these books should clumsily have recorded sayings, which on balance would seem to be authentic, in which Jesus is quoted as saying that his mission is to 'the lost sheep of the house of Israel'; that he has no desire to throw the pearls of his wisdom before the Gentile pigs. In another place he is quoted as saying that the Gentiles were dogs.

Jesus would seem to have shared the views of many Jewish contemporaries that the world was about to come to an end and that God would redeem Israel and bring to pass a new era in which the rule of the Gentiles would be smitten and driven away. Since the end of ages was at hand, and the Gospels record Jesus as predicting as much, it is hard to imagine why Jesus would have entertained the quite incompatible belief that several thousand years of human history stretched ahead in which a new 'religion' would be necessary. As far as the historical Jesus was concerned, it seems overwhelmingly likely that he did not think there was any future for the human race at all; that is, in so far as we can deduce any interest in the 'human race', as opposed to the fate of the Jews or more narrowly of his own followers, in the recorded sayings of Jesus.

Some little while after the death of Jesus, his followers in Jerusalem grouped themselves around his brother James. We are told that they continued to observe the Jewish law, and to worship in the temple. These testimonies from the New Testament reveal to us the rather puzzling information that Jesus's closest friends and followers, and indeed his family seemed to know nothing about the 'fact' – taken for granted by so many of us – that Jesus, or 'Christ', was the 'originator' of a religion called Christianity.

We assume that this fact is so obvious that merely to question it sounds cranky – as if a pet theory is going to be advanced. The simple truth, however, is that the New Testament documents themselves do not bear out Tacitus's notion that 'Christ', if we take him to be the same figure as Jesus, was the 'originator' of Christianity, if we take that word to refer to the set of beliefs normally regarded as Christian – belief in the Divine Saviour and his resurrection, belief in the Eucharist. If there is any single individual who can be labelled the 'originator' of Christianity in this sense, it would be Paul.

Christianity is the product of Judaism – that is a commonplace. It is also the product of the Roman world in which it came to be born. It achieved its cohesion because the Empire chose to persecute it, and it finally broke with its Jewish parent-stem in large measure for political reasons: less because church and synagogue could not agree and more because the Romans had destroyed Jerusalem and made contact between 'Jewish Christians' and their Gentile counterparts impossible. The Empire provided Christianity not just with the necessary boost of early martyrs, but with all the practical opportunities needed for a burgeoning movement: roads of a kind which the world had never known, an influx of Orientals into its capital, with its inevitable bundle of eastern wisdom and mystery religions. The Roman Empire also added to the huge and gullible slave class and allowed, by the trade routes opened up, for the commercial class to which Paul belonged to reach these masses of people.

It also provided, together with Judaism, a method of storytelling, a way of describing itself to itself without which no movement or political party or religion could survive. This is not the place to decide who wrote the Gospels, or when; who wrote the Acts of the Apostles, or where, or when. But whoever did so had already made Paul into a story, and in so doing he had used earlier stories, not necessarily Christian stories, to help him. He made Paul's conversion into a story of divine possession, which many of his contemporaries might have recognised from, say, going to the theatre; just as he makes Paul's journeyings seem like the recognisable Odyssey to which lovers of the Homeric tales would be able to respond.

But, before trying to explain the way in which Paul is important to history, a word about chronology. Readers of the New Testament, a collection of miscellaneous writings of questionable date, which were written in the first century but compiled as a single collection in the second century, over a hundred years after Paul's death, might be tempted to view the events of Christian history in a linear progression. First, the life of Jesus; then, his suffering and death; then (if you believe it) his resurrection and glorious ascension; then the founding of the church; then the coming of the Holy Spirit at Pentecost; then the conversion of Paul; and so on.

In Paul's lifetime, and Nero's, there was no such thing as the New Testament – even though some of its individual writings (perhaps all of them in some primitive form) could be dated to before the fall of Jerusalem in AD 70. The 'real' order of events, if we can speak in this way, could easily be reversed. It might make more sense to read the events, or at least the documents which relate to the events (and these, after all, are all that we have), in a notional rather than a linear pattern. In terms of their historical significance, this is certainly the most helpful way to read them. For our purpose, then, the most significant 'event' is the conversion or apocalypse, as he calls it, of Paul, his discovery of the Living Christ. It coincides with a period when other Jews, among them those who knew Jesus, and those who did not, were also proclaiming a number of religious experiences relating to Jesus, or a number of Scripture-interpretations of the End of Time which relate to Jesus. The old prophecies have been fulfilled – the Son of Man (from Daniel) is about to appear! The Lord's Anointed has come (or is about to come) to rescue and redeem Israel. The Gentiles will call upon God's name. The temple of Herod will be replaced with the old temple of Solomon. The Romans are to be driven out of Palestine.

Out of this set of experiences, which includes the old messianic belief that the dead have been raised, or shall be raised, there springs the teaching of this community of disparate believers – some of them practising Jews within the mainstream of Israel, Pharisees, temple priests and others; some of them Hellenistic Jews; some of them converts to Judaism; and some of them 'god-fearers', Gentiles who were not converts to Judaism but who had an affiliation of sorts to it. For them, the story is not (as it would be for a modern reader of the New Testament) a story which starts with the birth of Jesus, or even a story which starts with the old prophets. It starts with their own anticipation of the End of Time. Human beings, with as yet unrealised aspirations and dreams, they reinterpreted events in the light of the unfinished, uncompleted End. The death of Jesus, for instance, itself becomes a fulfilment of those Prophecies which are their synagogue reading. They tell and retell it, in spoken and eventually in written form, through quotations from the Jewish Psalms and Prophetic Books. His teachings are told and retold not as a modern historian would want them told, with an attempt to remember them accurately, but in an attempt to make them increasingly applicable to the coming End, to the Judgement.

Out of this set of beliefs, and out of the disparate communities which start to spring up around the shores of the Mediterranean and in Rome itself, there begins to emerge what they called the Good News or the Gospel – a word which both meant the spoken message of those who spoke it and, in time, the written book in which this message was contained. Once written, in whatever primitive form, the Gospel becomes a part of the history. Whatever the historical Jesus was like, and whether modern historians can ever hope to reconstruct the facts about him, the world now, at this stage in the history of the Christian idea, begins to have a much more durable figure than the historical Jesus: we have the Jesus of the Gospel, or Gospels. We do not know exactly how these books evolved and a purely textual account of their development, any account which has one 'author' copying and collating the papyri of another, is making the 'linear' anachronism and failing to see that the emergence of this written literature about Jesus is itself part of the story.

Even within the lifetime of this community itself, however, it does not make sense to view history as a purely linear progression. We see it all backwards – from the perspective of the cataclysm occurring in the year 70. We see a group of enthusiasts, broadly within the community of Israel, looking for a consummation of their hopes which were not fulfilled. Then we see the Roman War, and the destruction of the temple, the greatest catastrophe to befall Judaism since the Babylonian exile and arguably the most 'traumatic' event in Israel's history before the Holocaust 1900 years later. We see the 'inevitable' separation of Judaism and what has by now become 'Christianity', and we see all the 'events' in the New Testament leading up to that. The failure of the messianic hope (in the first generation, at least, the Christ did not return); the brutal Roman destruction of Jewry's most sacred shrine; the virtual elimination of the Sadducean, priestly sects of Judaism, and the inevitable triumph, out of disaster, of the Pharisaic or rabbinic school; the absolute separation which came to be drawn between this school and those other survivors of the first-century Holocaust, the Christians: this is an 'end' to the story which we know but which no one who was depicted in the pages of the New Testament knew! They were not – it is an obvious point but it is so easy to forget – viewing their own experiences in this linear way. Their immediate imaginative and religious hopes, experiences and aspirations, were far more important to them.

When Oscar Wilde was an undergraduate at Oxford, he had to undergo, as all classical students did, a *viva voce* examination to test his knowledge of Greek. Sensing an effete and 'difficult' young man, his examiners set him the most 'difficult' passage, from the translator's viewpoint, in the whole New Testament, namely the 27th chapter of Acts, with its many nautical terms. It tells of the shipwreck of Paul on his way to Rome, and his rescue, together with the crew of a ship, off an island which turns out to be Malta. 'That will be all, Mr Wilde,' said his astonished examiners, hearing Oscar (who was brilliant at Greek) make his effortless translation. 'Oh, please!' expostulated Wilde.

'Do let me go on – I am longing to know how the story finishes!'

Like many of Wilde's jokes (perhaps like all of them) it contains a great profundity. How the story finishes is the essential question, both for the characters within the Acts of the Apostles, and for its readers. It ends, in fact, in the most puzzling manner, with Paul having lived in Rome 'in his own hired house' for two years without having succeeded in having his case heard before the emperor. In our end is our beginning. We might attempt to tell Paul's story, or Peter's, or that of the first believers in Jesus the Christ, in a purely linear progression, but we should be constantly interrupted if we did so by our ignorance of how the story ended (for them as individuals) as well as by our knowledge of what happened in 64, what happened in 66, and what happened finally in 70. We read the story with the knowledge that Nero – seen by Paul as God's representative on earth – would make human torches of the Christians to amuse the crowds in the Vatican gardens. We also know that the Romans – seen by the Sadducees and the high priests as the only protectors of Herod's temple and city against anarchic insurgents – would, in 70, level the Holy City to the ground, change its name and build a new Roman city on its ruins. The year 70 marked a new beginning of a kind, but it also defined an 'end' of the variety which Wilde and all other intelligent readers of Luke have sought, and sought in vain. The present book is written for those, like Wilde, who long to know how the story ends. It is written by someone who shares that longing but who, after twenty years of thinking about it, can not really decide even the rather simple question of how it begins.

II

SAUL OF TARSUS

THAT PAUL WAS born in Tarsus, the capital of Cilicia, is not impossible; but we owe our knowledge of the fact not to Paul himself but to Luke,[1] a Gentile Christian who wrote two books, the Gospel of Luke and the Acts of the Apostles, and who claims to have accompanied Paul on his final journey to Rome. Theologians, who do not wish to be burdened with too many facts about Paul's life, have tended to discount Luke's testimony, and indeed the authenticity of his claims; historians, who wish to have as much evidence as they can reasonably muster, have tended to believe the assertion that Saul/Paul was a Roman citizen, born in Tarsus.

Tarsus was the splendid city on the Cydnus where Antony first met Cleopatra, thirty or more years before Saul/Paul was born. (No trace of ancient Tarsus survives in the modern city of the name.) The celebrated passage of Plutarch, rendered into English by North and into verse by Shakespeare, in which Cleopatra made her splendid water-pageant and 'burn'd on the water', all happened within the traditional birthplace of Paul.

Even this story, which seems so romantic, starts out with a dubious political pedigree. Christianity does not own a monopoly in myth-making. The great historian of the Augustan Age, Syme, was probably right to say that Augustus (Octavianus as he was during the civil wars) did his best to discredit Antony in the eyes of his enemies in Rome by picturing him as a doting fool, throwing away military and political advantage for love. Syme points out that in 33 BC, Cleopatra was 'neither young nor beautiful'.[2] Marcus Antonius chose at Tarsus to placate her rather than to depose her, and he did so in ways which were not irrelevant to the story of Paul and Christianity which began a hundred

[1] For shorthand, I refer to the author of the Gospel of Luke and the Acts of the Apostles as Luke without necessarily subscribing to any view about his actual identity.
[2] Ronald Syme, *The Roman Revolution*, p. 274.

years later. By forming his alliance with Cleopatra, Antonius was able to retain a Roman hold on her dominions in the Near East.

Marcus Antonius found himself in the East as the vanquisher of Brutus and Cassius at Philippi, the decisive battle between the assassins of Julius Caesar (and supporters of the old Republic) and the supporters of the new order. It is questionable whether Antonius, or anyone else at that stage of history, was fully aware of the fact that, after a period of rule by a Triumvirate, the Roman people and their dominions were to become the subjects of one Imperial Dictator, Octavianus, known to history as Augustus. On one level, however, the civil wars and constitutional problems of the Roman people during the hundred years 33 BC–AD 77 derived from the semi-accident of territorial expansion which had made the Romans the masters of the known world during the time of Julius Caesar. From Gaul, which Caesar himself had conquered, to Judaea, into which Pompey had blundered almost unintentionally in 63 BC, the Romans found themselves with responsibility for governing and administering a bewildering and dangerous variety of peoples and expanse of territory.

Cilicia, the easternmost region of southern Turkey, abutting Syria, was in the middle of all this and its history is symptomatic of what was happening in further-flung parts of the Empire. Its acquisition brought Rome as many problems as spoils. Julius Caesar gave Tarsus such favours that it temporarily adopted the title Juliopolis. It was a splendid city, known as Antioch on Cydnus. As it had been a *polis* in the Greek Empire, Antonius gave it the title of a *civitas libera*.

The simplest and most obvious legacy left to the Tarseans by the Romans was the road system which, a hundred years after Antonius and Cleopatra had consummated their cynical or romantic alliance (depending on whether you believe Syme or Shakespeare), still enabled a man such as Paul to travel freely. The overland route through Asia Minor could be followed even in the winter months when sea travel was impossible. The trade route went from Troas to Pergamum, the capital of Asia, and on to Sardis. The road passed through the high mountain range called the Cilician Gates, through Galatia to Tarsus. Tarsus was therefore linked with the main roads westward, and hence to the great Hellenistic and Roman centres of Ephesus and Corinth, as well as with Syrian Antioch and Jerusalem to the south and the east.

But as the story of Cleopatra reminds us, Tarsus was also a great port and the story of Paul is of one of the most indefatigable sea-voyagers of ancient times. By his own account he was 'three times shipwrecked', and he wrote that before the shipwreck described in Acts. In the summer months, sea travel was rapid – more rapid than it had ever been in history. In AD 193 the accession of the emperor Pertinax was proclaimed in Rome on 1 January and was not announced in Alexandria until 6 March because the news had to travel 2,420 miles by road, and necessitated two days' risky crossing of the Adriatic. The accession of Galba, by contrast, was proclaimed in the summer (9 June) and was known in Alexandria a mere 27 days later. It does not sound fast by modern standards but until the existence of the Roman Empire, the Mediterranean lands were not truly linked up at all, and travel between its separate parts was certainly not easy. The Romans did not merely encourage and revitalise the commercial and business centres of the Aegean world such as Corinth and Ephesus; they made it possible for commerce to flourish by means of transport. The names on the great commercial roads which link these centres are the names which echo in the life of Paul as the centres of his 'churches' – Ephesus, Pisidia, Iconium, Derbe, Tarsus, Syrian Antioch and Caesarea. 'Each of these was a knot where roads of a whole district met, and where its trade and intercommunication and education found a centre. Thus this great artery was the channel in which the lifeblood of the empire mainly flowed. It was not the route along which goods mostly moved, but it was the route of those who directed trade, as well as of thoughts and inventions.'[3]

Like any great port, Tarsus had a mixed population. The ancient writers speak of Tarseans as pirates, seafarers and worshippers of Mithras.[4] It was probably Pompey's soldiers, in their Eastern campaigns, who first introduced this cult to the Roman people. It became especially popular in the army, most of whom, in the first century, were Asiatics. Archaeologists show that Tarsus was a centre of keen Mithraic worship until the downfall of the Empire. The most distinctive feature of Mithraic worship is that the initiates either drank the blood of the sacred bull or drank a chalice of wine as a symbolic representation of blood. The steer would be held over a platform and ritually slain. Under the platform stood the initiate, who would be literally bathed in the blood which dripped down from the platform. He would rub the blood in his eyes, ears and nostrils. The *taurobolium*

[3] W. M. Ramsay, 'Roads and Travel', in *Hastings Dictionary of the Bible*.
[4] Franz Cumont, *The Mysteries of Mithras*.

as the Roman called it, like the sacred meals of other cults, symbolized the transfer of life and power. 'From the blood bath, he emerged confident that his was now the invincible might of the bull.'[5] If Paul's parents were Jewish, they would have been disgusted by the idea of the cult of Mithras, since the drinking of blood is one of the most fundamental taboos in Jewish life. But for those who practised the religion of Mithras, it was a commemoration of the life-principle itself. From the bull slain by Herakles, for example, flowed not merely blood but life, corn, plenteousness. It symbolised the springing up of new life beyond the grave.[6]

The Mithraic rites and the worship of Herakles might therefore have had much in common, and it would have been perfectly possible for a citizen of Tarsus to worship at both the shrines of the bull and of his slayer.

Any child born or brought up in Tarsus could not fail to have been impressed by the great religious ceremonies which took place there in honour of Herakles. Devotions to particular gods often took localised form. Just as in later ages there was Our Lady of Lourdes and Our Lady of Fatima, so the cult of the demi-god hero Herakles had its own local flavouring wherever it flourished. The Tarsean Herakles had probably begun life as a vegetation deity called Sandan, but Dio Chrysostom tells us that he was worshipped with all the honours normally accorded to Herakles. The cult owes much to the dying and rising to life again of other Mediterranean vegetation gods – the Syrian Adonis, the Babylonian Thammuz, the Egyptian Osiris. Every autumn in Tarsus the boy Paul would have seen the great funeral pyre at which the god was ritually burnt. The central mystery of the ritual was that the withering heat of the summer sun had brought the god to his death but that he would rise to life again in the spring, at about the time when the Jews were celebrating the Passover. From inscriptions in Tarsus we know that Herakles, in his dying and descent into Hades, was regarded as a divine saviour.[7] The Tarseans worshipped saviour gods (*theoi soteres*). From the stories we know of Herakles, this is not surprising. In the *Alkestis* of Euripides, for example, Herakles volunteers to go down into 'the sunless palace' of Persephone and

[5] Royden Keith Yerkes, *Sacrifice in Greek and Roman Religions and Early Judaism*, p. 43.
[6] Robert Grant, p. 72.
[7] H. Bohlig, *Die Geisteskultur von Tarsus im augustischhen Zeitalter mit Beurteilung der paulinische Schriften* (Heidelberg, 1913), quoted by H. J. Schoeps, *The Theology of the Apostle Paul in the Light of Jewish Religious History*, p. 17.

Pluto to ask for Alkestis, the lately dead wife of his friend Admetus. The scene in which Herakles returns and hands over to Admetus the veiled and silent figure of a woman whom he does not recognise, does not dare to hope, to be his lost Alkestis, is one of the most powerful and moving in the whole of Greek tragedy. At the heart of this myth is the most primitive fear – that of death – and the most primitive hope – of immortality. Admetus asks Herakles how he brought her out of darkness and into light. The son of God (Zeus) replies, 'I joined a struggle with the Lord of Spirits', that is, with Death itself. As the Chorus concludes, the Gods manifest themselves in many different forms (*pollai morphai ton daimonion*).[8]

Paul was to develop into a richly imaginative, but confused, religious genius who was able to draw out a mythological and archetypical significance from the death of a Jewish hero, Jesus of Nazareth. In the town where he grew up, as in all the towns of the ancient world (save Jerusalem), 'the gods were not jealous . . . They insisted that they must be offered punctiliously all honours due to them but they did not worry about what honours were paid to other gods or to men.'[9]

It is perhaps necessary at this early stage of a story which concerns a religious genius to point out one very obvious fact about religions in the ancient world, and that is that they were mutually tolerant of one another, and that worshippers were eclectic, moving from one shrine or cult to the next without the slightest feeling of inconsistency. In twentieth-century English it is possible to ask the question, 'What is your religion?', expecting the answer, 'I am a Presbyterian' or 'I am a Moslem'. It is highly debatable whether such a sentence, with such a sense, could be translated into Latin or into Greek, for the words *religio* and *eusebeia* do not in the imaginative worlds inhabited by Latin or Greek speakers encompass or denominate some exclusive set of values or beliefs of a kind which would be the equivalent of a modern Christian or post-Christian religion. Before the birth of Jesus, it is reported that the Maccabees 'were bravely and honourably fighting on behalf of Judaismos'. Not God, but Judaism or Jewishness. 'This is

---

[8] *Alkestis*, 1159. When Alkestis returns from the dead, she is 'consecrated' to the gods of the nether world and may not speak for 'three days'. Anthropologists do not necessarily believe that the story of the strong hero, wrestling with the black demon death, was part of the original Admetus and Alkestis myth, but since it had been part of the story since at least 438 BC there is no reason to doubt that it was still part of the story in first-century Tarsus. See A. M. Dale (ed.), *Euripides' Alcestis* (Oxford, 1954), p. viii.

[9] J. H. W. G. Liebeschuetz, *Continuity and Change in Roman Religion*, p. 198.

the first time in history that religion had a name.'[10] The Gods had different names, but there were not particular names in the Gentile world for the worship of those particular Gods; and it is only by the most painstaking and speculative researches that modern scholars can piece together what ancient religions were like, even though we are aware, from reading Homer, of what the Gods were like. Judaism itself only became an -*ism* in the minds of some of its adherents during the Maccabean period, a hundred years before Paul. It is misleading (though it is a convenient modern shorthand) to speak of paganism as though this were some alternative 'religion'.

It would be hard to exaggerate the importance of Paul's being a Greek speaker. Greek, not Latin, was the lingua franca of the Empire – anyway of the Eastern Empire, but to a large extent, as inscriptions testify, of Rome itself. To be able to write and converse in Greek was essential for any kind of trade or communication. When Jesus and his rustic friends went into a Hellenistic city such as Tiberias or Sepphoris they could probably sell fish in pidgin Greek, but there is no reason to suppose that it was a language in which they were intelligently conversant. It was Paul's first language and, though he spoke and wrote in *koine* (the common Greek rather than the classical language of Thucydides or Plato), he was therefore immediately, and by the simple virtue of the language he spoke, part of the great world, at one with Plato, Homer, Euripides and Sophocles even if he did not read them, in a way that Jesus never was and never aspired to be. Paul was not a peasant. He wrote with a vigorous and very distinctive Greek prose style. Any history of Greek literature which omitted him would be an incomplete work. 'He is certainly one of the great figures in Greek literature'; 'a classic of Hellenism' – these are not extravagant judgements, nor were they made by Christians.[11] Paul thought in Greek. He wrote in Greek. Together with Philo of Alexandria, he is the great conduit through which Jewish concepts and stories and patterns of thought came to the Gentile world. As these ideas came through the channel, they passed into a new intellectual world; the attempt to translate Hebrew ideas into a Gentile setting, above all a Greek setting, meant using words either with new senses or with great boldness.

[10] Wilfred Cantwell Smith, *The Meaning and End of Religion* (1978), p. 72, quoted by Don Cupitt, *After All*.
[11] Gilbert Murray and Ulrich von Wilamowitz respectively, quoted by F. F. Bruce, *Paul: Apostle of the Free Spirit*, p. 1.

Jesus could have been speaking of the art of translation (but was not) when he said that if you put old wine into new wineskins, they would burst. Even if we reject the idea of Paul's Roman citizenship, he was, as a Greek speaker, the inhabitant of a universe infinitely larger than that of the Aramaic-speaking Jesus of Nazareth.

The tutor of the future emperor Augustus, Athenodorus, became the governor of Tarsus and instituted reforms. During this period, the lifetime of Saul's parents, Roman citizenship could be purchased for 500 drachmae – the equivalent of two years' wages for the average day labourer.

We read in Acts that Paul was a tentmaker, and it would seem likely that in this he followed his father's trade. If Paul's father, or grandfather, bought citizenship, he must have been a man of some substance. Tents in the ancient world, where inns were filthy or non-existent, were for the wealthy, or, more commonly, for the Roman legions on the march. It would seem reasonable to accept the speculation of those scholars who have suggested that the tents on which Paul's fortunes were founded were no flimsy camping equipment but the huge and extremely expensive gear used by the legions for their winter quarters. Over ten Roman square feet in capacity, they housed eight men. Pieces of tent leather unearthed in this century at Newstead, Birdoswald and Valkenburg are variously identified as goat or calf (not pig). It would therefore have been possible for a Jew to have carried out the trade of tanning and tentmaking without infringing the sacred requirements of religion. The tents were rolled into huge sausage-shapes and carried by the soldiers on mules or ponies.[12]

The Acts of the Apostles tells us that Paul was born a Roman citizen, that is, that his parents had this privilege. Perhaps they were granted this privilege in exchange for helping Antonius with providing winter quarters for his troops. If Paul was a citizen, then he would have borne a Roman name, or rather the three names (*tria nomina*) to which such privileged status entitled him. Only guesswork could supply what these names were. The name Paulus, which means small, would probably have been his cognomen, an allusion to his size. (How else could he fit in the basket by which he escaped down the walls of Damascus?) Since it was Julius and Augustus who had enfranchised the citizens of Tarsus before Paul's birth, some recognition of this

---

[12] G. Webster, *The Roman Imperial Army of the First and Second Centuries AD*, p. 167.

might have been shown in his name, which could well have been Gaius Iulius Paulus. It should be noted, however, that by the time of the early Empire, when Paul was born, the *tria nomina* were being reduced to two names, and that in the cases of individuals who had some ethnic or localized name, this might be used in addition to the formal Roman name. In the Jewish catacombs in Rome, for example, we find the epitaphs are written in either Latin or Greek. Most of the names are single names with the addition of a *supernomen* or sobriquet. The formula would seem to have been 'x *and* y' or 'x *called* y'; and this seems to have been the pattern of New Testament names: Simeon called Niger (Acts 13:1), Jesus called Justus (Colossians 4:11) etc. So Paul of Tarsus would, among his Jewish coreligionists, perhaps have been known as Paul and Saul (*Paolos kai Saolos*).

That is to assume that he was a Jew.

It is a question which might seem surprising and indeed impertinent, considering the passages of autobiography with which Paul fills his letters, and in which he attests not merely his Jewishness but his ultra-Jewishness, if there is such a thing. Writing to his fellow-believers in Philippi, for example, he went out of his way to assert that he was 'circumcised on the eighth day, a member of the people of Israel, of the tribe of Benjamin, a Hebrew born of Hebrews' (Philippians 3:5).[13]

It would seem eccentric at this period of Roman history to boast about being Jewish unless you were Jewish. From the period when Cicero had contemptuously dismissed the Jews as 'a nation born to servitude' (*nationibus nati servituti*) the Jews and the Romans had enjoyed a relationship which could be viewed as rocky. Paul writes these boasts ten years after Claudius has banished Jews (albeit temporarily) from Rome, and ten years before a bloody war between Jews and Romans. For all the enthusiasm which the Gentile 'god-fearers' might have felt for the religious traditions of Israel, to boast about being a Jew was a sign that, if nothing else, Paul was a man who liked living dangerously.

Modern Jewish scholars are puzzled, however – and some are more than puzzled, they are enraged – by Paul's further claims that he underwent a thorough rabbinic training in the Pharisaic schools; 'as to the law a Pharisee'.[14]

If such a claim is true, how does it come about that he appears to have read the Scriptures, not in Hebrew, as any rabbinic scholar would

---

[13] He repeats the claim in Romans 11:1, and 2 Corinthians 11:22.
[14] Philippians 3:5.

have done, but in the Greek translation known as the Septuagint (hereafter, LXX)?[15] Or are we asking this question too rigidly from the perspective of modern Jewish scholarship, schooled in the traditions of rabbinic Judaism, which might in a prickly way wish to exclude Paul but would not wish to exclude the greatest Jewish philosopher of the ancient world, Philo, who read the Bible in Greek, and who, as far as we can infer, barely even knew Hebrew?

As we have seen, Paul's profession of tentmaker is not strictly speaking forbidden to a Jew, but the texts written by rabbis only a few hundred years later suggest that, if not actually incompatible with Judaism, tentmaking was a questionable activity for the devout. Tanning leather, even the leather of animals that were not pigs, was forbidden to Jews, and there would have been a risk of uncleanness in the very trade in which Paul made his living. In the Mishnah we read the story of a tanner who died and left a brother, who was also a tanner. 'The sages held that his (childless) widow had a right to plead, Thy brother I could bear but I cannot bear thee, and so in this case the woman might refuse to marry her husband's brother.' If a Jewish man became a tanner, this constituted grounds for his wife to divorce him, an understandable provision since, as well as contracting corpse impurity, the tanner would presumably have been very smelly. It is interesting that Peter should visit a tanner, shortly before his 'conversion' in Acts[16] to the idea that Gentiles should be admitted to the congregations of Israel, and that the dietary laws are not important.

Certainly, if we were to take a purist view of things, Paul would seem to have been a very strange sort of Jew. But it would be a mistake to forget the words of a wise scholar who wrote, 'Paul's Letters are *sui generis* for the simple reason that he was a very unusual person and we know of nobody remotely like him.'[17]

The difficulty arises from two facts: one is that the sources we possess

---

[15] Ptolemy Philadelphus (285–246 BC) ordered a Greek translation of the Hebrew Scriptures for the great library at Alexandria and commissioned 70 scholars for the work. (Hence, Septuagint, or 'the seventy'.) It was believed that the translation was made under divine guidance and the words of the LXX were as sacred to Jews as those of their Hebrew original. In fact, the translations, if dictated by the Almighty, were not all done at once, and there are many variants. James Barr, 'Paul and the LXX. A Note on Some Recent Work', in *JTS*, 45 (1994), pp. 593–601, expounds the difficulty of establishing which text(s) of LXX Paul actually read.
[16] If Paul's account of the quarrel with Peter is true then Luke's account in Acts of Peter's 'conversion' to a non-kosher diet can be dismissed as fiction.
[17] Henry Chadwick, *The Enigma of Paul*, p. 19.

are few. The other is, that, though some of those sources were composed before the destruction of Jerusalem in AD 70, we have no means of guessing what other sources must have been destroyed during that conflict.

Only a few decades ago, scholars, both Jewish and Christian, felt confident to pronounce about the 'Jewishness' or otherwise of certain New Testament writings. The Fourth Gospel, for example, with its great myths of a conflict between Light and Darkness, and its identification of Jesus with the Eternal Logos was clearly 'Hellenistic'. But Philo of Alexandria, a Hellenised Jew contemporary with Paul, spoke of the Divine Logos. And after the discovery of the Dead Sea Scrolls, we found that there were other Jews, contemporary with the First Christians, who spoke in terms of the Light/Dark cosmology and conflict. The more that twentieth-century scholarship has been able to uncover, the clearer it becomes that there were many 'Judaisms' flourishing in Palestine before AD 70. The destruction of Jerusalem must have led to the elimination of most of the evidence, and it is only prodigious archaeological strokes of luck, such as the discovery of the Scrolls at Qumran, which give us an inkling of that variety.

Generalisation is, however, inescapable if one is to say anything; and if one bears in mind the hazardous nature of generalisation, one could say that only two strands of 'Judaism' were sufficiently vigorous to survive the destruction: Pharisaism and Christianity. The discovery of how much they had in common, why they fell into conflict, and why Christianity chose to demonise the Pharisees has been one of the great achievements of twentieth-century scholarship. Pharisaism evolved into the rabbinic Judaism which produced the great literature of the Talmud and the Mishnah. Christianity developed along its own distinctive lines.

But, as we know from the survival of that sect called the Ebionites, there were other Judaisms, other Christianities, and because they have been eliminated, or all but eliminated, we do not take account of them. History is written by the victors. The religion of the Ebionites can be discovered from reading the letter of James in the New Testament. They were Jewish Christians, based in Jerusalem, and in the early years of Christianity, before the eruption on to the scene of Paul, it could be said that the Ebionites represented the mainstream Christian view − not that the word Christian was applied to them. Jesus's brother James was their leader, and we can assume that other members of Jesus's family belonged to this sect; hence, perhaps, the fact that the Gospels (written by Christians hostile to the Ebionites) represent Jesus as perpetually at odds with his family. Snatches of 'Ebionite' teaching survive, willy nilly, in the pages of the Acts of the Apostles. It is they who form the Jerusalem 'Church', who in Acts chapter 15 have a debate with Paul about whether Gentiles can be admitted to the 'Church'. The account given here must be a gross distortion of what, if anything, actually happened in history. But even Luke, with his pro–Paul bias and his ignorance of Jewish religious views and customs, registers the fact that these, the first followers of Jesus, see no need to admit Gentiles into the 'Church'. Of course, the whole notion of there having been a 'Church' at that date is itself an anachronism. The first followers of Jesus were Jews who worshipped in the Temple. (Again, this is information which we owe to Luke.) The Ebionites did not believe that Jesus was a divine being, or that he had been born of a virgin – they were his brothers and sisters, who knew that he was a fully human being and that he was an observant and devout Jew. They thought of him as a great prophet, who had come to tell the Jews that the End of Days was at hand. It is difficult to tell whether they believed in the Resurrection of Jesus as something which had already happened or whether it was something which would happen, when he arose to lead his faithful (Jewish) followers to behold a new heaven and a new earth in a rule of Holy Ones in the New Jerusalem. But they almost certainly did believe that Jesus, in the likeness of Daniel's Son of Man, would return on the clouds when the time was ripe to greet his true-believing followers. After the destruction of Jerusalem, most of the 'Ebionites' or 'Nazarenes' were destroyed also. Some, however, survived, into the Christian centuries, when they understandably fell foul of those Gentiles who were preaching a quite different message – that Jesus was a Saviour-God who had condescended to visit the earth to redeem the Gentiles and abolish Judaism. This distortion of the original message of Jesus by the Gentile Church was something for which the Ebionites directly blamed Paul.

The Israeli scholar Shlomo Pines has established that in a tenth-century Arabic manuscript at Istanbul, the work of 'Abd al-Jabbar, there is an interpolation of work from a fifth-century 'Jewish Christian' source – that is, from the work of the Ebionites. According to this source, Paul's Christianity was little more than 'Romanism'. He did not convert Romans into Christians; rather, he converted Christians into Romans. The writer even blames Paul himself for the destruction of the temple at Jerusalem.

It is not until the fourth century, in a writer called Epiphanius, that we come across references to what the Ebionites thought about Paul, so our evidence comes 300 years old. Since the Ebionites had every reason to hate Paul, it is necessary for the modern reader to take this judgement with a pinch of salt. Epiphanius, himself orthodox, informs us of the Ebionite 'heresy' that the Holy Apostle Paul was not a Jew at all, but a Greek who went up to Jerusalem for the purpose of marrying the daughter of a priest. In order to get his girl, he underwent circumcision and became a Jewish convert. Then, when he failed to get the girl, he flew into a rage and wrote against circumcision and against the Sabbath and the Law.[18]

Guided by these historical hints, the modern Jewish scholar Hyam Maccoby has advanced the theory that the Ebionites might have been right. In the very period when Christian scholars are beginning to appreciate how necessary it is for them to understand Paul's Jewish roots, before they can hope to understand Paul,[19] Maccoby upsets the applecart and asserts that Paul was probably not a proper Jew at all. 'Instead of the respectable Pharisee of unimpeachable Jewish descent, the friend and peer of James and Peter, we can sense through Epiphanius's garbled account something of the real Paul – the tormented adventurer, threading his way by guile through a series of stormy episodes, and setting up a form of religion that was his own individual creation.'[20]

No student of the subject can afford to neglect Hyam Maccoby's book.[21] Even if one were to concede that Maccoby's theories are right in every particular, however, there is one highly puzzling factor which does not entirely make sense of this picture of Paul as a goy interloper wishing to destroy Judaism. It is this. All the evidence we possess – and we are able only to use this evidence as intelligently as we can, conceding that it may mislead – is that Paul's custom was to attempt to preach his Gospel in the synagogues of the Mediterranean. The other Christians too, even those who did not necessarily have anything to do with Paul, such as the author of the Fourth Gospel, speak of a confrontation within the synagogues. The Jesus of the Fourth Gospel tells his followers that they will be thrown out of the synagogues, not

[18] Epiphanius, *Panarion*, 30, 16, 6–9.
[19] e.g. E. P. Sanders, *Paul and Palestinian Judaism*, or W. D. Davies, *Paul and Rabbinic Judaism*.
[20] Hyam Maccoby, *The Mythmaker*, p. 183.
[21] See also Hyam Maccoby, *Paul and Hellenism*.

that they will throw the Jews out of their own, newly-created Christian assemblies. Paul boasts that he was punished for heresy by his fellow–Jews – being beaten with thirty-nine strokes no less than five times.[22] If you dismiss this testimony as a lie, then you must logically dismiss all Paul's letters as fantasies which are incapable of yielding any historical information whatsoever. That is a point of view. But, as it stands, the claim that Paul was prepared to entreat his fellows in the synagogue to understand him, at the risk of dreadful floggings, suggests a profound involvement with Judaism which he was unwilling to forsake. No Jew, whether a 'Jewish Christian' such as Jesus's brothers or the Ebionites, or a twentieth-century scholar who has witnessed the calamitous consequences of Christian anti-semitism in our own memories, can view Paul with detachment. And though I have known Jews who have amusingly described Paul's religion to me as 'Judaism for export' there is a natural Jewish hostility to Paul as the greatest cuckoo in the nest in the history of the Jewish race. But as far as his religious history is concerned, it begins, even if it does not end, within the bosom of Jewry.

[22] 2 Corinthians 11:24.

III

JERUSALEM

ARRAIGNED FOR STARTING a riot, and for trying to take Greeks – that is non-Jews – into the temple in the year 57, Paul is reported to have said, 'I am a Jew, born in Tarsus in Cilicia, but brought up in this city' – that is, Jerusalem –'at the feet of Gamaliel, educated strictly according to our ancestral law.'[1]

The conflicts which are observable in almost every page of Paul's writings, between the broad experience of the Hellenised Mediterranean world and the obligations incumbent on anyone professing a belief in a revealed religion, are not necessarily to be sought in Paul's psyche, interesting and tormented as that must have been. They could be seen in Jerusalem itself, one of the most splendid and one of the most 'Hellenised' of all the cities in the ancient world. We see the Jews as a people who have been subjected to genocide in the twentieth century, persecuted in the name of Christ for twenty centuries in between and defeated by the Romans in a glorious but calamitous patriotic war in AD 70. Judaism has very understandably been embattled for two millennia; for without a stockade built around itself, it would not have been able, so heroically, to survive. The siege mentality of Judaism, undoubtedly there in the writings of the Qumran sect and in the heroics of the Maccabees,[2] for example, was not the whole story in the reign of King Herod (known as the Great) and his descendants. The invasion of Palestine, by Greeks and Seleucids and Romans, had caused outrage among Jewish patriots, but it had also brought the Jews into contact with a world from which they drew

[1] Acts 22:3.
[2] Even of the Maccabees, a modern scholar can write:'The emergent Jewish state differed little, in broad political outline, from those of Parthia or Armenia. Even the monotheistic religious ideology underpinning Judas Maccabeus's resistance movement had a more or less exact precedent in the priestly opposition to Alexander the Great maintained by the Persian Magi, in the name of the one God Ahara Mazda.' Peter Green, *Alexander to Actium: The Hellenistic Age*, p. 499.

much and to which they gave much. Post Masada, post 1900 years of persecutions, exiles and pogroms, post the Holocaust, post the embattled State of Israel and the last 45 years of history in the Middle East, it is difficult to think back to a world where the Jews were more like the rest of us than their own self-mythologising would want them to believe. To read many Christian scholars of the nineteenth and twentieth centuries, equally, you would think that Judaism was a single fixed theological position, defended by bigots and concerned wholly with trivial matters, such as whether eating-vessels are unclean or whether it is lawful in the eyes of the Almighty to eat shrimps. This is a travesty of Judaism, pre- or post-destruction of the temple, and if in its brightest luminaries, such as Jesus or Gamaliel, Judaism were such an Alice-in-Wonderland affair it would not be believable that so many thousands of Gentiles – including the empress Poppaea herself – should have been drawn to its fund of riches and spiritual teaching; nor would it be comprehensible that the grandest synagogues of the Mediter-ranean world, in Ephesus for example or in Rome, had large seating arrangements for the sympathetic 'god-fearers'. Christians like to think of Jesus as a man, or a God-man, who abolished Judaism and who quarrelled with the Pharisees because they were trying to make true spiritual religion into a matter of laws and regulations. Even a slight acquaintance with the actual teachings of the Pharisees shows that this was a grotesque misjudgement and that the Pharisees were teachers, such as Jesus himself, who believed that the teachings of the Jewish Scriptures were not a dead letter, written in stone, but a divinely-given insight into how to live, written in the heart; a teaching which applied in a vibrant and relevant way to the everyday lives not merely of Jews but also of Gentiles. It was, as even the Gospel of Matthew tells us,[3] the Pharisees who were the missionaries, the proselytisers of the Jewish world. If a charge of 'narrowness' can be brought in the conflict between 'church' and synagogue, one would have to say that the Christians seem in almost all cases to be the bigots and the Jews the more broadminded. (Compare the views of the Early Church Fathers and those of the rabbinic literature on such subjects as eating, military service or sex.) But the idea of a separation between two religions – Christianity and Judaism – is totally anachronistic and should, if it is possible, be forgotten for at least the first half of this book. Jesus did not come to start a 'new religion' and nor, exactly

[3] Matthew 23:15.

speaking, did Paul, though a new religion came about partly as a result of Paul's endeavours.

Throwing off, then, the sense of the Jewish religion as something which is in all circumstances defensive and inward-looking and suspicious of the Gentile world, and realising that it is, and was, something rather different – a calling to understand the will of the Almighty in a culturally diverse world – let us return to the city of Jerusalem as Paul might first have seen it when he went there as a boy or a young man in (what?) the 20s of the first century.

'Easily the most outstanding city of the east,' according to Pliny the Elder.[4] By the time Herod the Great (73–4 BC) had rebuilt it, one can see why it became one of the great tourist attractions of the Mediterranean world and why Gentiles poured in to it to see its hippodrome, its aqueducts, its palaces. There was an amphitheatre just outside the city where the shows rivalled those of Rome itself, with athletic contests and gladiatorial combats. Foreign visitors were excited and delighted by naked wrestling, the races and the fights between men and beasts, even though they offended the sensibilities of some Jews.

Herod, an Arab from the southern Palestinian province of Idumea, was one of the great builders of the ancient world. The prodigious desert fortress of Masada, whose name has been synonymous with Jewish patriotism, was actually built by Herod as a refuge against his Jewish subjects, many of whom had reason to hate him. Anyone who has struggled up the 2,000 feet in broiling sunlight to the ruins of this structure will have wondered how, even in the days of slave labour, so vast an edifice could have been constructed so ingeniously in the rock face at such a height. The great seaport of Caesarea had been splendidly rebuilt by Herod, with its astonishing harbour. As at Masada, one feels that Herod could overcome Nature itself, this time by building an artificial harbour. 'Notwithstanding the totally recalcitrant nature of the site, he grappled with the difficulties so successfully, that the solidity of his masonry defied the sea while its beauty was such as if no obstacle had existed.'[5]

As a client-king of the Romans, who had been given the governorship of the Jewish race as a reward for his loyalty, toadyism, call it what you will, it was not surprising that Herod should have named this harbour Caesarea. Though nominally a convert to Judaism, he

[4] HN, V, 70.
[5] Josephus, *BJ*, I, 411.

was eclectic in his religious tastes; in Sebaste (modern Sebastiyeh) in Samaria, he built a magnificent temple to celebrate the divinity of that bank manager's grandson, the emperor Augustus, a superb Corinthian affair with twenty-four steps leading up to the altar of the Divine Emperor, whose statue was its focal point. In addition to his palace in Caesarea and his fortress at Masada, this Arab genius built the most superb of palaces in Jerusalem, named this time after his hero Marcus Antonius.

The Antonia was, as has been rightly said by the most engaging of all modern historians of Herod,[6] like the Tower of London, 'a fortress, a palace and a prison'. It was, however, much larger than the White Tower in London. Its southern front was 375 feet long, about the same as Buckingham Palace. Its three towers rose up from a massive building which contained the great pavement, or Gabbatha, used by Pilate as a Hall of Judgement from which Jesus was led away to be crucified in the year 30 or thereabouts. The interior was encrusted with rare and costly marbles, and the rooms of the Antonia were filled with magnificent paintings and statues. Silver and gold was everywhere. On the outside the visitor would have been delighted to see porticoes surrounded by carved pillars. Fountains played and bright patches of green lawn and shady groves were watered by the ingenious aqueducts which Herod had constructed.

But if Jerusalem amazed by its beauty and magnificence, the greatest and most splendid building in its midst was unquestionably Herod's temple. The old temple, which had been a restoration built from the ruins of Solomon's temple after the Babylonian exile, had been largely rebuilt by Herod in 20 BC. This was not just a question of rebuilding a single edifice. 'The temple' was contained within a huge complex of courts, cloisters and outer buildings, all of which Herod embellished on a huge scale. Jesus's followers were not the only visitors to Herod's temple to exclaim, 'What large stones and what large buildings!'[7] The size of these perfectly cut stones can astonish a twentieth-century visitor who has seen the Manhattan skyline just as it amazed the rustic Palestinian Jews of the first century.

Herod's motives for building this stupendous monument to the Jewish faith were no doubt mixed up with a love of self-aggrandisement and with that peculiar form of compulsion or egomania which

---

[6] Stewart Perowne, *The Life and Times of Herod the Great.*
[7] Mark 13:1.

makes some rulers – the emperor Hadrian, or Louis XIV, or Stalin, for example – into obsessive builders. But he also wished to placate his Jewish subjects and to show that whatever tributes he might offer to Caesar they were as nothing to the tribute which he paid to the Unnamed and Ineffable God of Israel.

He constructed his temple, therefore, on the same holy site as its predecessors, that is to say on a platform at the highest point of the hill now occupied in Jerusalem by the Dome of the Rock. The construction of the temple proper had to follow the dimensions of Solomon's temple, so that the central part of the building was a tall, T-shaped structure with the sanctuary and the Holy of Holies running east–west to form an upright and an enormous flat porch with the façade 150 feet square across the eastern end as the horizontal. This part of the temple was so holy that the masons at work on it had to be consecrated as priests. Architecturally, it was an oddity, though one of the most splendid oddities ever constructed. Herod would probably have preferred to redesign the temple of Yahweh as he had built the temple of Augustus at Sebaste, on purely Grecian lines, but the religious Jews would never have tolerated this. Herod concentrated his creative efforts on lavish embellishments of the temple building, and a splendour in the enclosures and surrounding courts which quickly established this building as something which men and women would cross the world to see. The doors of the temple were of a size which beggared belief, surmounted with a golden vine, with grape clusters as big as a man. The inner walls were hung with enormous Babylonian tapestry. The outer walls were white marble, plated with gold so that the pilgrims and sightseers, as they approached the city from the main road, from the south, would look up and see it gleaming on the hill like something which had come down from heaven itself. It seemed to such travellers, if they arrived at the right time of day when the sun was catching the solid gold embellishments of these outer buildings, as if the city was all of gold.

The building work continued long after Herod's death in 4 BC. It was still in progress thirty years later during the adult lifetime of Jesus; and it had barely been finished before the Romans levelled it to the ground.

But this enormous building, built by a man who was not born a Jew, and so attractive to Gentiles of all nations that they came in their thousands to see it, embodied the paradox of Judaism at this date. On the one hand, like the gilded temple on the hill, the Jews saw themselves as the conscience of the human race, a light to lighten the Gentiles. But on the other hand, having lured the Gentile tourist to the very courts of the temple, they confronted him, or her, with this inscription: 'Let no Gentile enter within the balustrade and enclosure about the holy place and whosoever is caught shall be responsible to himself because death follows.'[8] The sanctity of the temple was taken very seriously indeed, both by Jews and by their Roman overlords. Pompey had violated, by the mere act of entry, the old temple in 65 BC, when he invaded Palestine and began that fateful century-long Roman occupation which would change the history of the world. He set foot, as no Gentile could possibly do without defiling it, into the Holy of Holies itself and was amazed to discover that it was empty. Subsequent generations of Romans had been more sensitive, and there are cases of Roman soldiers who failed to obey the inscription and strayed beyond the outer court being put to death.

Jesus is said to have exclaimed in exasperation, 'My house shall be called a house of prayer for all the nations. But you have made it a den of robbers.'[9] Many Jews, particularly the Pharisees, could have echoed these words in Herod's temple. For this was not the temple of Solomon, the temple 'not built with hands'; and those Jews who looked for the fulfilment of the Messianic promise expected, as some of them still do, that Solomon's temple would miraculously be reconstructed on its old site. (Hence the claims put into the mouth of Jesus by the Evangelists, that the temple of Herod will be replaced in three days with a new temple.)

The paradoxes embodied by the temple of Herod would be felt by any Jew, whether one who stressed the exclusive or one who stressed the universal aspect of the Jewish faith. For here was a building which attracted pilgrims from all nations, but which shut out anyone who was not a Jew. And here was a building which proclaimed the moral and religious superiority of the Chosen Race to all other nations, but which had been built for them by an ambitious Arab with money from the Romans. In what, then, did the uniqueness of the Jewish people, the Jewish religion, consist? How could it both live in the Gentile world and not be of the Gentile world? Was it hugging to itself tribal taboos and arcane rites which were kept hidden from the eyes of the uninitiated? Or was it uniquely privileged to know the

[8] Now in the Istanbul Museum.
[9] Mark 11:17.

teachings of the great God Yahweh which were entrusted to Moses on Sinai, not for the instruction of the Chosen Seed alone, but for the entire human race?

These paradoxes, from which the religious thought and heroic life of Paul of Tarsus were to be born, are all to be seen in that great gleaming marble and gold edifice which stood on the top of the hill as the visitor approached Jerusalem.

The outer court – called by modern archaeologists the court of the Gentiles – was surrounded by a continuous colonnade of lofty Corinthian columns with carved cedar-wood ceilings. These would have provided visual delight to the visitor, as would the aqueduct (water came from Jericho ten miles away, and, to satisfy the priests, the water in this aqueduct was for the exclusive use of the temple functionaries). Standing in this courtyard the visitor could look southwards through a huge royal portico, and see the monumental stairway which led down to a broad street that ran along the foot of the western wall. A curious Gentile, however, would have felt a peculiar fascination with the inner courts, which were meant for the Jews only.[10]

Had he been brave or foolish enough to risk death by breaking the taboo, and to visit the temple itself, what would the Gentile visitor have seen? He would have found a large, functioning religious edifice whose life and customs were largely familiar. The similarities between this temple and any other temple in the Mediterranean world would have greatly outnumbered the differences. Perhaps one of the secrets which the Jews wished to guard from the Gentile world was that their temple, and their method of appeasing the wrath or disapproval of the deity, was much like anyone else's. The primary function of a temple was religious sacrifice; the secondary function was purification.

The ancient rituals of the 'olah' – the matutinal and evening slaughter of lambs, bullocks and rams – may be read in the book of Numbers.[11] It continues to form part of the morning prayer in the synagogue; and modern Jews continue to rehearse in punctilious detail the rubrics of slaughter for a temple which was destroyed over 1900 years ago. It is questionable whether these animal holocausts took place as frequently in the temple of Herod as they had done during the days

[10] For all the above, see E. Mary Smallwood, *The Jews Under Roman Rule*, pp. 93–7; Kathleen Kenyon, *Jerusalem*; A. H. M. Jones, *The Herods of Judaea*.
[11] Numbers 28:1–15.

of Solomon;[12] but there would certainly have been plenty of thanks-offerings made of doves and lambs during the purification rituals – we read of these at several points in the Gospels – and at the Pesach (Passover) lambs would have been slaughtered here on a prodigious scale.

The Gentile of Paul's day who came to the outer court of the temple and saw the Jews buying their animals to be killed inside the sacred precincts would have seen nothing strange. The same sort of rituals would have been performed in temples of Jupiter or temples of Apollo all over the ancient world. You paid some money, you took an animal to the priest, who killed it in accordance with a formula; your duty was done; the god was satisfied. In all temples, rites were offered to atone for human sin or to cleanse human impurity; in all temples, as in the Jewish temple, thanksgiving (in Greek, eucharist) was made by rites and cults devised by the priestly hierarchy. An observant Gentile, if he penetrated the Jewish temple area and witnessed any of the animal offerings, would perhaps have noted the Jewish abhorrence of blood-consumption. Whereas, for example, in a temple of Mithras, the faithful would be encouraged to drink the blood of the slaughtered bullock, the Jews would be merely sprinkled with the blood of lambs in order, for example, to cleanse them from the impurity ensuing from having accidentally touched a dead cow, or from having given birth.

The temple, for all its marble and gold, was really a magnificently constructed abattoir designed to ease, and ritualise, relations between humanity and the Unseen.

Many Christians are under the impression that the temple occupied a comparable position in the Jewish religion to the Vatican in the Roman Catholic Church, and that the high priest was a figure like the Pope to whom all his coreligionists looked as a Father in God. In Paul's lifetime, this was not really the case. The temple was indeed under the jurisdiction of the high priest, and the hierarchy of priests and Levites was largely drawn from the Sadducee party within Judaism, who in turn made up the bulk of the Jewish administrative assembly or Sanhedrin. But far from being revered by all the Jews who came to the temple to worship, the high priest was regarded with a mixture of distrust and open hostility. Just as the temple was not Solomon's temple but a showy replacement built by a hated Arab client-king; so the

[12] Royden Keith Yerkes, *Sacrifice in Greek and Roman Religions and Early Judaism*, p. 145.

high priest was appointed by the Romans, and in the period following the death of Herod the Great he was in effect a client ruler exercising power on behalf of the Empire. Many Jewish patriots would have taken part in the worship of the temple for religious reasons, but would have considered their integrity compromised if they had entered into the service of the high priest. It was the high priest, for example, who was responsible for maintaining discipline in the temple at festival times, and he had to answer for it to the Romans if there was any public unrest or demonstration. The high priest's guard had the authority to arrest any patriotic troublemakers and to hand them over to the Romans for punishment or execution; and this is in all probability what happened to Jesus after he had caused a demonstration in the outer court of the temple, at Passover time in the year 30.

There were many Jews who did not regard the high priest, nor the Sadducees, as truly representative of the prophetic traditions of Israel; and it was not merely a matter of political stubbornness which made them view the high priests with distrust. Most Jews did not belong to any of the parties or groups within Judaism who have been named Sadducee (the conservative group from whom the high priests and the bulk of the Sanhedrin, or assembly, were generally drawn), Pharisee (the missionaries and educators) or Essene (ascetics). Between the Sadducees and the Pharisees there were profound religious differences in their entire attitude to the Torah – that sacred Jewish word which is so misleadingly translated, in the Greek version of the Scriptures, as *Nomos*, and so, into English, as *Law*.[13] It is hard for us, nineteen hundred years after its destruction, to realise that, outside the heart of each individual Jew, and his home and meal-table on the Sabbath, the temple is the *only* Jewish place of worship (hence the significance to modern Jews of the Western Wall of Solomon's temple); and that synagogues are schools or meeting-places which are in no way the equivalent of Christian churches. The Judaism which would be expounded by the rituals of the temple and the teachings of the Sadducean temple-priests would be very different from the Judaism of the synagogues.

Torah means teaching, at first any kind of teaching given to anyone by anyone else, but more particularly teaching given by God to the human race. For the Sadducees, the Torah was something which had been given on Sinai when Moses was told the teachings of the Lord.

[13] R. Travers Herford, *Judaism in the New Testament Period.*

The obligation of the Jew was fulfilled if he held to these teachings and if he observed the ritual requirements of him in the temple, and in particular the annual pilgrimage to Jerusalem at the time of Pesach.

For the Pharisee, however, each individual should imagine *himself* in the divine presence on the Holy Mountain where the Torah was first delivered. (So sacred and so immediate was the Pharisees' belief in Torah that they would bless themselves with the sacred letter T, tracing it from forehead, to breast, and across from shoulder to shoulder – a custom which was understandably discarded when it was taken up by the Christians and called 'making the sign of the cross'.) Paul (in Acts) tells us that it was in this sublime and strict school that he learnt his Jewish faith.

Though the parties in Judaism were distinct, we must not think of them as separate denominations such as obtain within the modern Christian Church. A Jew could dip into and taste the wisdom of the different sects without necessarily 'belonging' to one or the other. For a Sadducee to attend a rabbinic school, run by Pharisees, was not the equivalent of a Quaker becoming a Russian Orthodox. Many Jews, for example, must have attended synagogues (many of which were dominated by Pharisees) without themselves being Pharisees. Synagogue attendance was not compulsory, however, and a serious young Jew who wished to explore his faith might prefer to spend some time in the caves of Qumran among the Essene sect. Josephus had a spell with the Essenes, though he came from an upper-class priestly (Sadducee) family. He also attended the Pharisaic schools.[14]

Such schools were plentiful in Jerusalem. We can not know exactly what was taught in them. After the fall of Jerusalem, it was the Pharisees, in their schools and synagogues throughout the Diaspora, who ensured the continuity of Judaism as a religion. They were the spiritual ancestors of the rabbinic authors of the Talmud. But all the rabbinic writings we possess come from the third century or later; and although much of what they wrote is probably based on very old traditions, and can give us some clue about the nature of rabbinic or Pharisaic thought in the first century, there is a danger of anachronism if we make too many assumptions. No one would try to draw an accurate picture of the eighteenth-century Christian Church by

[14] 'I thought that after a thorough investigation I should be in a position to select the best. So I submitted myself to hard training and many exercises and passed through the three courses.' *Vita*, 422.

reading books or newspaper articles by twentieth-century Christians. 'We cannot transfer the reports about the teachers, the "rabbis", which have been handed down to us in written sources beginning in the third century directly and without further reflection to the Pharisaic school in Jerusalem at the start of our era.'[15]

In the Acts of the Apostles we read of the family and followers of Jesus forming themselves into a cell, or cells, to share a common life and to expound the Teachings in the light of their religious experiences. We learn that they were an exclusive sect even within Judaism – 'no one from outside their number venturing to join with them' even when they met in the temple precincts.[16] There were probably many such sects or holy assemblies. (The Greek word *ecclesia*, translated as church, like the Greek word *synagogue*, simply means an assembly or a congregation.)

Like Jesus's companions, the Pharisees formed close communities. They were members of a religious association to fulfil their interpretation of the Law.[17] Nor were these groups restricted to Palestinian Jews. A Greek inscription found in Jerusalem and probably dating from the late 60s reads, 'Theodotus, son of Vettenius, priest and archsynagogus, son of an archsynagogus, grandson of an archsynagogus, built the synagogue for the reading of the Torah and instruction in the commandments, also the lodging, the guest room and the water-system to provide for those in need coming from abroad. The foundation stone was laid by his fathers, the elders and Simonides.' Vettenius is a name which suggests a Roman origin. Since the inscription is in Greek, we can safely assume that the expounding of the Scriptures, if not the very Scriptures themselves, were, in this particular cell, in Greek. Paul, whose first language was Greek, would perhaps have been educated in such a place. Probably, the common pattern of Jewish education which we find in later centuries would have been pursued with the young men who attended such an informal 'academy' – the Jewish equivalent of the Greek 'triad': Gk. *sophos*/ Heb. *hakam*; Gk. *grammateus*/ Heb. *soper*, Gk. *suzetes*/ Heb. *darsan*. That is, the young man learnt to become a wise man, a scribe and a debater. In one of his letters, written much later in life,[18] Paul alludes to this 'triad': 'Where

---

[15] E. P. Sanders, *Jesus, Paul and Judaism* and *Paul, the Law and the Jewish People*.
[16] Acts 2:42; 5:13.
[17] Joachim Jeremias, *Jerusalem in the Time of Jesus*.
[18] 1 Corinthians 1:20. See Martin Hengel, *The Pre-Christian Paul*, p. 40.

is the one who is wise? Where is the scribe? Where is the debater of this age?'; and they are all designations from the Pharisaic school, the *bet midrash*. By this stage of his life, Paul has come to view this 'wisdom' as 'foolishness'; but his allusion to the threefold pattern of learning suggests that there is some truth in his claim elsewhere to have been taught as a Pharisee.

Luke claims that Paul's master was Gamaliel. The later rabbinic texts do not say much about this rabbi (known as Gamaliel I), nor about his son Simon, who would have been Paul's age. Gamaliel II (fl. 90–100) is much better known, and those critics who believe in a very late dating of Luke's writings have speculated that the portrait of Gamaliel in Acts is an anachronism, a projection into pre-70 Jerusalem of Gamaliel I's much more famous grandson.[19]

Of Gamaliel himself, we learn in the Mishnah that he was given the title 'Rabban' and that he was a leading sage, one of the great exponents in his day of the Torah.[20] In the Mishnah his opinion is given about such matters as whether a plate which has accidentally broken is clean or unclean; and whether it is allowable to cover hot food on festival days. He also gives his views on the size of bread which should be baked: 'Said Rabbi Gamaliel, "Never in my father's house did they bake large loaves, but only small ones." 'This widely-revered leader of the Pharisaic party also gave his mind to the question of whether it was permissible to use wineskins which had belonged to a Gentile, and he opined that much depended on the tear in the wineskin: 'When the tear in the hide is round, it is prohibited. If it is straight, it is permitted.'

He thought it was permissible for Jews to eat meats which had been *intended* as a sacrifice to an idol, but not meat which had in fact been sacrificed to an idol. Paul, when he came in contact with the idolatrous Corinthians in the 50s, was to address the identical question and come to very similar conclusions.

Those who look in the rabbinic texts for helpful thoughts about life or an uplifting 'philosophy' will be disappointed. What the rabbis were doing in their painstaking way was trying to see how the will of

[19] E. P. Sanders, *Jesus, Paul and Judaism.*
[20] Mishnah Fourth Division, 3:9, p. 648. The word 'Mishnah' means 'repetition' in Hebrew; hence, 'instruction'. It is a method of exegesis of Scripture. It describes the way in which exegetical material was collected in its own right, as opposed to *midrash* in which the material was attached to scriptural texts. Various collections of *mishnayot* were made, culminating in the authoritative *Mishnah* attributed to Rabbi Judah ha-Nasi (c. 135–c. 220).

God could be discovered in every detail of life. It was because they believed that the love of God was so wide that they appear so narrow – the divine interest descends even to pots and pans, just as Jesus believed the very hairs of our head are numbered. The fact that the rabbis minded – and mind – about meat, wineskins, square holes and round holes, should not allow Gentiles in their loftiness to suppose that devout Jews were or are little better than the inhabitants of Swift's Lilliput debating whether to eat boiled eggs from the Big or the Little End. These debates are not the core of the rabbis' religious faith. They are the consequence that grows out from the fundamental faith, which is found in the Torah and in the Prophets, the belief that the Universal Creator and Lawgiver had revealed himself to mankind, and called mankind to himself to worship Him and serve Him. To judge Judaism by these obscure passages in the Mishnah would be like judging Christianity by the petty rules pinned to a convent notice-board about when the novices should do the laundry. The universalist faith of the 104th Psalm, where God is seen animating, informing, enlivening and enriching all forms of terrestrial life, birds, trees, seas, land, men and mountains, underlies the apparently bizarre belief that He is fascinated with the details of domestic trivia. 'Man goeth forth unto his work, and to his labour until the evening.' There are many ways in which the later teaching of Paul diverges from that of the Pharisees; so much so, that – as we have stated – some scholars would altogether dispute his claim to have been taught by the Pharisees. But it would be a travesty of the Pharisaic and rabbinic teaching to suppose that Paul abandoned it – still more that he abandoned Judaism, which he never did! – on the grounds that it was too 'petty' and that he wished to set out on his own. His cavalier attitude to the details of Pharisaic teaching did not derive from a 'modern' notion that such things do not matter; and of his surviving writings, a substantial part is in fact devoted to questions such as eating, drinking, haircuts, head-covering and sexual intercourse – humdrum or private matters for the rest of the human race, but very much up the street of the rabbis.

Considering the fact that Luke wrote in order to impress the Romans and to reassure them that the Jews were the real troublemakers in the Empire, not the Christians, he gives a remarkably generous press to Gamaliel in the Acts of the Apostles. When the high priest has the friends of Jesus arrested as potential troublemakers, it is Gamaliel the Pharisee who speaks in their defence.

'Then he said to them, "Fellow Israelites, consider carefully what you propose to do to these men. For some time ago Theudas rose up, claiming to be somebody, and a number of men, about four hundred, joined him; but he was killed, and all who followed him were dispersed and disappeared. After him Judas the Galilean rose up at the time of the census and got people to follow him; he also perished, and all who followed him were scattered. So in the present case, I tell you, keep away from these men and let them alone; because if this plan or this undertaking is of human origin, it will fail; but if it is of God, you will not be able to overthrow them – in that case you may even be found fighting against God!" '[21]

We can take leave to doubt whether Gamaliel actually said these words *circa* AD 33, not least because the revolt of Theudas took place in 44–6, eleven or twelve years *after* the Rabban 'remembers' it.[22] Luke has made one of his characteristic muddles over ages, names and dates; but there is no reason to doubt that he gives a roughly accurate picture of what a leader of the Pharisees would have said in the early 30s about the followers of Jesus. Much later, in 62 when Jesus's brother was put to death by stoning at the behest of the Sadducees, it was the Pharisees who led the protest.[23] Stoning is the punishment for blasphemy, but the fact that the Pharisees defended James against the quisling Sadducean authorities shows that the motive for his death was really political. This is what makes us believe that Luke has probably retained some vestige of the truth in believing not merely that Gamaliel spoke up for the followers of Jesus, but also that he likened them not to religious visionaries but to political rebels. (Judas the Galilean inspired an anti-Roman rebellion in the year 6 when Augustus tried to depose the Galilean ethnarch Archelaus. What Gamaliel would have been saying, when he wonders whether the new Galileans are 'from God', is that they might be the instruments by which the Roman empire could be cast down.)

Given the fact that Gamaliel, even by the Christian account of Luke, is broadly on the side of Jesus's disciples, how did it come about that Gamaliel's pupil Paul first comes to our attention in Acts as a persecutor of the Christian church? This is not a question which can be ducked, but nor can it satisfactorily be answered. One merely has to leave it, and underscore it at the very beginning of the story. It is

[21] Acts 5:35–9.
[22] Josephus, *Ant*, XX, vi, 97–9.
[23] Josephus, *BJ*, XX, ix, 1.

presumably of the utmost significance, but there are simply not enough details available to the historian to enable us to make up our minds decisively about it.

We know that many of the minor employees of the temple (as opposed to the senior priestly hierarchy) were Pharisees and we also learn from Luke that the Christian movement itself began to expand within the temple: 'and a great many of the priests became obedient to the faith'.[24] If this were the case it would have been a cause of particular concern to the Sadducean authorities, to the high priests who were answerable to Rome, for they clearly believed that the new followers of Jesus were seditious. How could it not be seditious to revere as a great prophet, and more than a prophet, a rustic troublemaker who had suffered a Roman criminal's punishment, crucifixion?

And yet, we find that Paul, or Saul as he is first named in Acts,[25] appears first, not as a religious seeker, nor even as a Pharisaic disputant, but as a member of the temple police, employed by the high priest to stamp out the followers of Jesus and his 'Way'. He appears in the narrative – at the point where Stephen the Deacon is testifying to his faith in Jesus – as the young figure supervising the killing of the first 'Christian martyr'. While some passages of Acts must be disputed or discarded, this idea of Paul as a temple 'policeman' corresponds exactly to what Paul tells us himself about his career. 'I was violently persecuting the church of God and trying to destroy it.'[26] It is certainly very surprising that a Pharisee should find himself in this position; and it is hard to believe that Paul was ever a very thoroughgoing Pharisee. Only once in his letters does he claim to have been one (how much has been built on that one phrase, 'as touching the law, a Pharisee'!). More likely, Saul of Tarsus was someone, like Josephus, who attended a Pharisaic school. Unlike Josephus, he was not a priest, so what was he doing with employment in the temple?

A clue might lie in the temple itself.

We have seen that approximately 20,000 sheep were slaughtered each year at Pesach in the temple. This required a fairly intensive nurturing of sheep in the surrounding scrubby hill country. As we are reminded, 'there never was a city more unfitted than Jerusalem to be

[24] Acts 6:7.
[25] Acts 7:58.
[26] Galatians 1:13.

the home of industries.'[27] Perched on the hills in far from fertile country, and closely-inhabited hills at that, this was no place for a timber-yard or a metal-workshop, or a clay-pit and its attendant potteries, or a dyers' factory dealing in pigment. Jerusalem has never been a manufacturing city, which is why, except when artificial foreign injections of cash have come its way (as happened during the time of Herod the Great's rebuilding programme), it has always been a poor city, as it remains to this day. (Paul, after his 'conversion', devotes his energies to collecting money from his own Mediterranean converts to help out the poverty-stricken Jerusalem 'church'.) There were, however, markets in Jerusalem – horse markets, poultry markets, caravans carrying luxury imports such as pepper.[28] And one can only assume that in a city where 20,000 sheep were slaughtered in a single day there was a lively trade in sheepskin and other leathers. A useful place if you happened to make your money converting animal hides into tents. If you were also a tentmaker with a religious obsession, where better to spend some years of your youth than in Jerusalem?

The New Testament gives us the 'religious' side of Paul's life, with only the occasional glimpses into how he made his money. But in his letters he boasts of being entirely self-sufficient. If Luke's account of Paul's trial in Jerusalem is even remotely accurate we can only assume that Paul was very prosperous. Though we are taught that all Paul's journeys were 'missionary' journeys and though we are asked to view all his journeyings – he says himself that he was 'in journeyings often' – as part of a religious quest, the prosaic question asks itself: how, exactly, was his money made? Had there been a contemporary of Luke's with no interest in religion, he might well have been able to write a short book – The Acts of Paul, Commercial Traveller in Sheephide; Tentmaker By Appointment to the Imperial Army.

Such a Jew of Tarsus, having built up a smattering of learning in some Pharisaic academy, and having secured a good deal with the priests to buy so many thousand sheephides for the family business, could well have found himself involved with the pressing question of security in the Holy City.

'Paul, destined to become Jesus's most influential spokesman never

[27] George Adam Smith, *Jerusalem*, vol. 2, p. 372.
[28] Jewish Encyclopaedia I, 2.

met him.'[29] This is a succinct rehearsal of the view entertained by one of the most eminent of modern New Testament scholars.

It is strange that so many scholars, who differ about so much else, should be agreed about this paradox. Why should Paul have devoted perhaps thirty years of his life to being the 'spokesman' for a man he had never met? It does not make sense. To say that he was a spokesman is something of an understatement. As we have seen, Paul himself claims, at various points in his writings, that he has been five times flogged within an inch of his life and imprisoned for his belief in Jesus. He has undertaken innumerable hazardous journeys, more than once being shipwrecked, in order to take the name of Jesus to those who have not heard it. He writes obsessively and repeatedly, in those few writings of his which we possess, about the way in which Jesus met his death. He even, on a number of occasions, quotes the words of Jesus. One key passage where he might possibly allude to the earthly Jesus and his, Paul's, knowledge of him is ruthlessly reinterpreted by the modern translators. The Greek has '*Ei kai egnokamen kata sarka Christon, alla nun ouketi ginoskomen.*'[30] The Authorised Version translates, quite literally, 'Yea, though we have known Christ after the flesh, yet now henceforth know we [him] no more.' This translation allows Paul's original words to remain mysteriously themselves, and we can make what we will of his assertion that 'we' have known Christ 'after the flesh'. The New English Bible tells us what we should think: 'Worldly standards have ceased to count in our estimate of any man: even if once they counted in our understanding of Christ, they do so now no longer.' It is possible that this is what Paul means by saying that we once knew Christ 'after the flesh'; but it is rather typical of the modern translators that they have intruded their own interpretation into the text. If one were going to do this one could have translated it, 'though we knew Jesus when he was alive we no longer see him physically'. This would make just as good sense, when Paul then goes on to say that anyone who is 'in Christ' is a new creature. The much more accurate translation of the Jerusalem Bible is: 'Even though we did once know Christ in the flesh, that is not how we know him now.'

To assert, then, that Paul never met Jesus is to argue from a negative. True, in the surviving New Testament writings, there is no record of such a meeting, but this really does not prove anything. There are

---

[29] E. P. Sanders, *Paul*, p. 10.
[30] 2 Corinthians 5:16.

almost no 'life records' of the historical Jesus, and though there are more of Paul they are far too scanty for the purposes of a modern biographer.

But we do know that he devoted the second part of his life to proclaiming that Jesus, though Crucified, was the Messiah, and we also know that, in the earlier part of his mission at least, Paul was convinced that Jesus was going to make an imminent reappearance on to the earthly scene, bringing the present pattern of things to an end and establishing a rule of the Saints.

He must have heard such talk among Jesus's followers, the ones whom he was delegated by the 'high priests' to round up and cast into prison. If we were to summarise the beliefs of these first Jewish followers of Jesus in Jerusalem we should say that they were as follows: God has decreed that the End of Days is near; Israel is to be redeemed; the long succession of prophets and holy men in the scriptures had pointed to a coming Anointed One – Messiah; God has appointed Jesus as this Messiah; as a sign of this fact, he raised Jesus from the dead, even though, in fulfilment of prophecy, the Gentiles, that is the Romans, raged and plotted against him and put him to death with the connivance of the quisling high priests; this putting to death and rising to life were the mere prelude to the new age of hope which would dawn for Israel; Jesus had gone to heaven but he would return imminently to inaugurate the promised rule of the Saints.

It is obvious why the high priest and the leading members of the Sanhedrin should have objected to this view of the life and death of Jesus. Josephus tells us of a number of such figures who were the focus of political discontent. Any breach of the peace was the responsibility of the high priest. If the high priest with his guard did not put down such disturbances the Romans exacted reprisals: during the time of Pontius Pilate these reprisals were cruel and horrible. Much better, as with double irony the high priest remarks during Jesus's trial in the Fourth Gospel, that one man should die for the people. We find Paul, when he makes his appearance in Acts, in the hire of the high priest. It does not seem unreasonable to suppose that he was in the same position in the temple guard when Jesus was arrested.

There is no need to be fanciful about this. We do not need to reconstruct a melodramatic scene in which Saul of Tarsus is taking part in the scourging or the mockery of Jesus. But it does not seem so very unreasonable to suppose that if Paul was employed by the high priests in their 'guard' or police in the year 33, then he might have been so employed two or three years earlier at the date of Jesus's crucifixion. If he was employed by the high priest to arrest and imprison men called Stephen and Peter and John, might he not reasonably have been supposed to have taken part in the arrest and execution of Jesus, the Galilean troublemaker?

We are told by the Fourth Gospel that Jesus was arrested by the temple guard, and we are told by Luke that Paul was employed in the temple guard in some capacity.[31] One does not need to impress the point nor to insist upon it. If readers of the New Testament choose to believe that Paul never set eyes on Jesus and that he had no psychological interest or compulsion to inspire him throughout the thirty years in which he preached Jesus Christ Crucified other than the testimony of the friends of Jesus, whom he had barely met, then that reader is entitled to his or her point of view.

The accounts of the death of Jesus in the Gospels are ritualised. They have already been informed by theological beliefs about the significance of the death; influenced among other people (above all, one might say) by Paul. It could be argued that in some senses Paul was the Ur-author of the Passion Story in Mark, in so far as that Evangelist has absorbed into his narrative Paul's concept of Christ as one who became weak so that his weak followers could become strong – he saved others, himself he could not save. All the details of the 'passion' – the vinegar to drink, the crying aloud to a God who has forsaken him – are taken from the Psalms or the other Jewish Scriptures, so that we can not look here for much in the way of historically verifiable narrative. The Gospels, as much as the other writings of the New Testament, such as Paul's letters, are first and foremost theology; though they are theology in a narrative form. If one had to define them as a literary genre it might be most accurate to term them 'theological novels'. They do not attempt to tell the truth in a post-enlightenment way, but they do attempt to tell the same truth which is being expounded in Paul's writings.

An underlying assumption in all the Gospel accounts of Jesus's crucifixion is that he is quite innocent of whatever charge it is which we suppose to have been brought against him. If he had truly been guilty of a blasphemy according to Jewish law he would have been stoned. Some of the old rabbis maintained, against all historical

---

[31] John 18:3; Acts 9:14.

indication and probability, that this had indeed been the fate of Jesus;[32] but we have it on the authority not only of the New Testament but also of Josephus and Tacitus that Jesus suffered at the hands of the Romans. Though the gospels might represent the Roman procurator wringing and washing his hands and asserting the innocence of his victim, they can not deny that Jesus died at the hands of the Romans. For the Jews, this should make him a patriot.

Pilate, after all, was a notoriously horrible man. Philo of Alexandria, Pilate's contemporary, describes him as 'a man of inflexible, stubborn and cruel disposition' and tells us of the 'venality, violence, robbery, assault, abusive behaviour, frequent executions without trial and endless savage ferocity' characterised by his period in office.[33] This was a terrifying time to be a Jew in Palestine (it has been likened to life in France during the German occupation of 1940–44) when comparable fears and tensions existed throughout the populace. Pilate was destined to be recalled to Rome by order of the legate of Syria, Vitellius, to stand trial for his vindictive savagery. He deeply offended Jewish consciences in the very first year of his procuratorship by wilfully parading the legionary standards in Jerusalem with emblems of the Divine Emperor. (To the Jews, the standards were idols.) Previous procurators, in deference to Jewish iconophobia, had removed offensive emblems from their banners and standards before entering specifically Jewish territory. Pilate had plundered the sacred temple fund to build an (admittedly much needed) aqueduct. In the popular demonstration which followed, he 'mingled the blood of the Galileans with the blood of their sacrifice'.[34] The final outrage for which Vitellius demanded Pilate's removal was perpetrated against the Samaritans, when Pilate put many of them to the sword for assembling on Mount Gerizim, their holy mountain, to see some vessels which had allegedly been buried there by Moses.

Paul, writing to his Gentile converts in Galatia, makes great play of the fact that Jesus's manner of death was a disgrace, which would have made it impossible for him to have been honoured by the Jewish race. In one of his more incomprehensible flights of imagery, Paul

[32] The idea is revived by J. Enoch Powell, *The Evolution of the Gospel* (Yale, 1994). It is impossible to determine from this gnomic work of scholarship why the author, in the absence of any legal transcriptions of the trial by non-Christian historians, assumes that Jesus's offence was blasphemy.
[33] Philo, *De Legatione ad Gaium*, 301.
[34] Luke 13:1.

asserts that 'Christ redeemed us from the curse of the law by becoming a curse for us – for it is written, "Cursed is everyone who hangs on a tree" – in order that in Christ Jesus the blessing of Abraham might come to the Gentiles.'[35]

People have derived comfort from this verse; they have reinterpreted the Christian faith in the light of its picture of Christ's vicarious suffering. But no commentator can explain it because it does not on any rational level make sense. How could the crucifixion of Jesus by one of the most notorious thugs in the history of the Roman Empire extend the 'blessing of Abraham' to the Gentiles? It could make some biographical sense if Paul had himself been part of the arrest or trial of Jesus; for then it could mean, 'I was so changed by the crucifixion of Jesus that I, after a series of visionary experiences, am now extending the blessing of Abraham by preaching to the Gentiles.' Some such psychological truth might lie behind Paul's incomprehensible words; but what they say is of course on a surface level quite untrue. In the eyes of most Jews, anyone who was put to death by Pontius Pilate would have been a hero. The idea that being crucified put you outside the Jewish 'law' or that it made you a thing accursed in the eyes of your fellow Jews is demonstrable nonsense. The Romans used crucifixion as their means of humiliating and torturing their enemies. Would the Jews give to their enemies the means not merely to torture the bodies but also to damn them in the eyes of God and the assembly of Israel? Hundreds of Pharisees were crucified and we never read of a single member of their communities fearing lest they were thereby accursed. It is in the eyes of the Romans that a crucified man would be accursed; it was in the Roman Lex and not the Jewish Torah that such a curse existed. It is Paul the Roman Citizen, not Paul the Jew, who addressed the Galatians.

This leaps ahead; Galatians was written some twenty years after the Crucifixion. We can not explain anything but we can offer tentative hypotheses. Paul's letters are written from a point of view of one who is racked by self-contradiction, whose life is pulled in two conflicting directions. He imagines the friends of Jesus saying of him, 'The one who formerly was persecuting us is now proclaiming the faith.'[36] Such paradoxes – the dead being alive, the weak being strong, the good that we pursue turning to evil – are wholly characteristic of

[35] Galatians 3:13–14.
[36] Galatians 1:23.

his distinctive view not only of his own character but of the human situation. We do not know anything about the inner psychology of Paul. We can, however, reconstruct the political and social setting from which his letters come. They are highly comparable to the histories of Josephus, that other Jew who 'came to terms' with the Romans, or as Jewish patriots would wish to say, betrayed his own kind. The 'scandal' of the cross, which casts its shadow across Paul's letters and becomes the ultimate paradox (the cruellest form of humiliating death becomes a sign of glory), is a Roman scandal.

The speech which Josephus claims he made to his misguided compatriots is an extraordinary document, which must be read alongside Romans 13.[37] Josephus went much further than to suggest that the Jews did not have a hope fighting against the most powerful army and the mightiest empire in the world. He does not argue merely from expediency. The Romans, he believes, had respected the sanctuary of the Jews and revered the temple. The servitude of the Jews to the Romans had come about as a result of Jewish wickedness. Impiety, disobedience to God, sedition and disobedience had brought about the Roman occupation, just as, in the past, God had punished his people by the Babylonian occupation of Judaea and the Jewish captivity. But Josephus went further, even, than this. He claimed that God was now on the side of the Romans. 'Fortune had on all sides been transferred to the Romans, and God, who had bestowed power on all the nations in turn, now rested over Italy.'

These words must have been easy to write from the comfort of Josephus's Roman apartment, when Jerusalem was a heap of rubble and the Jews had been utterly defeated. Paul, as a servant of the high priest, had in his youth contorted himself into similar intellectual knots. Neither the Homeric, nor the Vedic, nor the Nordic theological myths assume that perfect virtue, still less love, resides in the heart of the First Cause. The situation of the world in which the righteous suffer and the strong succeed, regardless of their goodness, provides no difficulties in such mythologies and creeds, which take it for granted that life is nasty, brutish and short.

The Jewish tradition, however, asserted the Justice and the Wisdom and the Goodness of the First Cause which, throughout the Wisdom writings[38] – the Book of Job and the Psalms particularly – troubled the Jewish conscience. How could a good God allow wickedness to

[37] *BJ*, V, ix, 3–4.

flourish? How could he desert his people? How could he allow a virtuous man to suffer a hideous death at the hands of secular, foreign powers?

If Paul had been a true Jewish patriot, rather than a man of the Diaspora with very divided loyalties, it would have been intellectually easy for him to answer this question. Everything that was wrong about the condition of Israel and Jerusalem could be put down to the Roman presence. Patriots of one sort or another in Josephus, before, during and in the very midst of the flames and destruction, continue to assert the righteousness of their own position. Four legs good, two legs bad.

Paul belonged to two political worlds, as did Josephus, thirty years his junior. He believed in Providence and he thought that 'God now rested over Italy'. The high priests, who wished to preserve the *status quo*, were on God's side; those zealots and patriots who wished to rock the boat were simple criminals and fools and had to be put down. Paul was only too happy to be a persecutor of such people.

But Paul had seen the Cross. It would be very hard to rove about in the Roman Empire and not see crosses. This terrible method of execution, which could, if handled with judicious skill by an experienced torturer, keep the victims alive for several days before they died of asphyxiation, was widely practised, particularly against political dissidents, rebel slaves and the like. Paul must have seen such gibbets outside the city walls of Jerusalem, as in the killing fields of other Roman towns. He would have passed them on any of his trade trips. They would have been as familiar a sight to him as milestones along the road. He knew very well how Jesus died, even if he did not actually witness that death himself; even if he did not give evidence which led to the arrest.

He knew that Jesus was a good man, and, to judge from his letters, Paul also knew what some of the teaching of that good man was. Jesus had numbered at least two political activists among his chosen twelve disciples: Judas Iscariot and Simon the Zealot. The very decision to elect twelve, after the number of the tribes of Israel, is a patriotic gesture which was not, perhaps, disengaged from the political struggle. We can not know at this stage of history. It was one thing for the police, to which Paul belonged, to arrest and execute criminals,

---

[38] The Jewish Scriptures divide into the Five Books of Moses, the Histories (telling the story of the people of Israel), the Prophets and those books which are generally called the Writings, proverbs, apothegms and definitions of the Good Life.

terrorists and thieves. What was the effect on Paul of ritually killing a man who was 'patient . . . kind . . . not envious or boastful or arrogant or rude'; one who 'bears all things, believes all things, hopes all things, endures all things'? What was the effect of watching a man like that die, or knowing that a man like that had died? How did such a death square with Paul's profoundly-held belief in the loving Providence of Almighty God? He knew what the Romans were like. He knew how cruel the soldiers were. He had seen for himself the licentious and uncontrolled immorality in the cities of the Roman Empire. It was these thugs who had killed Jesus, but it was Paul or temple guards like Paul who had handed over the Prophet from Galilee into their hands. Paul knew the sort of religion which was popular among the soldiers. They, like so many of the citizens of Tarsus, worshipped Mithras. They did not worship weak men like Jesus, who went to his death like a sacrificial Passover Lamb. They worshipped the Bull. As the blood flowed down from their victim, they derived strength from it, divine strength; and they were thereby initiated into secrets, buried long since in the depths of the earth and now made manifest.

The Crucifixion of Jesus was not, in Paul's eyes, simply a political tragedy, as it was for the immediate circle of Jesus's family and friends. The Crucifixion became the focus of Paul's obsessive religious attention. In the course of the next thirty years he would mythologise it and try to come to terms with its meaning. The most hideous form of torture became the cause of sublime, blood-curdling boasting. The one who died on the Cross was alive. Jesus lived. In the mind of the Romanised Jew, the tormented Pharisee, the temple guard and tentmaker for the legions, it was Paul himself who was nailed to that instrument of torture, Paul who died, Paul who suffered, Paul who rose.

IV

CONVERSION

To SPEAK OF the 'conversion' of St Paul is not a neutral description; it is an interpretation. In Christian mythology, a fervent Jew named Saul, passionately addicted to persecuting Christians, journeyed to Damascus to round up more of his enemies. Before he reached his destination, however, he saw a blinding light from heaven. If we are guided by the great Renaissance masters such as Tintoretto, we believe that Paul fell from his horse. He heard a voice – that of Jesus; he came to faith; and thereafter he 'became a Christian'.

The New Testament does not actually speak of the 'Conversion' of Paul. Only once does it record the usage of the word 'Christian' in a non-pejorative sense.[1] If Paul was 'converted' 'from' something 'to' something else, it certainly was not 'from' Judaism 'to' 'Christianity'. Paul continued to be a Jew to his dying day, a fact which most Christians nowadays choose to neglect and which many Jewish scholars find exasperating. What happens after the 'conversion' is an interior debate – interior within Paul, inward within the synagogues of Asia Minor and Greece and Rome – about the nature of religion itself; and the nature of the times in which Paul and his fellow-believers were living.

There are two basic accounts of the great change which took place in the life of Paul the temple guard. One is the account which he wrote himself to the Galatians, probably in 54.[2] The other is the narrative of the Acts of the Apostles, which tells the story no fewer than three times. The first time, the story is introduced as part of the narrative. In the other two passages, Paul himself tells the story – first to the Jews in Jerusalem 'in the Jewish language', and next to King Agrippa and the Roman governor of Judaea, Festus. Luke, who addresses his entire *oeuvre* to a senior Roman official, presumably

---

[1] 1 Peter 4:16. Even here it is used of persecuted Christians; i.e. it speaks of a situation where to be a Christian was not so much a new religion as an indictable offence.
[2] F. F. Bruce argues strongly for a date as early as 48.

intends his reader, Theophilus, to be aware that Paul is in a special position, *vis-à-vis* his fellow-Jews and *vis-à-vis* the Romans.[3] It suits Luke's purpose very well to tell us nothing about Paul in the initial chapters of Acts. He makes the dispute between the hard-line 'Jews' and the believers in Jesus a purely religious dispute, even though, in his clumsy use of sources, Luke can not disguise from us the fact that the Pharisees, supposedly the deadliest enemies of Jesus, actually speak up in *favour* of the new movement!

Luke tells an apparently neat story. The Messiah, having risen from the dead, rises into heaven in the very opening sentences of the book. Not long afterwards, on the feast of Shavuoth, Pentecost, the Holy Spirit is poured out on to the followers of the Way – as Jesus's movement within Judaism appeared to be called. In consequence, the curse of Babel, placed on the human race in Genesis is undone, and all the visitors to the feast can understand 'these Galileans', though they are speaking in their own language: 'Parthians, Medes, Elamites, and residents of Mesopotamia, Judaea and Cappadocia, Pontus and Asia, Phrygia and Pamphylia, Egypt and the parts of Libya belonging to Cyrene, and visitors from Rome, both Jews and proselytes, Cretans and Arabs – in our own languages we hear them speaking about God's deeds of power.'[4]

It is not clear from Luke's narrative whether the jabbering of Peter, James and others, mistaken by observers for drunkenness, is supposed to have been the phenomenon known as 'speaking with tongues' or glossolalia, or whether the miracle consists merely in non-Hebrew speakers understanding a different language – rather as participants in debates at the United Nations hear simultaneous translation through headphones into their own language of speeches by different delegates. The point of the story is not a difficult one to grasp. The new faith – the Way of Jesus – was to be a religion for all people, stretching across the Empire. The fact that visitors to a Jewish festival – 'devout Jews' we are informed – understand a speech in Hebrew is not likely to amaze modern readers; nor could we be surprised if in fact (were there such a thing) the Holy Apostles addressed the crowds in the

[3] We do not know who this Theophilus was, to whom Luke dedicated both his Gospel and Acts. He is addressed as 'your excellency', and it has been suggested that he occupied some official role at Nero's court. Those who find this probable have sometimes supposed that the 'biography' of Paul contained in the pages of Acts was a document put together for his legal defence when he had appealed to Caesar and went to Rome for trial.
[4] Acts 2:9–11.

common lingua franca which they all understood in any case – Greek. Luke is telling us a story about the power of this new phenomenon, the religion of Christ, which has come into the world through the Holy Spirit.

From the sermons which he places into the mouth of Peter, quite likely to be authentic recollections of the faith of the 'Jerusalem Church', Luke manages to neuter the dangerous and alarming features of 'the Way'. He retains (again, rather clumsily) the distinctly non-Christian theology of 'the disciples'. That is to say, he recalls artlessly, and therefore we can assume authentically, the fact that they had no sense of Jesus as a divine, or even as a quasi-divine being; merely as the figure whom God had chosen to anoint. Even the Resurrection of Jesus is not, in their teaching, a sign of anything particularly special about Jesus: for in the Jewish teaching the rising of the dead is a sign of the beginning of the messianic age. Jesus is only the first to rise.

Luke is also artless enough to recall that Peter and John are hauled before the high priest for their views. 'What will we do with them?' the 'Rulers of the People' and the 'high priests' ask themselves, 'To keep it from spreading further among the people, let us warn them to speak no more to anyone in this name.'[5] The Gospels and Acts are written against a background of decades – perhaps more – of disputing in the synagogues about the nature of the messianic hopes. The preservation of monotheism, and of their own national/religious integrity, was the Jews' most fervent need. They therefore did all in their power to punish and to exclude from their midst what they regarded as the heresies of the 'Christians'. Writing from this historical perspective of several decades, the Christians could make the Jews, in their narratives, figures who are religious persecutors of the embattled Christians. At the same time, Luke can not really quite hide, either from himself or from his readers, the fact that this is an anachronism. In the times which he describes, there is no division between Christians and Jews. The followers of Jesus are Jews, and persist in being Jews throughout the Acts of the Apostles. As the genial Pharisee remarks, there have been many 'false alarms', many messianic movements. Time alone tells how false they are. The religious claims of these false messiahs did nothing to damage Israel, and it is by no means clear that the Jews did regard Jesus either as a messiah or as a false messiah.

Why then, the summoning of 'the whole body of the elders of

[5] Acts 4:16, 17.

Israel','[6] as Luke slightly inaccurately calls the Sanhedrin, just to put
down a few religious eccentrics from Galilee? Peter tells this august
assembly: 'The God of our ancestors raised up Jesus, whom you had
killed by hanging him on a tree. God exalted him at his right hand as
Leader and Saviour that he might give repentance to Israel and
forgiveness of sins.'[7] Luke is trying to depoliticise the nature of Peter's
speech, but there was no separation of religion and politics for Jews
living under Roman occupation in first-century Palestine. The idea
that Jesus came simply to teach the Jews 'repentance' is a very mild
one, and at this distance of history we have no possibility of knowing,
for certain, what Jesus thought he was up to when he assembled five
thousand men in the desert for a foretaste of the messianic banquet
or upset all the money-changers' tables in the court of the Gentiles in
Herod's temple. We do not even know whether these events took
place, but if they did, we could be sure that Jesus's death by crucifixion
– the punishment for political troublemakers – would be just what
we should have expected during the time of Pontius Pilate.

Luke, in other words, retains the spiritual message of Peter, John
and James but deliberately fillets out the disturbing fact that anyone
causing public nuisance on the scale that Jesus allegedly did would
have been regarded as an enemy not by the Jewish people but by the
Romans and by the Jews who exercised power on behalf of the
Romans, namely the high priests.

In all this part of Luke's narrative – the first five chapters of Acts –
we hear not a word about the servant of the high priest, Paul. He
materialises after the next (self-contained) piece of narrative, chapters
six and seven of Acts – the witness and death of the deacon Stephen,
known to Christian tradition as the protomartyr. It is hard to know
how much of this story to believe. It begins with a squabble in the
early Jesus-movement. Luke's original Greek tells us that the dispute
was between Hellenists and Hebrews.[8] It is impossible to prove who
or what the Hellenists were, though it would seem safe to assume
that they were Jews from the Diaspora. You might expect such a quarrel
to have been about the interpretation of Scripture, with the Hellenists
perhaps siding with the neo-Platonic way of reading the Bible
popularised by the Hellenist Philo of Alexandria, and the Hebrews

[6] Acts 5:21.
[7] Acts 5:30, 31.
[8] Not, as NEB says, 'those of them that spoke Greek and those that spoke the language of
the Jews'.

sticking out for Jewish conservatism. But the quarrel seems less esoteric than that. The Hellenists found that although the followers of the Way held everything in common, some were more common than others. The Hellenist widows were getting less attention than the Hebrew widows. For this reason, the leaders of the group established a group of servants (Greek, *deacons*) to oversee this practical, charitable work.

Next, we read that while Stephen is responsible for 'great wonders and signs among the people' he falls foul of another sect – the Synagogue of the Freedmen (NEB) or the Synagogue of the Libertines (RV).[9] The Greek, significantly, is a loan-word from Latin (Libertine). This Latin word, *libertinus*, means a member of the slave class who has been liberated and granted the privilege of citizenship. It is difficult to see why such Jews, if Jews there were, should need a synagogue to themselves; so one sees the attractiveness of a fairly ancient emendation to the text here, which reads Libertinon as Libyorum, a synagogue not of Libertines but of Libyans!

Stephen's speech is meant to be an answer to a charge of blasphemy which has supposedly been brought against him. His speech consists of a fairly lengthy résumé of the familiar Jewish folk-tale of God appearing to Abraham, Joseph going to Egypt, followed by his father and brothers, Moses leading the Hebrews out again, Joshua being given the land, David having the idea for the building of the temple, and Solomon accomplishing it, though, as all Jews know and agree, no temple can contain the Almighty.

At the end of this speech, Stephen exclaims that the Jews have always persecuted the prophets and killed those who foretold the coming of the Righteous one. In a vision, however, he sees the Son of Man who had been foretold in the prophet Daniel. For some reason this makes the Jews stop their ears; they accuse him of blasphemy and proceed to stone Stephen.

It is easy to sympathise with those commentators who believe that all this is pure invention. We do not know how common it was for blasphemers to be stoned, though we do know from the Mishnah that the offender would be thrown from a great height and killed by having a single stone dropped upon him, not pelted with stones by a mob as Stephen supposedly was. We have no contemporary accounts of a stoning with which to compare the story in Acts, but, as it stands, it is hard to see where a 'blasphemy' has occurred. It would also seem

[9] Acts 6:8, 9.

at least possible that the Fourth Gospel is accurate when it tells us that the Jews were not allowed, at this period, to put their own citizens to death without the permission of the Roman authorities. It would be impossible to get much sense out of the story of the stoning of Stephen, but it does appear to retain memories of disputes in Jerusalem among the followers of the Way – Hebrews versus Hellenists, Hellenists versus Libertines or Libyans. Luke does not make sense of it because he is almost certainly writing at a time when the significance of these sobriquets has been forgotten. He would, in any case, be anxious to play down the differences between different followers of the Way, wishing rather, as a Gentile follower of Paul and his teachings, to suggest that from the beginning there was harmony in 'the Church' and a feeling of separateness from 'the Jews'. The political reality of the situation is not one which Luke would wish his first reader, Theophilus, to consider: that some of the followers of the Way were probably patriots who would if necessary take up arms against the Romans. And that even if this were not the case, their obscure disputations would have caused a public affray and constituted a prima facie case for arrest by the authorities. It is on to this confused scene that, without introduction or explanation, Luke chooses to introduce the hero of his narrative, 'a young man named Saul'.[10]

We are told that, having disposed of Stephen by stoning, Saul collects letters of authority from the high priest in Jerusalem, to be shown to the synagogues of Damascus, 'that if he found any who belonged to the Way, men or women, he might bring them bound to Jerusalem'.[11] It is true that two centuries earlier, there was a letter from the Roman consul to Rome's allies in this region requesting the extradition of troublemakers who had fled from Judaea; but the situation is rather different in Acts and many modern commentators have doubted whether the high priest in Jerusalem had any 'jurisdiction' over Damascus. Local synagogues were, it would seem, entitled to have their members flogged. Those modern scholars who feel able to believe that the high priest did indeed authorise Saul to go to Damascus, believe that it was in the nature of an 'undercover' operation. 'After all, successful, although illegal, kidnapping is not unknown even in well-policed twentieth-century society.'[12]

[10] Acts 7:58.
[11] Acts 9:2.
[12] R. P. C. Hanson, *The Acts* (Oxford, 1967), p. 113.

That Luke tells us the story of Paul's vision on the road to Damascus three times must emphasise the supreme importance which he attaches to the event not only in the life of Paul but also in the history of the Church. He is at pains to emphasise two aspects of the experience which are missing from Paul's own account of the matter. The first is that the vision earned Paul the immediate enmity of the Jews, who rather mysteriously 'plotted to kill him' as soon as he had arrived in Damascus.[13] (Why should having a vision make Paul so tempting a target for murderers? If the Jews did try to kill Paul in Damascus it was much more likely because Paul was a collaborator with the Romans than that he had met the risen Jesus in a vision on the road to Damascus.)

The other facet of the episode which seems very different from Paul's account of the matter is Luke's insistence that after his 'conversion' Saul (as he is still called at this point) instantly became a fully integrated and welcome member of the 'Church'. Only days after he had seen the light, heard the voice of Jesus, gone blind, and had his sight restored by Ananias, Saul is down at the synagogue 'proving that Jesus was the Messiah'.[14] This is followed by a visit to the Jerusalem 'Church', where he is introduced to the apostles. Saul stays with them and moves about among the Greek-speaking Jews until they, too, like the good people of Damascus, feel moved to attempt Saul's murder.

Again, it seems a rather strange introduction to Church life. Luke is a ham-fisted historian who attempts to put a shape on recalcitrant material, but can not avoid letting the cat out of the bag almost every time he does so. His aim is to persuade Theophilus that the Church, for all its differences of view, is essentially united, and that Paul was, after a little suspicion, welcomed by members of the Jerusalem Church. The picture he wants to paint is of Paul the instantaneously popular Christian saint. He can not help letting slip, however, that Paul was so popular in Jerusalem that he had to go home to Tarsus in secret lest someone murder him. When he came back to the Jewish capital twenty years later, we find that once again, in Luke's narrative, there is a price on his head. This is not what we should expect of the humble tentmaker and convert of Christian legend; it is very much what we should expect of a member of the temple police and supporter of the Roman regime against the Jewish people. Luke, who tries to tell a

[13] Acts 9:23.
[14] Acts 9:22.

purely 'religious' story to soothe Theophilus into thinking that the
Way is very different from Judaism, is actually making a strongly
political point.

When we turn to Paul's own account of how he changed from being
a persecutor of the Way to the most ardent disciple of Jesus, we find a
markedly different story. No 'Damascus Road experience' is mentioned,
although by implication we may infer that the visionary experience
did take place in or near Damascus. Nor does he mention the voices
from heaven, the blinding or the healing, though this does not mean
that they did not take place. The chief discrepancy between Luke's
account of the matter and Paul's is that whereas Luke makes the convert
immediately welcome in the circle of the Jerusalem 'Church', Paul
underlines the fact that the 'revelation' was unique and personal to
himself and that his experience of the Risen Jesus owed nothing to
the testimony of Peter, James or John.

> For I want you to know, brothers and sisters, that the gospel that
> was proclaimed by me is not of human origin; for I did not
> receive it from a human source, nor was I taught it, but I received
> it through a revelation of Jesus Christ.
>   You have heard, no doubt, of my earlier life in Judaism. I was
> violently persecuting the church of God and was trying to destroy
> it. I advanced in Judaism beyond many among my people of the
> same age, for I was far more zealous for the traditions of my
> ancestors. But when God, who had set me apart before I was
> born and called me through his grace, was pleased to reveal his
> Son to me, so that I might proclaim him among the Gentiles, I
> did not confer with any human being, nor did I go up to Jerusalem
> to those who were already apostles before me, but I went away
> at once into Arabia, and afterwards returned to Damascus.[15]

Luke's cosy picture of Paul being welcomed immediately into the
Christian family is contradicted in the subsequent sentences, in which
Paul specifically states that three years passed before he so much as
visited Jerusalem after his 'revelation', and that when he did so, far
from mixing with the assembly of believers (the Church), he met no
one except Peter and Jesus's brother James.

   Paul's religion, then, which was to have an incalculable influence

[15] Galatians I:11–17.

on history, was never based, and never claimed to be based, on the traditions which, we may assume, informed the teaching of Jesus's family and close intimates. It would seem, if the Epistle of James is representative of their piety, that they were more concerned to intimate the religion of Jesus himself, rather than making Jesus the focus of their religious feelings; 'Religion that is pure and undefiled before God, the Father, is this: to care for orphans and widows in their distress, and to keep oneself unstained by the world.'[16]

It was above all a shared and collective faith. 'They devoted themselves to the apostles' teaching and fellowship, to the breaking of bread, and the prayers.'[17]

Paul's distance from the assembly in Jerusalem – a distance which is quite clearly much more than a geographical one – can not be emphasised too strongly. For them, the patient waiting, in the city of Jerusalem, for the coming of the Lord. For him, a frenzied journey from place to place outside the Jewish world, to meet merchants (male and female), slaves, soldiers, philosophers, district governors, synagogue officials, wizards, sea-captains, artisans, and non-Jewish religious leaders. For them, a pious memory of Jesus's life. For Paul, an obsession with the manner of Jesus's death.

The short passage of spiritual autobiography which has been quoted above comes from the letter to the Galatians, written most specifically to attack the idea that, in order to make themselves acceptable in the eyes of God, his friends in Galatia must undergo circumcision and follow the dietary laws of Judaism. Paul has preached to them his own 'Gospel for Gentiles'. He tells them that, at a meeting in Antioch, he has quarrelled with Peter, chief of the apostles, because Peter 'was clearly in the wrong' in the matter of whether or not Gentile members of the congregation must observe the dietary laws. At one moment Peter appeared to be a liberal over this matter, and at the next, when his stricter friends came from Jerusalem, he had meekly toed the party line.

It is one of the supreme ironies of history that Christians have managed to make Paul's letters a blueprint for a new 'religion', whereas they are something infinitely stranger and much more radical than that. Paul did not exchange Judaism for Christianism, still less for Predestinarianism, Lutheranism, Calvinism or Catholicism. His

[16] James 1:27.
[17] Acts 2:42.

'revelation', or to use the Greek word, his 'apocalypse', was something deeper and more searching and more original.

We can speculate if we choose about the 'manner of life' which Paul had when he claims to have been 'in Judaism'; whether he was really a Pharisee, or whether, with his supposed zeal for the patriarchal faith, he was not quite suited to be the servant of the Sadducean high priest. If he never so much as met Jesus, never so much as heard his words, or set eyes upon him, then his 'apocalypse' of Jesus risen from the tomb is all the more remarkable.

Some of those modern Christians who sing hymns based on Paul's words might forget that, whether he himself had anything to do with the trial or death of Jesus, he lived in a world where crucifixion was common. He and his followers would almost certainly have seen, perhaps at close hand, the slow death of a criminal nailed through wrists and ankles up on a cross. He would in all likelihood have seen some crucified victim dying of asphyxiation, when the arms or legs grew too weak any longer to uphold the weight of the body and the rib cage finally pressed up against the lungs. Sweat, blood, pus, urine and excrement must have poured down the upright beam from the tortured body. No wonder that Paul should have been shocked and puzzled that God's Chosen and Anointed One, the Messiah of Israel, had undergone such a dreadful death. His letter to the Galatians, however, reveals to us the searching nature of Paul's genius. He is not a philosopher, he devised no system and he wrote no summa. And yet his apocalypse of Jesus reveals the crucifixion as a moment of glory. The 'curse' of the tree is something laid upon Paul himself, who is in a visionary manner 'crucified with the Messiah'. 'I have been crucified with Christ; and it is no longer I who live, but it is Christ who lives in me';[18] 'May I never boast of anything but the cross of our Lord Jesus Christ, by which the world has been crucified to me, and I to the world.'[19] If we believe that he was implicated in the crucifixion itself, or even if we simply acknowledge that, in the course of his work as a temple guard Paul was responsible for certain arrests which led to the prisoner being crucified, these words seem all the more extraordinary. Luke's account of the 'vision' on the Damascus Road in this particular seems plausible. You would think, after the so-called stoning of Stephen, that it was of that late death that Paul meditated as he went to

[18] Galatians 2:19, 20.
[19] Galatians 6:14.

Damascus. Instead, 'He fell to the ground and heard a voice saying to him, "Saul, Saul, why do you persecute me?" He asked, "Who are you, Lord?"The reply came, "I am Jesus, whom you are persecuting." '[20]

The apocalypse led to a complete reversal of the way Paul had been living. Just as the worshippers of Mithras, in his native Tarsus, could stand beneath a platform and catch the cascade of blood falling on them from the slaughtered bullock, so Paul could bathe in the blood of the crucified and find that the life of the Messiah had become his own. He was 'in Christ'. Just as Paul's contemporaries in Tarsus believed that the demi-god Herakles – with one human and one immortal parent – had, in his descent into the realms of death, become the saviour of his people, so Jesus 'gave himself for our sins to set us free from the present evil age, according to the will of our God and Father'.[21]

The revelation or apocalypse came upon Paul instantaneously, but we discern from his autobiographical reflexions that it took him at least three years for its implications to sink in; three years before he turned back to meet Peter and James in Jerusalem. He was not rejecting Judaism so much as coming to terms with its own most far-reaching implications. No Jew believes that Yahweh is a mere tribal totem. All Jews believe that they worship the Almighty, the Maker of Heaven and Earth, who inspires and enlivens all flesh. Perhaps the acrimonious sectarianism of Judaism struck Paul, in the moment of his apocalypse, as foolish and nauseating. Perhaps, though, the revelation was of a more positive character than that and he saw what it would be like if, and when, the promised messianic age dawned, and the peoples of the world could – as the Jewish Scriptures believe that they will – unite to worship the God of Israel.

'For in Christ Jesus you are all children of God through faith. As many of you as were baptised into Christ have clothed yourselves with Christ. There is no longer Jew or Greek, there is no longer slave or free, there is no longer male or female; for all of you are one in Christ Jesus. And if you belong to Christ, then you are Abraham's offspring, heirs according to the promise.'[22]

He was not putting aside Judaism but trying the contradiction which lay at its heart – that it both drew people to itself and shut them out.

[20] Acts 9:4, 5.
[21] Galatians 1:4.
[22] Galatians 3:26–9.

This becomes enwoven with the contradictoriness of the Cross. The great blessing in the life of a Jew, the Divinely-given Teaching (Torah) becomes in Paul's vision a Law which is a curse. The accursed thing, the Roman torture, becomes a blessing in which he 'glories'.

To return to, and make sense of, the world of the ancients, the modern person must attempt to regain the mythic habit of mind. The ancients perceived truth through myth. Myth 'is not of the nature of fiction . . . but it is a living reality, believed to have once happened'.[23]

It is all but impossible for post-Enlightenment humanity to comprehend a world where myth, thus defined, was the natural way of coming to terms with history and experience. The Greeks and the Jews and the Romans were in this respect far more like one another than they were like us. They would be puzzled by debates among modern Christians concerning the verisimilitude of the New Testament – the question whether this or that event, such as Christ's Ascension into Heaven, actually took place. The genius of Paul and the collective genius of the 'early church', which wrote the twenty-seven surviving books that we call the New Testament, was to mythologise Jesus. Paul, who had a much broader experience of life in the Mediterranean and was a witness to the religious experience of people other than Jews, had a richer language-store, a richer myth-experience, than some of the other New Testament writers, whose mythologies were limited to Jewish liturgy or folk-tale. One does not need to revive the old History of Religions School to see how obvious all this is. One is not saying that Paul crudely invented a new religion, but that he was able to draw out the mythological implications of an old religion, and the death of a particular practitioner of that religion, and to construct therefrom a myth with reverberations much wider than the confines of Palestinian Judaism.

The modern person can be dismayed as well as puzzled by what Paul has done. 'None of this happened.' In a sense, such a sceptic, viewing matters (as Paul would say) 'according to the flesh', is in the same case as the gallant modern 'believer' who would try to assert – 'Yes it did happen.' Both believer and unbeliever would be trying to apply post-Enlightenment standards of verisimilitude to stories which grew up in a different imaginative world; and therefore the modern

[23] Bronislaw Malinowski, 'Myth in Primitive Psychology', reprinted in *Magic, Science and Religion*, pp. 100–1. Quoted by M. I. Finley, *The World of Odysseus*, p. 22.

student of the New Testament finds herself reduced to the absurdity of asserting that bodies really did come to life or float through the clouds. Perhaps the greatest tribute which we can pay to the mythologising of Jesus, however, is that it guaranteed the survival of this faith in worlds which were quite alien, spiritually and geographically, to its native setting of first-century Palestinian Judaism. This is what is going on as these twenty-seven different books come to be written down. Just as Pharisaism was the only sect within mainstream Judaism equipped to survive the destruction of the temple in 70, so the heretical Jesus-religion, incorporating or battling with Paul's version of the Christ Myth by becoming an interior thing, an imagined thing and at last a written thing, was able to withstand the passing away of those who had known Christ 'according to the flesh', i.e. of those who could say, 'But this is not what Jesus wanted or meant at all!' The historicity of Jesus became unimportant from the moment Paul had his apocalypse. The striking thing about the New Testament is the way that the myth gave birth to so many manifestations of itself, so many different versions, of which perhaps the Fourth Gospel, the story of the Divine Logos, visiting the world (*kosmos*) as a stranger and enlightening his chosen few, is perhaps the most haunting. The modern Christian 'fundamentalist' who bravely continues to 'believe' in a real star of Bethlehem or an actual Garden Tomb in Jerusalem from which Jesus rose from the dead is making the same unimaginative mistake as Heinrich Schliemann when he dug in the sands of Hissarlik and thought he was finding Homer's Troy. Troy is in the *Iliad*, not in the sand. And because of Homer, not because of the sand, Troy exists in the collective consciousness of the human race. The young men, or angels, at the empty Garden Tomb in the different Gospels emphasise for the reader or hearer the same story: 'Why do you look for the living among the dead?'[24]

[24] Luke 24:5.

V

PAUL IN ARABIA
The Silent Years

IN *THE BACCHAE*, the last play Euripides ever wrote, Dionysus discards his divine nature and walks in the human world disguised. Pentheus, the king, is the representative in the play of cool reason, conservative government, the desire for rational human society to remain undisturbed by the hysterical forces of superstition. Dionysus is not just the god of wine whom we know from Roman statues of Bacchus. He touches on all that is wild and ungovernable in our natures – sexual passions, dark religious needs, violence, fear. The Bacchae are his frenzied, hysterical female admirers. In the middle of the play, the herdsman comes into the presence of Pentheus to give his terrified account of their behaviour, as they run through the mountains and hills in search of prey, full of preternatural strength. They have torn cows limb from limb, they have snatched children from their parents' houses, they have passed on from village to village – and 'there was the power of a god in that'. Euripides was a rational man trying to make sense of the irrational in his fellow-human beings. Within the next few hundred years, the cult of the Dionysian mystery became one of the most popular manifestations of Greek religion.

The mysteries promised to lead the initiate deeper in. A mystery was a religious ritual, enacted to take the devotee closer to the purposes of God, closer to the secrets of life and death. The most popular of the mysteries was a twice-yearly ritual held at Eleusis, thirteen miles west of Athens. The Eleusian mysteries continued into Christian times, having been celebrated for over a thousand years. The essence of the mystery was a ritual of rebirth. The soul, or inner being, of the initiate 'dies', or is killed when it comes into God's all-consuming possession. Then, like Persephone going down into hell, and coming up again in the spring, the believer came to new life in God. The mysteries promised the believer not merely a new spiritual life in the body but also after bodily death a new life in heaven.[1] One of the most popular of the 'mysteries' was that of Dionysus, and Euripides probably recalled, in his play *The Bacchae*, some of the liturgical language associated with the cult. Pentheus, the *homme naturel*, attempts to resist the cult: 'This outrageous Bacchism advances on us like a spreading fire.' He decrees that his soldiers should go out of the city fully armed to fight the mad women. But Dionysus, the god disguised in human form, tells him that his efforts to resist the new movement will be completely worthless; he is not contending against flesh and blood but against a god. 'You are mortal, he is a god. If I were you, I would control my rage and sacrifice to him, rather than kick against the pricks.'

The very phrase is used by Luke in his third retelling of the story of Paul's 'conversion' – the version in which Paul is defending himself before the Roman Governor Festus and King Agrippa, and speaking in his best Greek. Explaining that he had been in the hire of the authorities as a young man, not merely to imprison but, where necessary, to cast his vote in favour of killing the wild men and women of the Way, he added, 'I pursued them even to foreign cities. With this in mind, I was travelling to Damascus with the authority of the chief priests, when at midday along the road, your excellency, I saw a light from heaven, brighter than the sun, shining around me and my companions. When we had all fallen to the ground, I heard a voice saying to me in the Hebrew language, "Saul, Saul, why are you persecuting me? It hurts you to kick against the goads." I asked, "Who are you, Lord?" The Lord answered, "I am Jesus whom you are persecuting. But get up and stand on your feet; for I have appeared to you for this purpose, to appoint you to serve and testify to the things in which you have seen me, and to those in which I shall appear to you." 'After more testimony of this kind, Festus pronounced that Paul was mad: 'Too much learning is driving you insane.' In short, Paul was a *maenad*, the Greek word for one of the Bacchic women. '*Ta polla se grammata eis manian peritrepei.*' The mania into which Paul has been led, Luke wishes to suggest, is precisely comparable to that mania which took possession of the initiates into a mystery. Just like Pentheus confronted by a god-man, Paul could not kick against the pricks. Henceforth, he is possessed.

If only Paul had sat down to write a full autobiographical account

[1] Robert Garland, *Religion and the Greeks*, p. 17.

of it all! As it is, we have to rely on tantalising fragmentary allusions, tossed out from his letters because they must have been common knowledge to their first readers: those friends of his knew what Paul was like; what he looked like, what his voice sounded like. An apocryphal work of *circa* AD 160, written by an orthodox Christian and known as the Acts of Paul, contains the purported memory of an eyewitness. It might be based on a genuine oral tradition. Who knows?

> A certain man named Onesiphorus, when he heard that Paul was come to Iconium, went out with his children Simmias and Zeno and his wife Lectra to meet him, that he might receive him *into his house*: for Titus had told him what manner of man Paul was in appearance; for he had not seen him in the flesh, but only in the spirit. And he went by the king's highway that leadeth unto Lystra and stood expecting him, and looked upon them that came, according to the description of Titus. And he saw Paul coming, a man little of stature, thin-haired upon the head, crooked in the legs, of good state of body, with eyebrows joining, and nose somewhat hooked, full of grace: for sometimes he appeared like a man, and sometimes he had the face of an angel.[2]

The comparison must often have been made between the apparently unprepossessing appearance of Socrates, described by his friends as a Silenus or a satyr, and the diminutive, bandy-legged apostle.

If we have only the testimony of oral tradition to give us a hint of Paul's size and appearance, however, we have his own written words as evidence of his fiery and passionate religious nature. The conversion was absolute and sudden. At one moment, he was a persecutor. Thereafter, he had complete certainty that he was a changed man, a new being.

Just as the Pythagoreans and the followers of the mysteries believed it possible to ascend into the very heavens, so Paul in his new vision of Christ, had been caught up into Paradise, 'and heard things that are not to be told, that no mortal is permitted to repeat'.[3] By definition, there can be no explaining this strange 'boast', as he calls it. We can be quite certain, however, that whatever the nature of the experience, it left him forever altered. He writes not as a man who is searching but as one who has found; not as one who struggles for the truth but as

---

[2] *The Apocryphal New Testament*, newly translated by M. R. James (Oxford, 1924), p. 273.
[3] 2 Corinthians 12:4.

one who has heard it. He has known Christ, and he is in Christ. In the Mithraic cults which flourished in his native Tarsus, each grade of initiation corresponded to the seven planets or 'heavens'. Journeys from our present earth-bound condition to a different plane of consciousness were possible in the religious traditions of both Jews and Gentiles, and Paul makes clear that their authenticity and reality as spiritual experiences are in no way invalidated by the suggestion that the initiate might not have journeyed to outer space in person in order to reach the 'third heaven'. The point is not so much whether Paul did journey to space as that he believed himself to have heard unspeakable words. We can exaggerate Paul's differences with the other believers in the Way. The more distinct he became from the older followers of Jesus, the more urgently he would try to suggest that he alone had understood the implications of what they had been the first to believe, that they were all different limbs of one body, all parts of the same whole, all members one of another. Perhaps that was true. But we should distort the picture of Paul in the New Testament if we thought he was simply a 'convert' to a pre-existent faith. That faith was still being found and formed and fashioned by the followers of Jesus when Paul was converted. We can see it as an inchoate collection of hopes, not a single one of which would be fulfilled in the manner expected; Jesus did not return in the manner they predicted; the messianic age did not come to pass in their lifetimes; Israel did not triumph over the Romans.

There have been those who have asked themselves whether Paul's original vision, at the moment of Revelation, accompanied the onset of leprosy, or some hysterical disease. Paul himself gives the clue here, but it is only a clue, and he does not reveal it to us. He writes to his friends in Corinth as if they knew perfectly well the nature of his weakness. 'To keep me from being too elated, a thorn was given me in the flesh, a messenger of Satan to torment me . . . Three times I appealed to the Lord about this, that it would leave me, but he said to me, "My grace is sufficient for you, for power is made perfect in weakness." '[4] This sentence can be read alongside the famous boast, made to the Galatians, that, 'I carry the marks [*stigmata*] of Jesus branded on my body.'[5] Is Paul claiming that, like a mediaeval saint, he carries the very wounds of Crucifixion in his person, just as so many Franciscan

[4] 2 Corinthians 12:7–9.
[5] Galatians 6:17.

mystics have, by meditating on the Passion, been granted the wounded hands and feet and side of their crucified redeemer? This could be the case, but it is much more likely that Paul is making one of his profound revolutionary utterances about the very nature of physical frailty than that he is 'boasting' about some particular phenomenon in his own person. The 'mark', the *stigma*, would more appropriately, given his view of life, be a common but debilitating affliction, such as the chronic repetition of malaria or the constant fear of epileptic fits, rather than some freakish or miraculous sign. After all, had he received the *stigmata* in the mediaeval sense, this would not really have been a *weakness*. In the fourteen to seventeen years which Paul spent in obscurity following the Revelation to him of the Risen Jesus, he had time to ponder and evolve a whole vision of life, an understanding of the principles by which it was possible to envisage the strength of God at work in a world that had apparently turned away from him. The profound and mystic significance of God's son dying on a Cross had burned itself into Paul's psyche, like a brand on the flesh of a slave (which is another meaning of the word *stigma*). Since he had the mind of Christ, and had been invaded by Christ just as the Bacchae were invaded and possessed by their God, the very weakness of his own body became a book in which he could read the divine purpose. The reversal of earthly values, the cosmic paradox, was what had been revealed to Paul: that God who was all power and all strength had chosen to enflesh himself in weakness; that God who was all wisdom had chosen to reveal himself to fools. The Jerusalem Jesus-movement still looked to Jesus as to a conventional Messiah. They hoped for him as for a national deliverer from the hands of the Roman Empire, one who would come to redeem them from the legions. Paul's own thinking about this was to evolve to the point where, in the second generation of his followers, the word 'Christ' had lost any of its militant associations and had become a purely interior thing. Already, by the time he emerged from his wilderness years, Paul's 'Christ' is someone very different from the conventional or Scriptural Jewish Anointed Warrior-King. Power is made perfect in weakness. Those who have nothing possess all things.

If we had that autobiographical work from Paul's hands, which we have not, we should know what effect his encounter with the Risen Jesus had upon his worldly prospects. Towards the end of the story, when Paul returns to Jerusalem after two decades as a Christian missionary, Luke leaves tantalising hints in the narratives which suggest that there had been difficulties after the original vision. No sooner is it heard that Paul is in town than a riot ensues. We learn, moreover, that he has, or had, a sister in Jerusalem. But what of the parents, what of the employers in the temple?

We must guard against parallels with modern Jews who have become 'Christians' and been disinherited. In the year 33, or whenever we date the conversion, Paul was simply a Jew who had an ecstatic experience; he was not a Jew becoming a Christian. The very word did not exist when he had the experience. We know from his own testimony, however, that he changed at once from being a persecutor of the Way to being a follower of the seditious Jesus of Nazareth. We can assume that he would no longer be welcome in the police office at the temple. And perhaps, too, his family, cut him off? In the 50s he writes as if he is a man who was once much richer than he now is, indeed, as a man who has become enslaved, and humiliated by the need to undertake manual work. If this is the right reading of the relevant texts, then we can assume that, having been as it were the director of the family tentmaking business, he was thrown back on the necessity to work as an actual tentmaker in other people's business enterprises. The appearance of the risen Jesus to Paul had one very immediate consequence. It compelled him to work.[6]

As Cicero put it, a workshop can in no way be an appropriate place for a free man.[7] In 2 Corinthians 11:7 Paul says that he 'demeaned himself' by working in trade, but that he did so in order to 'exalt' his converts. He has left the world of the temple civil service, left the rabbinic schools and taken to the road, taken on the status of a common labourer. He has gone into exile.

The word that Paul uses for his willingness actually to work at, as opposed simply to profit from, his tentmaking, is nevertheless revealing. He says that he is enslaved (*douloun*) to his work. With his zest for paradox, he could see that it was this very slavery which made him free. By pursuing a trade as a tentmaker, he was able in his Christian life to be free, independent of all men (*eleutheros ek panton*).[8] In rather the same way, Socrates could boast 'Who among men is freer than I, who accepts neither gifts nor fee from anyone?'[9] It was for this reason that Paul worked with his hands in later life.

[6] I Corinthians 4:12; I Thessalonians 2:9; I Corinthians 9:19.
[7] Cicero, *De Officiis*, quoted by Ronald F. Hock in *JBL*, 97, 4, p. 555ff.
[8] I Corinthians 9:19.
[9] Xenophon, *Apology*, 1, 6.

There are examples in ancient literature of 'upper-class' men being reduced to manual labour. Agathocles of Samos followed his friend Deinias into exile on Gyara and worked as a purple-fisher.[10] Dio Chrysostom in his exile worked at a variety of manual jobs – planting, digging and drawing water. Musonius, who belonged to the equestrian order, worked on a farm.[11] We should not necessarily suppose, merely because Paul's life took him into artisan circles and forced him to work, that this was the class to which he had originally belonged. The indications are that he was rich, certainly that he had been 'born into the purple of commerce', and that he had not expected to demean himself by working at a trade.[12] The alleged practice of rabbis engaging in manual work to pay their keep – which we were told about at school while we drew our sketch maps of Paul's missionary journeys – is without documentation in the Jewish literature of the period. Paul writes as if he had every right to expect that he would have enjoyed leisure and an income without working with his hands. Work came to him as a necessity (*anagke*), not because he believed in a 'work ethic'.

Whatever it was that Paul was doing before his Apocalypse, there follows a long period after the Apocalypse or revelation of Jesus to Paul – up to seventeen years – in which the convert is removed from our gaze. The Acts tell us nothing about these years, and we have only a passing allusion to them in the letter to the Galatians. He tells us that he 'conferred not with flesh and blood' after the conversion, but went away 'into Arabia', and then returned to Damascus, a period which lasted three years. After that, he visited Jerusalem, where he met Jesus's brother James, and Cephas, better known as St Peter. After a fortnight in Jerusalem, Paul took himself off again, this time to the regions of Syria and Cilicia.

It would be a mistake to imagine, when Paul tells the Galatians that he went into 'Arabia', that he was taking himself off to the desert as contemplative figures such as the Essenes might do. Paul is an essentially urban figure; his religion an essentially urban phenomenon. The religion of Jesus was sustained by stories of sheep, lambs, plants, trees, fishing, sowing, reaping, harvest. The scenes of Jesus's activity were in the small towns and villages of the Galilee, and he eschewed

[10] Lucian, *Somnium*, 13, quoted by Ronald F. Hock in *JBL*, p. 562.
[11] *ibid.*, 31.
[12] Ronald F. Hock, 'Paul's Tentmaking and the Problem of his Social Class', in *JBL*, 97, 4, p. 555ff.

PAUL

the big cities such as Sepphoris or Tiberias, which were to be found
in the region. Paul was an urban man and his first converts, when he
began to make them, belonged to urban classes.[13] But for the better
part of twenty years, we do not know whether he was trying to make
converts in these regions, or simply mingling with them, pursuing his
trade as a tentmaker, attending the synagogues in whichever towns he
happened to be residing and having his own powerful experiences of
the love of Christ.

We can not date Paul's sojourn in Damascus, but whenever he was
there, he would have been walking into a political trouble spot, if not
a war zone. Gospel-readers will remember the vivid incident – almost
the only story in Mark's Gospel which does not concern Jesus – in
which John the Baptist denounced Herod the Tetrarch (son of Herod
the Great) for adultery with his niece and sister-in-law Herodias. John's
temerity cost him his head, presented in a grisly fashion on a charger
at a banquet to gratify the blood-thirsty humour of the lady in question.
In order to marry Herodias, Herod Antipas the Tetrarch divorced his
Arab wife, the daughter of the ethnarch Aretas IV. She fled to her
father's court in Petra. Aretas IV awaited his moment. In AD 36, when
Antipas had been ruling over the province of Galilee for forty years,
and when his ally the emperor Tiberius was in his dotage on the Isle
of Capri, Aretas exacted his revenge, invading and annexing Antipas's
territories. He routed the Jewish armies and established himself in
the northern kingdom of Syria. Damascus, which had been under
Roman control since the time of Pompey, was now under the
dominion of the Arabs; and it looks likely, though historians differ
about the length of time Aretas held on to Damascus, that he did so
for the next few years. (There is a gap in numismatic evidence, though
we do know from coins that Damascus was back in Roman hands by
AD 62.) Tiberius, when he was told that his protégé Antipas had been
humiliated in this way, ordered Vitellius, then prefect of Syria, to
capture Aretas and send him dead or alive to Rome. Vitellius collected
two legions stationed at Antioch (which had been for some years the
Syrian capital) and proposed to march them, with some light-armed
infantry and a regiment of Asiatic cavalry, on Petra. The Jews rendered
his campaign impossible. The route from Antioch to Petra would have
involved a march within the sacred precincts of Jerusalem, and the
Jews were so horrified at the idea of the idolatrous Imperial Ensigns

[13] Wayne A. Meeks, *The First Urban Christians: The Social World of the Apostle Paul.*

polluting their holy soil that Vitellius withdrew rather than find his legions in a position where they had simultaneously managed to antagonise both the Jews and the Arabs. Tiberius died in 37. We know from Paul that (whatever the date of his conversion) he managed to irritate Aretas by his preaching, and that he had to escape from the walls of Damascus hidden in a basket.

One brief allusion in 2 Corinthians to this fact suggests the world in which Paul was moving at this time. 'In Damascus, the governor under King Aretas guarded the city of Damascus in order to seize me, but I was let down in a basket through a window in the wall, and escaped from his hands.'[14] There is no evidence to support the notion, dear to the early fathers of the Church, that Paul was in some kind of monkish 'retreat' for the lengthy period between his conversion and his emergence as the most dynamic missionary for Christ. He was moving about in towns, he was almost certainly continuing to engage in trade, and he was probably confronting the political uncertainties of the times in a much more immediate way than Jesus, in his village ministry, would ever have done. Paul, even if we do not accept Luke's claim that he was a Roman citizen, was someone whose life was made in the urban activity of the Graeco-Roman cities; and to this extent at least he was very much a citizen.

The death of Jesus at the hands of the Roman authorities, those very authorities with whom, as the servant of the high priest, Paul was colluding so vigorously, was a political event which Paul transformed in his imagination into a moment of cosmic religious significance. It was within the political structures of the Empire that he would see the working of divine redemption, for God, who shall be all in all, is the father not of the Jews alone, but of all men and women – Greek, Arab, Jewish and Roman. He was not looking for a political synthesis nor even perhaps for an 'explanation' of this state of things. But he could not view what was going on politically without realising that God's purposes were painted on a universal canvas. In Syria and Arabia, Paul saw cities threatened by anarchy because of the ethnic, religious and political conflicts which were inherent in the fabric of life in the Roman Near East: Who governed? How should men and women determine what is right and wrong? How should the powers of this world, the emperors, kings and potentates, govern the lives of their subjects?

[14] 2 Corinthians 11:32–3.

You could do worse, if you wanted to plumb the mind of Paul, than look up the words he used for 'righteousness' and 'love' – both divine attributes – in a Greek lexicon. Whereas for the generality of seekers after truth, since Plato, righteousness or *dikaiosune* was a human quality, a skill to be learnt, for Paul it was a quality possessed by God alone – dispensed or withheld from the universe as God chose. *Agape*, too, a word that Paul did not exactly invent but which he made his own, is love which is one way. It is God's love for his chosen, not the other way round. Paul seldom speaks of human beings loving God. It is open to question whether he believed they could, or even whether they should. *Pistis*, or faith, is the proper attitude of a human being in the presence of the Almighty in Paul's vision of things. The surrender to God in his Apocalypse had been absolute. He was to evolve, in his thinking, a system of out-and-out determinism so total that few in later Christian generations were able to match or to follow. A few names, all of them great names, stand out in Christian history – Marcion, Augustine, Luther, Calvin, Kierkegaard – of thinkers bold enough to attempt to apply Paul's vision of God, to make it their own, to draw from it a system. Most have been only too happy to select a few favourite passages from Paul's letters and to ignore the disturbing, the devastating, implications of the whole. That is, that the human will has no freedom whatsoever; the human endeavour to pursue the good is at best foolish, at worst a sort of blasphemy outside the Covenant. And the Old Covenant of Sinai has been done away and replaced by the New Testament, the revelation of God in Christ to Paul. In Paul's poem about the universe – it is too ecstatic, too jagged, too hither and thither to be described in his writings as a system – the sheer terribleness of God's justice, the absolute ruthlessness of it and its arbitrariness are set against the Cross. He makes of the dying Jesus as it were a Prometheus to challenge the cruelty of the First Cause; but unlike those who take comfort in the Prometheus myth, Paul never once suggests that the First Cause has any reason to show love and mercy. 'For the wrath of God is revealed from heaven against all ungodliness and wickedness of those who by their wickedness suppress the truth.'[15] Only the 'love' of God, and the love of God alone – Paul has to invent a new word for it – can provide hope. That hope can come only with the complete surrender of will, mind and heart to Christ.

[15] Romans 1:18.

No wonder those who have pondered it most deeply have said, 'No one has ever understood Paul, and the only one who did understand him, Marcion, misunderstood him.'[16] Or, 'I doubt whether there is a single one of us capable of having to do personally with a personal God in the old Christian or Jewish sense. In comparison with those heroes, we are mere rags and tatters, one of a series, we come in dozens, like shoals of herring.'[17]

John Henry Newman,[18] who began as a hero and then joined the shoals of herring, reminds us that the emperor Nero banished magicians from Rome not because they were politically dangerous. He was afraid of them. In a post-Enlightenment world, we assume that power is something which human beings can manipulate and seize for themselves. For the ancients, this was not necessarily so. Magicians who could control, or placate, or summon up the 'powers' which govern the universe might have more 'power' than a mere general or politician. The figure of Apollonius of Tyana reminds us that itinerant preachers were a familiar feature in the ancient world. It was a line of business in which the Jews by no means held a monopoly. Apollonius travelled even further than Paul did in his missionary endeavours, visiting Ethiopia and Egypt and, in his eastward meanderings, reaching as far as India, though his chief area of operation was the Mediterranean, and Asia Minor in particular. A long-haired vegetarian of considerable eloquence, he would seem to have been gifted with miraculous powers on a scale to rival, if not to outstrip, those of the apostles – casting out demons, raising the dead, and healing the sick. The most eloquent Christian essay on Apollonius describes him as 'an ordinary Pythagorean, which may be comprehended in three words: mysticism, travel and disputation'.[19]

Paul's life could be similarly described. And for the first seventeen years after his conversion we have no reason to doubt that all three tastes were indulged to the full. Travel, whether for commercial reasons or a combination of commerce and inner restlessness, was a constant feature of Paul's life. He tells us that he went off, after the conversion,

---

[16] Franz Overbeck in tabletalk with Adolf Harnack, the great historian of Dogma in the mid 1880s, quoted in Albert Schweitzer, *The Mysticism of Paul the Apostle*, p. 38.
[17] Søren Kierkegaard, *Journals* (The Last Years XI A.35), edited and translated by Ronald Gregor Smith, London, 1965, p. 200.
[18] J. H. Newman, *Historical Sketches*, vol. 1, p. 311.
[19] *ibid.*, p. 126.

to the kingdom of the Nabateans, where he would have visited the flourishing cities of Philadelphia (modern Amman), Jerash and Petra (the capital of Aretas).

We do not know whether, on these journeyings, Paul preached his new-found 'Gospel', or whether the Gospel was something which was at this time growing within him like the mustard seed preparing to become a great shrub. It was during this period that he left the kingdom of the Nabateans and made his way back to Damascus, and it was on this journey (almost certainly) that he met Cephas – that is Peter – in Jerusalem. The encounter lasted a couple of weeks, and it is extraordinary that this new convert to the love of Jesus was not introduced on this occasion to any of the other followers of the Way except for Jesus's brother James.

Presumably, he was afraid of confronting those whom he had so lately persecuted, afraid of the tumult which would ensue, and perhaps afraid of assassination? It would be fascinating to know what was discussed by Peter and Paul and James at this preliminary meeting, or series of meetings. What was their shared faith? If they had been arrested by a Grand Inquisitor during that two-week period, what account could they give of the distinctive doctrines of the Messianic Reform Movement to which they now held allegiance?

First, they would agree that the End was Near. The promised time, the messianic age, when God would fulfil his purposes for the human race, as revealed in the Prophetic books of the Scriptures, was upon them. At any moment, the present order of things would be wound up.

Secondly, this destiny, which was something understood by many Jews to be part of the divine scheme, was uniquely linked with the person and mission of Jesus of Nazareth. Whether Jesus himself had claimed to be the Messiah, and whether Jesus himself believed that the End of Days had come, we shall probably never know for certain.[20] But we do know that his brothers and his friends, after the Crucifixion, believed that Jesus was the Messiah, the chosen one of God. They believed that God had set his seal on his purposes by raising Jesus from the dead and they probably believed that this Jesus was to be identified with the Son of Man in Daniel, who would soon come on the clouds to rescue the redeemed of Israel.

Thirdly, it hardly needs to be said that this was an all-Jewish

[20] J. A. T. Robinson, for instance, in *Jesus and His Coming*, believes that the disciples misinterpreted Jesus's teaching about the End.

movement. It began among the Jews. Jesus was a Jew. All the movement's terms of reference come from the Jewish Scriptures. And yet – the paradox which we have already rehearsed when discussing the temple – the Jewish inheritance was not given to the Jews alone. Even the most rigidly sectarian Jews today do not believe that the God of Israel is a tribal God. They believe he is the God of the whole earth and therefore the Creator and sustainer of the whole human race. In the coming messianic age, would this ever-merciful God cast aside those who were not born of the inheritance of Israel? On the contrary. We find in the prophecies the assurance that the Holy Spirit of God will be poured out on all flesh.

Paul might have accepted this primitive and threefold creed, but he brought to the movement a much more capacious imaginative inheritance, filled with a wide variety of myths, and a memory of customs which he had seen along the trade route from Ephesus to Antioch. He did not originally seek to alter the messianic beliefs of Peter; but we can assume, from an early stage, that the two men were at variance over the matter of the admission of Gentiles to full membership – not just of their own particular holy group, but to the family of Israel, that is, to the company of the redeemed. It is possible that the seeds of this division were present even in the earliest meeting between the prince of the Apostles and the Apostle of the Gentiles. Acts tells a story, directly after the conversion of Paul, about a vision given to Peter. It was as if he saw a great sheet in the sky, containing all the animals of earth, including all the beasts forbidden in the Scriptures. A heavenly voice told him that it was now lawful to consume anything he liked, and that, in effect, the ancient Jewish dietary laws were null and void. Even assuming that the vision took place, as Acts avers, in the house of a tanner (that is to say, in the house of a man whose trade put him in a dubious position *vis-à-vis* the Jewish Law, in constant danger of corpse-contamination), the story of this 'vision' is surprising, given the fact that we find Peter several years later adopting a very ambivalent attitude towards Jews eating with Gentiles. The 'vision' would seem to have been supplied by the inventive imagination of St Luke, who uses it as a prelude to the baptism by Peter of a Roman god-fearer, a centurion called Cornelius. While these seem more like stories made up to cheer a later 'church', where Jews and Gentiles worship together, than they seem like history, the stories might contain, at their conclusion in Luke's narrative, the nugget from which they grew. 'The Holy Spirit fell upon all who heard the word. The circumcised believers who had come with Peter were astounded that the gift of the Holy Spirit had been poured out even on the Gentiles.'[21]

So much for the hopes of Peter and James. From the beginning, however, while embracing these hopes, Paul made of them something personal and distinctive. For he relates the saving story of God's work in the world to his own story, and by doing that, he allows every single believer to partake of that inner drama. 'I have been crucified . . . and it is no longer I who live, but it is Christ who lives in me. And the life I now live in the flesh I live by faith in the Son of God, who loved me and gave himself for me.'[22]

Acts tells us that after praying in the temple (presumably during this fortnight's trip) Paul fell into a trance and was informed that his visions would not be acceptable to the former victims of his persecutions. The voice told him, 'Go, for I will send you far away to the Gentiles.'

Paul found himself, after a journey through Antioch, back in his old home town of Tarsus, a place that, according to Apollonius, was a 'city of wags and bullies, where fine stuffs are more valued than science is at Athens'. The inhabitants lolled by the river-bank 'like so many water-fowl'.[23]

If, as Pliny says, Tarsus displayed 'the infinite majesty of the Roman peace', was this true for the Tarsean Jews at this time? The accession of Gaius (nicknamed Caligula or Little-boots) in 37 introduced a sinister and terrifying chapter of history for the Jews.[24] The comparative geniality or cynicism of earlier emperors had allowed the Jews, for the most part, to retain their civic and religious loyalties without contradiction. The new emperor, to all appearances, actually believed in his own divinity, which placed an intolerable stumbling-block in the path of the devout monotheist.

For the Jews of Alexandria, the reign had started badly with riots against the Jews to which the praetorian prefect Flaccus (his own position very precarious *vis-à-vis* Caligula) turned a cautiously blind eye. There had been some unfortunate blunders, among them the failure of Flaccus to send to Rome the *politeuma* written by the

[21] Acts 10:45.
[22] Galatians 2:19–20.
[23] Philostratus, *The Life of Apollonius of Tyana*, I, vii.
[24] E. Mary Smallwood, *The Jews Under Roman Rule*, pp. 238–45.

Alexandrian Jews in the new emperor's honour. The largest Jewish population outside Palestine had thereby placed itself in bad odour with the most capriciously cruel and megalomaniac of the emperors. The worst of the anti-Jewish riots broke out when Agrippa I passed through Alexandria on his way to Judaea in 38; and things reached the point where the Greeks actually deprived the Jews of the use of their synagogues. A massacre took place in the Jewish ghetto; Jewish shops and houses were looted and abandoned; Jewish refugees from Alexandria found themselves huddled in the cemetery with nowhere else to sleep.

With considerable courage, Philo, one of the richest and certainly the wisest Jew of the period, and four other Jews, led a delegation to Rome during the winter of 39–40 (when travelling conditions were at their worst) to remonstrate with the emperor and to insist that civil rights were restored to the Alexandrian Jews.[25] When they arrived, they found the emperor away on his campaigns in Gaul. It was late August before he had returned and the delegation had managed to secure an interview.

'So you are the people who refuse to acknowledge me as a god', was how he greeted them. Philo and his friends endeavoured to draw the distinction between offering sacrifices in their temple for the emperor (which they did) and the blasphemy of offering sacrifices *to* him. Caligula's next question was 'Why do you not eat pork?' When the hearing was ended, he made the dismissive statement, 'I think these men are lunatics rather than criminals for not recognising that I am god.'

Had Caligula not been murdered in 41, it is doubtful whether Philo's embassy to Rome would have been of much effect, or whether the lot of the Alexandrian Jews would have been improved. In 39–40 trouble broke out in Jamnia, some thirty miles to the west of Jerusalem. The Greek population of the town, as an act of deliberate provocation against the Jews, erected a statue in honour of the Imperial cult, and a Jewish mob promptly tore it down. The emperor, when he heard of this outrage against his divinity, announced that he would exact a terrible revenge. He commissioned a giant statue of himself dressed as Jupiter and commanded Petronius, the governor of Syria, to have it set up in the temple at Jerusalem. The temple would from henceforth be dedicated to the Imperial cult.

[25] Philo, *De Legatione ad Gaium*, 307.

PAUL

Even to moderate Jews, disinclined to open rebellion against the authorities, such a proposal must have called to mind the blasphemy of Antiochus Epiphanes, who, in 168 BC, had erected a statue of the Olympian Zeus in the Holy of Holies – this was the Desolating Sacrilege, the Abomination of Desolation.

It was a sign of the End in the mind of at least one Jewish apocalyptic writer. 'When you see the desolating sacrilege set up where it ought not to be (let the reader understand), then those in Judaea must flee to the mountains; the one on the housetop must not go down or enter the house to take anything away; the one in the field must not turn back to get a coat.'[26]

An enormous delegation of Jews walked to Ptolemais to meet Petronius and to plead with him to desist from the insane scheme. The mob chanted that they were prepared to die for the Torah. Petronius silenced them:'Will you, then, make war on your emperor?' The Jews replied that they offered sacrifices twice a day for the emperor and for the Roman people, but that if he set up his statue he must sacrifice the entire Jewish nation. As a result of this debate, Petronius sensibly withdrew the legions to Antioch until the following spring, by which time, mercifully, Caligula had been killed.

These events must effect our reading of the New Testament, and they must have had their effect on Paul, as he waited, in what for us is silence, to emerge on to the scene. In the early first century, the mythology of the Maccabean period did much to sustain the spirit of the Jewish nation, whose freedom was curtailed by the legions and whose religious sensibilities were challenged and upset by the existence of the Herodian temple itself, and by the threat of actual blasphemy

[26] Mark 13:14–16. D. E. Nineham, *Saint Mark*, pp. 352–4, discusses the likelihood of this being a Jewish apocalypse from this date which was incorporated into the Gospel tradition and placed as a prophecy into the mouth of Jesus by the evangelists. Some commentators take this 'apocalypse' as a reference to the Roman siege of Jerusalem in 68–70. If so, it is surprising, when they placed this passage on to Jesus's lips as an *ab eventu* prophecy, that none of the evangelists emended it to make it fit the situation of 68–70 more plausibly. When Titus besieged the city in 68, he had already taken care to occupy the surrounding hill-country, and those who were caught in the siege had no possibility of fleeing to the hills. Besides, when Titus reached the sanctuary, he did not, as Caligula had wanted to do, set up a blasphemous idol therein. He set it on fire and gutted it. Much the likeliest date for this passage must be the period when there was an actual possibility of the Abomination of Desolation being set up in the temple. Since nearly all commentators believe that this passage started life as a piece of Jewish apocalyptic which has been incorporated into the Gospel narrative, it remains possible to believe in a 'late' date for the Gospel and an early date for the apocalypse, though there is no logical necessity for this.

on the part of the Imperial powers. From such events grew the messianic hopes that the Deliverer of Israel, the Avenger, the Messiah would come – a military figure. Babylon in the old 'prophecies' of Daniel becomes Rome. The Desolating Sacrilege becomes emperor-worship. When the Gospels came to be written down, for a readership who could certainly have included Roman magistrates, censors or soldiers, the compilers went out of their way to emphasise how fiercely loyal to the Empire Jesus and his friends had been. We have stories of John the Baptist blessing Roman soldiers, popular centurions building synagogues in Galilee, and Jesus commending the faith of one centurion as greater than anyone's in Israel. We even read of a Roman army officer at the foot of the Cross exclaiming that Jesus was the Son of God. Responsibility for the death of Jesus is attributed firmly, by these writers or compilers, to 'the Jews', as though Jesus himself was not a Jew.

The truth is, however, that, whatever Jesus proclaimed about himself, his followers were using politically emotive language in describing him as Messiah. It is not just a 'spiritual' title. Even if we do not believe that Jesus was a freedom fighter against the Romans, the Gospels themselves are artless enough to let us know that some of his disciples were precisely that. The persecution of the 'early Christians' was, as we have seen, almost inevitable, given the position of the temple, the high priestly families, the tense situation in Jerusalem during and immediately after the procuratorship of Pontius Pilate. The reign of Gaius might have prompted the more resolutely military-minded of religious Jews to believe that the End was Near, and that the End would be hastened by those prepared to revive the Maccabean spirit and take up the sword. The Maccabean spirit was not the only one alive in Jewry. Philo had shown not only that there was the way of robust verbal self-defence against Gentile aggression, but, in his philosophical writings, a great assimilation between Jewish and Graeco-Roman ways of looking at the world. Josephus, later in the century, was a Jewish traitor, if viewed from a purely Maccabean point of view; but that was not how he saw himself. He saw the wish of the Jews to fight the Romans as suicidal and pointless. From the position of old age, and an extremely comfortable 'grace-and-favour' residence in Rome, Josephus could write the history of his people and recommend the way of political expediency and accommodation.

If we regard Paul as little better than a hired police thug, whose head happened to be buzzing with religious dreams and fantasies, then it is perhaps not surprising that he should come down so firmly, particularly in his letter to the Romans, against the notion of resistance to the 'powers'. For me, however, this analysis of Paul's nature, as it breathes out of the page, does not quite make sense. Admittedly, this is the territory of subjective 'feeling' where nothing can be proved; but the surviving writings of Paul do not to me read like those of a quisling or a traitor or a thug or a crook. And yet we do not hope to understand him unless his writings are viewed in the context of their age. And perhaps the most troubling passage in all his writings is the thirteenth chapter of Romans: 'let every person be subject to the governing authorities.'

Paul's politics, if we may call them that, grow out of his vision of Christ's glory, but it would not be impertinent to say that his theology, in part, grows out of the conflicts in his world. Having returned to Tarsus, where he spent the best part of a decade, a decade of tremendous turbulence in the history of the Jewish race, he must have had time to ask himself how his 'apocalypse' affected this world around him; how did it change the relations between the Jews and the Romans which were so violent, so tense? Reading and rereading the Scriptures, interestingly enough in Greek, Paul must have been forming the questions which occupy his mind in his written work: at what point did the manifestation of God to his people turn itself into a 'religion'; at what point did the faith of his fathers become an 'ism' – Judaism? How could such a grotesque travesty of the meaning of the Scriptures, the changing of a universalist creed into an embattled sect, have come to pass? How did it come to pass that the Messiah, who died on a Roman cross, could be the Man for Others, the Saviour of the World? What happened to Paul in his 'apocalypse' – whether it all came to him at once or dawned on his mind gradually – was 'the revelation of the mystery that was kept secret for long ages'. He had become that slightly alarming figure, the man who could *explain everything*. But while by the banks of the Cydnus he sat with the Tarsean 'water-fowl' hearing them bargain over the price of linen, his fellow-Jews in Rome, both those who did and those who did not follow the new Way, were living face to face with dilemmas which to him were largely notional. Rome, the ultimate destiny of Paul, though he was not to visit it for twenty years, is where we must go for one chapter.

VI

THE CHURCH OF ROME

THE PERIOD WHILE Paul was thus at large – more than fifteen years after the Damascus apocalypse – was one in which the relations between the Roman Principate and the Jews in different parts of the Empire became more tense and more difficult. The tension between differing branches of Jewry reflects this much larger, underlying, political situation. When Paul received his revelation from the Risen Jesus, the emperor was still Tiberius. By the time Paul emerged again into Luke's narrative (*circa* 45+), the emperor Caligula (37–41) had finished his lurid and murderous reign and been replaced by his uncle Claudius. The very status of the province of Judaea had changed three times – from a divided group of territories ruled over by tetrarchs and Roman procurators, to being, for a brief moment, a quasi-independent kingdom once more, and back to being a divided province ruled directly from Rome. The capital itself of Judaea was changed from Caesarea to Jerusalem and back to Caesarea. Jews were uncertain where they stood in relation to the Roman authorities; and those authorities themselves became increasingly uncertain, and edgy, about the position of the Jews.

Above all, perhaps, the most important fact in Christian history took place during these years of Paul's silence in the regions of Arabia, Syria and Cilicia. That is, the messianic movement which proclaimed Jesus as Lord reached Rome. The whole of Paul's later ministry, as it is described for us in the surviving Christian documents, is worked out in the context of the fact that the people of Rome have already heard the Good News. We need to remind ourselves constantly that for the followers of Jesus the world was coming to an end, history was finishing. For them, the arrival of believers in the centre and capital of the Empire was not to be seen as a spiritual Aeneid, as later generations of Christians were to see it. They knew nothing, and were in no position to know anything, at the beginning of the 40s, of what Rome would be in the Christian mind from the moment that

Nero lit his grotesque fires in the gardens of the Vatican in 64. They knew nothing of the heroic sanctity displayed in the catacombs, nor of the catalogues of the martyred dead, the establishment of a 'Church', with orders and doctrines, the conversion of the emperor Constantine nearly three centuries hence, the unthinkable banishing of the old gods, the replacement of Rome's great temples with Christian basilicas, the accretions of pious legend in the minds of pilgrims about the apostolic origins of the Roman Church. All that lay in the future.

In Paul's lifetime, the 'Roman revolution', started by Augustus, the change from a republic ruled by a senate to an Empire ruled by a dictator, was far from complete; nor could any of those caught up in its ineluctable processes fully understand each and every implication of the transition from republicanism to despotism which Augustus had set so ruthlessly in hand. Even the divine Augustus himself could not have predicted to what degree and in which areas of provincial life of a now enormous Empire the transition would affect or disrupt the populace. Would the Macedonian farmer notice, or the Ephesian medical man, or the Alexandrian professor, if the Roman Senate and people, though preserved in name, were the creatures of a military despotism? Would it change the lives of Greek merchants, Asian sailors or the ragged Gaulish or British huntsmen in their damp forests, if the established traditions of republicanism were displaced in the Italian capital? The answer must in most of these cases be 'yes and no'. But there was one race and one group within the Empire for whom this political development, from republicanism to despotism, was to have catastrophic effects.

It was a transition from a government, in effect, by aristocracy (at least, in its accurate Greek sense) to the perilous experiment of placing the autocracy in the hands of one man and his usually appalling family, dependent for their survival and power on the whims of the army and the favour of the masses. Every Roman value for which Cicero had stood, a century before, seemed to be publicly disregarded. The expansion of the Empire (using the word to mean territory) went hand in hand with the extension of Empire (in its sense of the autocratic rule of the Princeps; not for nothing does the title *imperator* mean a military general). How far the two things, the expansion of territory and the increase in the Emperor's autocratic powers, were linked to one another, or even grew out of one another, was something which each individual emperor, together with his advisers, was to discover or invent, as he proceeded. There was no blueprint in history for an Empire of this kind or this scale. In hindsight one could say that as a political entity and concept it contained so many contradictory elements that it was destined to destroy itself, even had it not contained so many anarchic and irreconcilable elements. Certainly one vital element in what led to the crisis in Judaism and the separate development of Christianity was, precisely, the novelty of the Roman political innovation. This was not an Empire which had always been as it was and would always continue the same. It was a Frankenstein's monster, a political experiment which had grown out of hand before it came to birth, a semi-accident of the Civil Wars between Caesar and Pompey.

By the end of the 30s, in deference to an old childhood friendship with Agrippa I, Caligula had the vagabond Jew shaved and dressed like a king and made ruler of the ancient kingdom of Judaea. By the end of the 40s, Judaea was partitioned, Caligula was dead and Claudius was expelling the Jews from Rome. The shadowy figure of St Peter, the legendary first 'Bishop of Rome', is caught up nebulously in this drama. All these matters require consideration before we encounter Paul again, back from his travels *circa* 49.

Claudius, that most paradoxical and difficult of the emperors to understand, was an assiduous practitioner of the old Roman religion. Under his principate, the College of Haruspices was restored, the Augurius Salutis was repeated, the Saecular Games were revived (in 47). The emperor himself made frequent, and often ostentatious, visits to soothsayers, astrologers and augurers. But in all this apparent conservatism 'the desire for preservation was no more than superficial'.[1] The *pietas* felt towards the old divinities, who had preserved the republic, was directed towards the person of the princeps himself; and the government of Rome attracted to itself not merely the political loyalties but the religious devotion of its people. Religion had always been a department of state as far as the Romans were concerned, but now the state took upon itself the qualities of divinity.

This development came about partly through the design (in the case of Gaius, as we have seen, the actual lunacy) of the emperors themselves, partly as a result of the movement of peoples. In the first four decades of our era, Asiatics of all varieties – slaves, freedmen, military, merchants – migrated into Rome. For many orientals, the concept of monarchy was essentially a religious one. Thinking of their

[1] Arnaldo Momigliano, *Claudius: The Emperor and His Achievement*, p. 47.

emperor as their monarch, their *basileus* (an idea which would have been as ludicrous as it would have been offensive to old republicans such as Cicero), was perfectly natural to the Levantine, Greek and Asiatic mishmash who now swarmed into the Roman slums. For them, a monarch was, almost by definition, a divine being. There was no more difficulty in believing that Claudius was a god than in attending a sacrifice at the temple of Herakles, or offering a prayer to Osiris. The growth of such concepts went hand in hand with Claudius's apparent conservatism, and he did nothing to discourage the idea, in the popular mind, that he was a God. There were many within the Empire who might view such a development as ludicrous, but there was perhaps only one group, and that a substantial one, for whom it was inherently dangerous: and that was the Jews, the fundamental tenet of whose faith was that there was but one God and that they should have none but Him.[2] The question which affects certain religious groups within the United States today, or devout Muslims trying to live within a secular Western state such as France or Great Britain, was one which most urgently faced the Jews of the first century. Most political thinkers who have considered the matter have taken the view that the state has a duty to decree the religious customs of its subjects. It is axiomatic to Plato, as it is to Hobbes, that private religion is the greatest likely source of sedition and anarchy. Marx's essay 'On the Jewish Question'[3] could have been written about the Jews in the Roman Empire rather than about those of Germany in 1843, for it poses essentially the same questions as faced Philo, Josephus and Paul. If a state is to be fully a state (and no one can doubt that the Empire of the first century would fit Marx's iron definition of a state very fully) why should it brook dissidence on allegedly religious grounds? So long as the religious allegiance did nothing to interfere with an individual's loyalty to the state, then it could do no social harm; but if you emancipate a religious group or a race within a cohesive political setting, that setting ceases to cohere; the state ceases to be a state in so far as the religion is allowed to be a religion. Marx, of course, as a secularist, believed that 'Judaism continued to exist not in spite of history, but owing to history'. It is in so far as they agree or disagree with him that the Jews of the first century, as it were, line up. Josephus, the Sadducees, and, one might guess, the great majority of

[2] Exodus 20:3.
[3] Karl Marx and Frederick Engels, *Collected Works*, vol. 3 (1975), pp. 146–74.

Jews being only too happy to see themselves as 'products of history' rather than rebels against it;[4] the Pharisees, the Zealots and the patriots of other kinds standing firmly against the *saeculum* and regarding their own laws, the laws of religion, as being the ones which bound them, rather than the laws imposed by Caesar. The gnomic utterance ascribed to Jesus that the Jew should render to Caesar those things which were Caesar's and to God the things which were God's begs all the deepest political and historical questions of this period, as far as the Jewish race is concerned. For it was precisely in deciding which things were Caesar's and which things were God's that the tension between the Jews and the Romans arose. In order to understand why St Peter might, even by the wildest stretch of unlikelihood, have been in Rome in the early 40s, or even in order to understand why the Christian legends might have developed the suggestion of such a thing, we need to remember the kingdom in which he lived, Judaea, and the vicissitudes through which it was passing in the lifetime of King Agrippa I.

Agrippa I (b. 10 BC) was perhaps the only grandchild of Herod the Great to inherit the genius and dynamism of that potentate. Unlike his grandfather, however, he had the gift of rubbing along well with a wide variety of people, and he was in the unique position in the first century of being accepted as a king by the majority of the Jews and as a responsible leader by the Roman authorities. Agrippa (one quarter Jewish, the rest Idumean, with notably lively Arab features as we see from his coins) had, like Herod the Great, spent much of his life in Rome. He was brought up at the court of Tiberius and was the companion in youth of the future emperor Caligula. No man in those days anxious for political power could avoid risking his neck. Agrippa took extraordinary risks, leading a more or less pirate existence in order to raise the enormous sums of money necessary, when the time came, to bribe his way into favour with the insane Caligula. Tiberius and Caligula both had reasons to doubt Agrippa's trustworthiness, and Caligula actually had him imprisoned. But Agrippa led a charmed life. After a series of adventures and scrapes which have been pertinently likened to *The Thousand and One Nights*[5] he became the king of Judaea, contriving to oust from power all his relations who clung on to puppet titles and local governorships. At first, Agrippa accepted (from Caligula)

[4] Though perhaps unable to echo Marx's view that 'the Jew is perpetually created by civil society from its own entrails'; *op. cit.*, p. 171.
[5] Stewart Perowne, *The Later Herods*, p. 58.

the client-kingship of the region of which his uncle Philip had been the tetrarch. By the time Caligula was dead, however, and his old childhood friend Claudius was emperor, Agrippa was able to see off all his former rivals and enemies and to become the king of the Promised Land. For the first time in that century, the land of the Jews was united under one leader.

On the death of Caligula, the Jews of Alexandria had broken out in a violent riot which amounted to an armed insurrection against the Empire. The riot was quelled, but Claudius accompanied this pacification with an edict in which he reiterated the special and privileged position of the Jews within the Empire. He admitted that Caligula had been insane[6] and conceded that 'it is therefore right to permit Jews throughout the empire to keep their ancient customs without let or hindrance'. It would have been a very naive Jew who read this edict without realising that there were now very strong conditions attached to the privilege and that the 'auld alliance', established by Julius Caesar between the Jews and the Roman Empire, was in danger of coming apart.

Having issued this edict, Claudius reappointed Agrippa to be the king of the Jews. Agrippa returned to Jerusalem and demonstrated the fervour of his quarter-Jewish credentials by undergoing all the appropriate ceremonies in the temple and by paying for the Nazirites[7] to have their heads shorn. The golden chain that had been donated to him by the mad emperor Caligula he had suspended from the temple treasury as a thank-offering, an appropriate symbol, since he owed his elevation partly to luck, but certainly as much to the divine Roman emperors as to the God of Abraham, Isaac and Jacob.

Like his friend Claudius, Agrippa was a politician. While capable of being fervently Jewish among the Jews, he was happy, in other parts of his dominions, to be a cosmopolitan Roman governor. His territories included Syria and the modern Lebanon. It was he who was largely

---

[6] Josephus, *Ant*, XIX, v, 2.

[7] More properly, Nazirites, a body of Jews specially consecrated to the service of God, as Samson had been – *vide* Judges 13:5ff. – by abstaining from eating or drinking the product of the vine and by avoiding contact with the dead. They also demonstrated their holiness by refusing to cut their hair. If they accidentally suffered defilement by the death of someone beside them, they were compelled to undergo a purification ritual by shaving and burning the hair and renewing their vows. *Vide* Acts 21:23–6 where Paul appears to have demonstrated his loyalty to Judaism by joining with certain fellow-believers in Christ who were contemplating such vows; F. L. Cross, *The Oxford Dictionary of the Christian Church*, p. 957.

responsible for the expansion of Berytus (Beirut), where, safely distant from the Jewish patriots and their fervour, he provided lavish musical festivals in the high Roman manner and gladiatorial contests in which 1,400 condemned men were obliged to fight to the death. The crowd loved it, undeterred by the fact that in organising such an event, their king was infringing the sixth commandment of the Decalogue.

For all his cynicism, Agrippa I was a ruler who suited both sides of the argument which was set to develop between Jews and Romans. The patriots could believe that for the first time since Herod the Great the Jews had their own system of security (the legions had temporarily withdrawn), their own laws, their own taxes, even their own coinage (though the extremists would not have approved of Agrippa's quasi-idolatrous placing of his own head on a coin). The Land belonged once more to the Jews. Moderate Jews and realists were aware that Agrippa really only held his kingdom on sufferance from Rome. The price he had to pay for his crown was a price that it was to his advantage to pay, namely the stability of the kingdom. The hothead factions, the Zealots, the sicarii, the messianic Freedom Fighters of whatever name, sect or persuasion, were to be suppressed whenever they were found.

It is not surprising, therefore, that Agrippa should have chosen to suppress the messianic movement associated with the followers of Jesus. He had James arrested and executed (that is, James, son of Zebedee the Fisherman, not the brother of Jesus who now led the group in Jerusalem).[8] Luke tells us that this was a popular action: 'it pleased the Jews'.[9] Since the decapitation of Galilean fishermen might be thought a very easy way for an absolute monarch to keep the populace in a good humour, Agrippa ordered the arrest of another of the band, Simon Peter. The king had reckoned without the intervention of an angel, who, we are informed, secured the Apostle's miraculous release from prison. From this time (Pesach 42?) we can date the peregrinations of Peter, who appears to have set off to Syrian Antioch, a place which was destined to become a (the?) major centre of the new movement's strength. It was in Antioch that the word 'Christian', or as we might say Messianist, was first coined.[10]

For any unfervent citizen, anxious to do no more than pursue his

[8] Acts 12:1–2.
[9] Acts 12:3.
[10] Acts 11:26.

or her lawful occasions, the frenzy of the messianic movements must have been highly uncongenial. But there are additional reasons why Agrippa's decision to persecute the Christians might have been met with a particular welcome both from Jews and Romans. Not only was the new movement supposed to preach sedition against the high priests and against the Jewish hierarchy,[11] but they also proclaimed that the present order of things would soon be dismantled altogether to be replaced by a messianic age in which Jesus would return as King to rule over a new heaven and a new earth. To believe this with fervour would hardly be compatible with good citizenship, and the temptation in some quarters to hasten the time when the Lord would gather his elect to himself would have been strong. Magistrates as well as priests would have no reason to trust the Jesus-movement, however loudly it proclaimed its peaceful intentions.

The authorities in Rome, even more than the quisling Agrippa in Jerusalem, had a further reason to be suspicious of the new messianic movement: its powerful attraction to Gentiles. If our analysis has been correct, the more authority that came to be invested in the person of the princeps, the more dictatorial the Empire became and the harder it was to maintain the comparatively genial tolerance towards religious dissidents which had obtained in the days of the republic. The more power the state gathers to itself, the less tenable *any* religion which dissents from that power, the less plausible it is that a distinction may be drawn between private and public morality. The emperor would have agreed with Marx that a Jew who asks for religious liberty is claiming a political right for himself with which a secular state can not comply without undermining itself. 'The groundless law of the Jew is only a religious caricature of groundless morality and right in general.'[12] The last thing a dictatorship would welcome would be the spreading of this 'groundless' religious faith to non-Jews, the creation, within Rome itself, of a body of people who, like the Jews, owed no primary allegiance to the secular powers, but to another king.[13] The paradox becomes most striking in the writings of Paul, who tried in his own person to be a contradiction in terms:[14] a good Jewish citizen of the Empire who wished to admit Gentiles into his new-found

[11] Acts 4:1, 2; 5:17–21; 5:29; 6:11; 23:4.
[12] Karl Marx, *op. cit.*, p. 172.
[13] 'They are all acting contrary to the decrees of the emperor, saying that there is another king named Jesus.' Acts 17:7.
[14] 1 Corinthians 9:22.

faith. But the nature of the paradox is much bigger than Paul's divided selves. All first-century Jews had to struggle with it; all the emperors in deciding what to do about the Jewish question, and later with the growth of Christianity, had to face it. Philo, Josephus, Agrippa I himself, were all in their differing ways responding to the new political realities of the first century, to an unfolding tension which had its own inexorable logic ('the social emancipation of the Jew is the emancipation of society from Judaism'),[15] but which many individual players in the game would much prefer to have opted out of. The Philo who wrote the *Legatio*, the Josephus who at the end of the century wrote *Contra Apion*, would certainly have wished to be out of it. So, too, in all likelihood, would the Claudius who issued the edict of 49; for the tension that the men of the 40s were feeling was what led the next generation into the Jewish War. The last thing which any civil authority wanted during this time of tension was the growth of a new Jewish movement which attracted Gentiles. Gentile adherents of such a sect might start claiming all the Jewish privileges, such as freedom from military service. They would be citizens of two empires, the Roman *saeculum* and the 'egotistical' or 'groundless' (to use Marx's words) inner empire of their own religious faith. Jesus was supposed to have said that no man could serve two masters.[16] The Caesars would have agreed with him.

It was not long, according to the Acts of the Apostles, before God exacted a revenge for his saints. The beginning of August 44 found Agrippa at his seaside palace of Caesarea, and it was here that the annual celebration of the emperor's birthday was held (rather as the highest point in the social calendar in British embassies abroad is, or used to be, the official birthday of the sovereign). On the second morning of the festivities, Agrippa, nothing if not flamboyant, entered the amphitheatre at dawn, wearing a splendid costume made entirely of silver. The early morning rays of the sun caught this wonderful garment, so that 'it glittered in a surprising manner'[17] and inspired his flatterers to cry out that Agrippa was a god. A solemn rereading of Exodus 19 (the encounter between Moses and the God of Sinai), or the sight of the faithful united in prayer in a mosque might be able to make us aware of how profoundly shocking the Jews would have

[15] Karl Marx, *op. cit.*, p. 174.
[16] Matthew 6:24.
[17] Josephus, *Ant*, XIX, viii, 2.

found this exclamation. It is perhaps tedious to reiterate that the gods were a less serious order of being for non-monotheists than for Jews. The reading of almost any classical text, from Homer to Horace, would make one realise that gods were as easily encountered in their world as the fairies in Shakespeare's England.

It is one of the great divisions of the human imagination; difficult for us to envisage if we have been born neither into a great monotheistic faith such as Islam, nor into a polytheistic faith such as Hinduism, but into a post-Christian culture.

Even as the sycophantic crowd called out that Agrippa, in his silver 'creation', was 'divine', an owl, a bird of omen, swooped through the air and settled on a rope above his head. Years before, when an owl had flown over Agrippa when he was the prisoner of Caligula, it had been seen by his fellow-captives as a sign of good luck. This second visitation by the Athenian bird was less happy. Agrippa was seized by an immediate attack of violent dyspepsia and made a speech whose sincerity there is no need to doubt, but which could not have been better calculated to pacify Jewish fears that he was in danger of apostasy. 'I whom ye call a god, am now commanded to depart this life; fate thus reproving the lying words you just now said to me; and I whom you just now called immortal am now hurried off to death.'[18] Acts gloatingly records that he was smitten by an angel (whose presence on this occasion was something which Josephus neglected to mention) and that he was 'eaten by worms'.[19]

While in the short term, the death of Agrippa must have been cheering to those who, for whatever reason, revered the memory of the fisherman James, son of Zebedee, or respected the authority of the fisherman Simon Peter, the death of Agrippa I can be seen, from a broader perspective, to have been a disaster in the history of the Jewish race.[20] His combination of wiliness, cynicism and political acumen was unusual:'He had the virtue, almost unknown in the Levant, of being able to see that a question had two sides.'[21] The quarter century which elapsed between the death of Agrippa I and the sack of

[18] Josephus, *Ant*, XIX, viii, 2.
[19] Acts 12:23.
[20] 'If only Agrippa had lived! It is one of the tragic "ifs" of history. Would he have continued to keep the balance? Could he have prevented the growth of Zealot intransigence, of Greek resentment, of Roman exasperation? We cannot tell; we only know that in his own brief day Agrippa had shown that it could be done.' Stewart Perowne, *The Later Herods*, p. 82.
[21] *ibid*.

Jerusalem by the legions of Titus witnessed a decline in political life precisely in those qualities which Agrippa had in such abundance – moderation, pliability, common sense. From now on, a deadly mixture dominated public affairs in the Roman Near East: a growing violence and recklessness among the Jewish terrorist organisations; an increase of hostility towards the Jews by the Roman authorities at the highest level; weakness on the part of the Jewish leaders, both the puppet high priests and the puppet secular rulers whom Claudius shoved in, but who could not fill the place of Agrippa.

When the contumacious Greeks noticed that the Jews (*pace* Acts) were lamenting their king, they staged a demonstration of their own at Caesarea. They burst into the king's palace, bore off the statues of his daughters, placed them on the rooftops of the brothels and 'did such things to them as are too indecent to be related'.[22] They poured out libations to Charon, the ferryman of the river Styx, for joy that the king had crossed that river into the underworld. It was then that the inhabitants of that troubled region, Jews and Gentiles, could begin to see how fragile the brief period of 'Jewish independence' had been. Claudius, just back from securing a conquest which was also not without historical consequence (that of the island of Britain), imposed martial law in Palestine. Once again, as in the unpopular days of Pontius Pilate, the region became a Roman procuratorial province. Cuspius Fadus was told to put down the insurrection at Caesarea with severity. As a symbol of what had happened, more potent than any purely military conquest, Cuspius once more (as Pilate had done) took the high priest's vestments into custody. The atonement of their sins and the worship of Yahweh himself was now something vouchsafed to the Jews only with the permission of Rome.

At the end of the decade – almost certainly in 49 – Claudius expelled the Jews from Rome because they were causing 'continuous disturbance at the instigation of Chrestus' (a clear garbling of the word Christ).[23] An interest in Christian history can distort the contemporary importance of this act. As far as Suetonius is concerned, it is one tiny episode, conveyed by a mere parenthesis, in a reign crowded with incident. The single sentence which speaks of the 'disturbance' occurs during a chapter in which Claudius has reorganised the army, banned

[22] Josephus, *Ant*, XIX, ix, 1.
[23] Suetonius, *Claudius*, xxv.

travel in Italy except on foot (a classic despot's trick as Stalin's life reminds us), instituted proper fire brigades at Puteoli and Ostia, forbidden foreigners from adopting Roman names, granted the Trojans perpetual exemption from tribute 'as founders of the Roman race' (Claudius the sentimentalist and Hellenist), and attempted to transfer the Eleusinian Mysteries from Athens to Rome.

Still, Suetonius does mention the fact that the Jews, in their uncongenial, slummy quarters in what is now the Trastevere – the crowded region which they knew as Transtiberinum, where trades and minor crafts were carried on, linenweaving, leathermaking, perfumery[24] – were causing continuous trouble at the instigation of 'Chrestus'. Only the most perverse scholars have doubted that 'Chrestus' is Christ, a figure whom the Roman historian mistakenly supposed to be a Jew actually present in Rome and stirring up the rabble. In other words those very fears which we described above – that the monotheistic allure of Judaism should have affected the Gentiles – had already been realised *in Rome itself* by the middle of Claudius's reign. While Paul is still on his travels in the Near East, the Jews of Rome had found themselves divided over the new messianic reform movement in their midst. No certainty can be expressed about the exact nature of the quarrels, but we can have a number of intelligent guesses, both about the quarrel itself and about two matters of historical interest – whether St Peter came to Rome at this period and whether we can believe the early ecclesiastical folklore which states that it was from the testimony of Peter that we receive the first Gospel.

The puerility and grossness of public religion in Rome at this date (every time he concluded a foreign treaty, Claudius sacrificed a sow in the Forum) would be enough to explain the allure of monotheism among those of a serious disposition, just as the relentless incidence of bigamy, incest, murder and divorce in the highest places would be enough to explain the desire in some quarters for a more austere approach to existence. When sweet cakes and jam biscuits are the only items on the menu, the palate yearns for plain bread and butter. It is not surprising that there were many Gentile 'god-fearers' in the Roman synagogue(s), and certainly since the mid-second century BC there had been Jewish proselytisers in the city. (It was their activity which probably led to the expulsion of the Jews in 139 BC: 'Because they

---

[24] Wayne Meeks, *The First Urban Christians: The Social World of the Apostle Paul*, p. 29.

were converting many Italians to their customs', says Dio Cassius.)[25] Even during the Jewish Wars towards the close of the first century BC, the Flavians deemed it necessary to enact laws making it a capital offence for a Gentile to be circumcised.[26] This certainly suggests that Judaism retained a potent attraction for certain Romans, though how many males were actually prepared to risk blemish or death for the sake of religious curiosity must remain a matter of doubt. In spite of its popularity as a 'cult' it is uncertain how many full converts the Jews ever made in Rome – that is to say, how many adult males they persuaded to undergo circumcision and how many adult Italian women were persuaded to undergo baptism by immersion. There are 550 epitaphs readable in the Jewish catacombs in Rome and only seven of them belong to proselytes.[27] This suggests that when the chips were down, a literal willingness to save their skins took the better of the Roman god-fearers.

Judaism certainly offered both the austerity of a strict moral code and the simplicities of a monotheistic philosophy; but then, so did Stoicism, which was in a sense the most popular form of 'personal religion' at this date, and which could be practised without danger of mutilation. In order to discover what made Judaism so special in the eyes of many Gentiles, we need to remind ourselves of the superior potency, when compared with the other spiritual systems, of its magic powers.[28] This has long been recognised. Alexander the Great, for example, worshipped the tetragrammaton carved on the mitre of the high priest at Jerusalem, that is the four-lettered but unutterable name of the Jewish God, Yahweh. Magic derives much of its power from the manipulation and possession of names. The Jews had a God who could not be named and who was therefore very powerful. The mere whisper of Yahweh's name was enough to make Pharaoh drop dead.[29] There was a secret name for Rome; because he uttered it, the magician Valerius Soranus came to a sorry end. In addition, the names of the God of Israel's angels were of the greatest value and occasional efficacy to the magicians, who were easily able as 'god-fearers' to attend the

[25] E. Mary Smallwood, *The Jews Under Roman Rule*, p. 117.
[26] James Parkes, *The Conflict of the Church and the Synagogue*, p. 24. See also J. A. Hild, 'Les Juifs à Rome devant l'opinion et dans la littérature', in *Revue des Etudes Juives*, vols 8, 1971 (p. 11) and 11 (p. 39).
[27] E. Mary Smallwood, *The Jews Under Roman Rule*, p. 205.
[28] Wilfrid Knox, *St Paul and the Church of the Gentiles*, p. 40ff.
[29] Eusebius, *Praeparatio Evangelica*, 9, 27, 13, quoted in F. F. Bruce, *Paul*, p. 73.

synagogues and pick up an oral knowledge, or actual copies, of the Hebrew Scriptures for magical use. The incantatory application of God's name(s) and those of his angels could drive out demons, heal sickness and establish the magician who used such powers as a person of influence. In so far as the Hebrew Deity could claim to be the creator and mover of the planets, it was obviously essential for the astrologers to master the Scriptures. (All the Jews at this date, ranging from the Jewish Platonists of Alexandria to the Essenes of Qumran, would appear to have been obsessed by astrology.) Jesus himself was clearly in some senses of the word a magician, since he called upon powers outside himself to heal and to destroy.[30] He was, according to his followers, able to control the weather, to wither fig-trees with a word and to drive out evil spirits. It is quite possible that the followers of Chrestus, as Suetonius calls them, claimed a superior magical proficiency; and there are those who believe that it was precisely the question of magic which led to the foundation of the Church of Rome.[31]

The most ancient traditions of Christendom, preserved by Eusebius and Justin Martyr,[32] assert that one Simon, known as the Magus and who came from the village of Gitton in Samaria, had been proclaimed divine on account of his supreme magical powers. He came to Rome during the reign of Claudius and, having performed some impressive magic rites, was able to persuade the credulous of his divinity. Eusebius tells us that this Simon had, before leaving Judaea, fallen foul of another Simon – Simon Peter, who denounced him and, so the tradition asserts, followed him to Rome in order to defuse the effects of his magical influence. 'Not for long did his success continue; for on his steps in this same reign of Claudius, the all-good and most beneficent providence of God conducts the mighty and great one of the Apostles, Peter, on account of his virtue the leader of all the rest, to Rome against so great a corruption of life, who like some noble warrior of God with divine weapons, brought the precious merchandise of the light that had been manifest from the east to those in the west.'

In the eighth chapter of Acts, we come across Simon Magus at a slightly earlier stage of his career. In his native Samaria he is regarded

[30] For a discussion of this, see J. Morton Smith, *Jesus the Magician* (1978).
[31] George Edmundson, *The Church of Rome in the First Century*.
[32] Eusebins, *Historia ecclesiastica*, II, 13, 14; Justin Martyr, *Apologia*, I, 6.

as 'a great power', a phrase which suggests he was almost divine in the eyes of his followers. Seeing the superior power or magic of the Holy Spirit, which descended when Peter, Philip and the other Apostles laid hands upon the faithful, he offered money to receive the gift himself (the origin of the later word 'simony' to mean purchasing office in the church).

Justin Martyr also knew the tradition that Simon Magus was believed to be divine. Justin claimed that the Romans had worshipped Simon Magus as a God, and that there was a statue of him on an island in the Tiber, inscribed *Simoni Deo Sancto*. In fact, Justin had seen a statue to the Sabine God Semo Sancus and the inscription read *Semoni Sanco Deo Fidio*. Perhaps local pride (for like Simon Magus, Justin Martyr was a Samaritan) made him want to believe that one of his own countrymen had 'made good' in the capital of the Empire, even though, as a Christian, Justin abominated everything which Simon Magus stood for. Perhaps, simply, he did not know Latin very well. It is interesting, however, that these ideas of human incarnations of divinity should begin in Samaria, the probable seed-bed for the idea of the Christian Incarnation, and the creed of the Fourth Gospel that the Word was made Flesh.

Simon Magus certainly went to Rome. Of that other Simon, Simon Peter, we can be less sure. Although there is absolutely no proof that Peter – revered to this day as the first Bishop of Rome – ever set foot in the celestial city,[33] it has to be said that there is a strong body of later tradition that he did so. Throughout the second century, we have the testimony of Christian writers that Peter and Paul met a martyr's death in Rome and exercised an apostolic ministry there before handing on the episcopate to Linus. Though some of this

[33] Michael Grant keeps an open mind on the question, but in *Saint Peter* (pp. 147–9) lists eight cogent reasons why the tradition of Peter's residence in Rome, or episcopal status in the Roman 'church', should be treated with scepticism. Of these, the strongest must be those arguments based on the letters of Peter's contemporary, Paul. While the letter to the Galatians makes open references to Peter (Cephas) and his activities in Antioch, in the letter to the Romans, with its assertion that the Church of Rome had been founded by another man, Peter is not named. Acts, which eliminates any mention of the quarrel between Peter and Paul, tries to depict them as joint workers in a single endeavour. Had Peter been to Rome, or had there even been the extant legend that Peter went to Rome, Luke would surely have mentioned it in the concluding chapter of Acts when Paul arrives in Rome as a prisoner. In Romans, written in the late 50s, Paul states that he has never met the Christians in Rome. By then he had already met Peter and quarrelled with him. This documentary evidence makes it hard to believe the tradition, of a hundred years later, that the Church of Rome was founded by Peter.

testimony (for example that of Irenaeus) dates from the late second century, it was based on oral traditions and testimonies which were much older. Irenaeus (Bishop of Lyons, AD 177) had been a disciple of Polycarp, who had known the Apostle John. He had spent some years in Rome and would have known the grandchildren of first-generation Roman Christians. This does not prove anything. If you are a Roman Catholic, or sympathise with the Roman Catholic idea, you will be likely to believe it; if you are temperamentally Protestant, you will doubt it. Rome was the capital of the Empire, and the Christian Church intended to exploit the administration, transportation, roads and organisation of the Empire in order to create its own rival spiritual empire. What more natural, then, that the second or third generation of Christians, with their ambition to found the Catholic Church, should pretend that the Chief of the Apostles (whose centre of operations according to Acts was Antioch) had in fact been the first Bishop of Rome? Peter and Paul, by this view of things – witness Paul's expressed ambition, perhaps realised, to visit Spain – were making spiritual capital out of the conquests of the legions.

Again, however, although *we* know that Christianity was destined to become the dominant religion of the Empire, Irenaeus did not. When he wrote, the Christian faith, to which more and more people adhered, was still wrestling with many different religions and with the ethos of the civil powers. The Cross had not conquered. In the time of *his* mentor, Polycarp, who could remember the Apostolic Age, the Romans were seen as barbarous persecutors of the Faithful. And in New Testament times, Rome was seen by many Christians as Babylon. The claim to have visited Rome, or to have been the first Bishop of Rome, would not necessarily have been worth inventing, if you were a key member of that first generation of the Jewish messianic movement which believed that the world would end *in their lifetimes*. Jesus's brother James would not have thought it was anything to boast about, to have sojourned in 'Babylon'.

By the time the Church had become a dominating, and eventually the dominant, religion of the Mediterranean world, the tradition had developed that Peter's episcopate at Rome lasted twenty-five years. We can discount the *Chronicon* of Eusebius as a useful historical tool. In his lists of the 'bishops' of Rome he has merely modelled himself on a Greek work of chronology, the Olympiad, and assigned a period of time to each of the 'bishops' at his disposal on the list. To each entry in the Roman episcopal list there are twelve years, and it would seem as if Eusebius merely doubled this number when estimating the 'episcopate' of the Prince of the Apostles.[34] By counting backwards from the traditional date of St Peter's martyrdom (29 June 64) Eusebius arrives at the 'fact' that Peter arrived in Rome during the reign of Claudius. Nevertheless, while we should have to dismiss Eusebius's methodology (and of course it is quite anachronistic to think of Peter as a 'bishop' in any sense that Eusebius might have used the term!), it is not wholly inconceivable that the Galilean fisherman, driven out from Jerusalem by Agrippa's persecution, found his way to Rome. Jerome records that 'Simon Peter, prince of the Apostles, after an episcopate of the Church at Antioch and preaching to the dispersion of those of the circumcision who had believed, in Pontus, Galatia, Cappadocia, Asia and Bithynia, in the second year of Claudius goes to Rome to oppose Simon Magus, and there for twenty-five years he held the sacerdotal chair until the last year of Nero, that is the fourteenth'.[35]

To the positive testimony of the early Christians that Peter was the first 'bishop' of Rome, we must add the negative testimony which also points in the same direction. No other city ever disputed Rome's claim to be Peter's see; and, perhaps even more significant, given the huge importance attached by the early Christians to burial-places, no other city ever claimed to have St Peter's tomb. 'Probably never was any tradition accepted so universally, and without a single dissentient voice, as that which associates the foundation and organisation of the Church of Rome with the name of St Peter and which speaks of his active connexion with that Church as extending over a period of some twenty-five years.'[36]

Writing to the Roman followers of 'Chrestus' ten years after they caused trouble in the Trastevere trading districts, Paul emphasises the fact that it had never been his custom, as a missionary, to work in districts where the name of Christ had already been heard – 'so that I do not build on someone else's foundation'.[37] Those who suppose that Peter was the first 'Bishop of Rome' naturally interpret Paul's phrase ('allotrion themelion oikodomo') to mean what it says in the version just quoted. But allotrion does not even compel the sense of 'another

[34] Trevor Jalland, The Church and the Papacy (1944), p. 74.
[35] De Viris Illustribus, i.
[36] George Edmundson, The Church of Rome in the First Century, p. 51.
[37] Romans 15:21.

man's'; it could mean 'strange' or 'foreign'. Those who would argue against the likelihood of St Peter having visited Rome at this date would point out that, given Paul's readiness to name Peter (and to come clean about his differences with Peter) when he wrote to the Galatians, it is very odd that Paul should not have named Peter, or Cephas, in this context of his Roman letter. After all, the last chapter of Romans consists almost entirely of names.

The legend of Peter's martyrdom in the 60s is more substantial than the legend of Peter the missionary in the 40s. Perhaps more important than whether it was Peter himself, or another, or a group of others, who took the Word to Rome, is that there obviously was an early community of believers there, at odds within the synagogue. What made the difference in the case of the new movement, the followers of Chrestus? First, the movement was a messianic one. It believed that the great messianic deliverance (not merely from Rome in the case of Palestine, but from the 'rulers of this world') was momently to take effect. The secular power, with all its misguided polytheistic idolatrous ways and all its acceptance of sexual licence, would be brought to an end by the arrival of the Son of Man, the Deliverer promised in Daniel and identified by the new group with their hero, Jesus of Nazareth.

The possibility of such ideas turning into open sedition was obvious and would be disagreeable to the bulk of Jews, who, paradoxically (given their traditional distrust of politics and of monarchical institutions in particular as far as their own internal organisation has been concerned), have always tended, in the great numerical part, to adopt conservative and pro-establishment political standpoints wherever they have resided.

So, the messianic movement in Rome could well have been quarrelling with the more mainstream, conservative Jews who simply wanted to go to the synagogue and give alms and practise their business, but not to be involved in the belief that the Messiah was to come, or had already come.

If he had already come, which was one of the ideas that the new movement probably enshrined from an extremely early stage, then it followed that the prophecies concerning Messiah would be fulfilled in their very lifetimes, in their very midst.

Possibly, however, the row was caused by Simon Magus. Whatever the cause, it is in Rome, probably as early as the 40s, that we begin to see a separation between the synagogues and the households of faith represented by the likes of Priscilla and her husband the tentmaker Aquila – they will surface again later in this story, as business-colleagues and fellow-workers with Paul.

VII

ANTIOCH

THE JESUS-MOVEMENT in Jerusalem was known as the Way, but it did not seek to detach itself from Judaism. For reasons which are obvious, Gentile god-fearers who made the pilgrimage to Jerusalem could never hope to play a full part in the Jewish life of faith unless they were able to cross the Court of the Gentiles in the temple and attend the liturgy. For the uncircumcised, as we have noted, this was an offence punishable by death. So, it is perfectly clear why the Jerusalem Jesus-movement, which was based on the temple and drew most of its early converts from temple priests and temple officials, should be a purely Jewish phenomenon.

After the death of Stephen, however, the Hellenists, the Greek-speaking Jews of the Diaspora who had gathered in Jerusalem and around the friends and family of Jesus, were dispersed. There was a geographical as well as a spiritual division in the Jesus-movement; and the one division helped to exacerbate the other. That is to say, once they were away from the temple, there was much more possibility for Hellenist followers of the Way to pray with the god-fearers. Since in Syrian Antioch there was no temple guard to say, 'I'm sorry, sir, but you can't come in here', the new Gentile converts to the Way could enter into the full fellowship of prayer with their Jewish brothers and sisters. Philip, one of the Hellenists, took the word to Samaria and lived in the largely Gentile city of Caesarea Maritima. Probably, these Hellenist sorties into Samaritan country led to the development of that curious blend of high spirituality, loathing of the human race, and glorification of Jesus which we find in the Fourth Gospel. Other Hellenists went to North Africa and settled in Alexandria. But the centre of Hellenistic faith in Jesus, the place where this fellowship first came to be noticeable, was the Syrian city of Antioch, three hundred and fifty miles north of Jerusalem. It was here that the followers of the movement were first called Christians.[1] A Greek word for a Hellenistic concept. For it would seem extremely likely that before Paul, or the Fourth Gospel, had developed a 'christology' – a sense that the exaltation by God of Jesus had given to Christ a unique status among men, proclaimed him almost a divinity – this idea was being developed by the Hellenists. Most scholars now think it was probably the Hellenists who composed the hymn quoted by Paul in his letter to Philippi and which apostrophises Jesus:

> Who, though he was in the form of God,
> did not regard equality with God as something to be exploited,
> but emptied himself, taking the form of a slave,
> being born in human likeness.
> And being found in human form,
> he humbled himself
> and became obedient to the point of death –
> even death on a cross.
>
> Therefore God also highly exalted him
> and gave him a name that is above every name,
> so that at the name of Jesus
> every knee should bend, in heaven and on earth and under the
>   earth,
> and every tongue should confess that Jesus Christ is Lord,
> to the glory of God the Father.[2]

You might have thought that anyone capable of singing this ancient hymn had left behind the strictest tenets of monotheism. If it does not completely suggest the divinity of Jesus, it suggests something pretty close to it. Gentiles who heard the hymn, composed and sung in Greek, could readily translate its mental images into pictures that were far from Jewish. The figure of Dionysus who walked the earth concealing his own divinity replaces the actual or folk-memory of the Galilean preacher; the very concept of Messiah has become something both more internal and more universal than can be contained within the confines of Palestinian Judaism.

If the hymn is really as old as this, however, dating perhaps to less than twenty years after the death of Jesus, we are compelled to wonder and awe at the fact that out of this strict and monotheistic religion, there was born such an all-but-idolotrous worship of a prophet. The

---

[1] Acts 11:26.
[2] Philippians 2:6–11.

scholars can speculate about the origins of theological ideas, imagining, for example, where this or that 'christology' first evolved. Simple common sense, and decent reverence in the presence of such faith, is bound to ask, 'What can it have been about this man that inspired such thoughts?'

The Gospels are written from the point of view of faith, and are therefore to be handled cautiously as tools to answer this particular historical phenomenon. It will not do to say that Jesus in his early life went about claiming to be the Christ of a later generation's faith. For Jesus Christ in the Gospels is a product of such faith, and so our answer, from a purely historical point of view, is bound to be circular. The story, like that in Mark's Gospel, about Jesus stilling the raging of a storm on the Sea of Galilee, evokes the response, 'Who then is this, that even the wind and the sea obey him?' We, as believers of the 60s and 70s, buffeted in the little ship of the early church, and afraid that Our Lord is asleep, can be comforted by knowing the answer. 'They will have seen in the story evidence that Jesus was, if not actually God, undoubtedly the eschatalogical agent of God, entrusted with the plenitude of divine power for the protecting and saving of his church.'[3] This is not, however, quite the question we were asking. What was it about Jesus *at the time* of his earthly life which so impressed his followers that they could group together in his name and be convinced that even after his death he was the focus of Israel's hopes?

Treating the Gospel evidence with the mixture of reverence and caution which is likely to yield the most solid answer to this question, we can see that to his contemporaries in Galilee, the appeal of Jesus was twofold. First, like some of his other contemporaries, but much more than they, he was renowned as a healer and an exorcist. In that world, where illness was believed to come from the devil or to be the result of demonic possession, the two functions were the same. So it is that oral tradition, refashioned into written Gospel story, retains for us memories of the exorcist who went about Galilee healing those who were brought to him from the fishing villages and hill towns. Given the religio-political climate of the times, there was an inevitable association in the minds of the people between the man who showed such 'power' over the demons, and who could perform such miracles, and the Son of Man for whom they waited, their Jewish Deliverer, the Messiah.

There was, however, a second thing about Jesus. 'For he taught

[3] D. E. Nineham, *Saint Mark*, p. 147.

them as one having authority, and not as the scribes.'[4] It is very difficult in this area to separate what might have been the teaching of the historical Jesus and that of the early Church who cherished his memory.[5] The teaching belonged to that strand of Jewish belief which has been called the *imitatio Dei*.[6] Any Jew, however poor and humble – in fact, the poorer and humbler the better – could in the teaching of Jesus embody in their own person the divine nature of pity and purity and love. When the Judgment comes, Jesus taught that we shall not be asked to rail at God for having created a world in which there are hungry, poor unhappy people. He, by contrast, will have expected *us* to have incarnated his virtues; he will expect us to have been 'God' towards our unfortunate neighbours; for he will have been hidden within them. 'For I was hungry and you gave me food, I was thirsty and you gave me something to drink, I was a stranger and you welcomed me, I was naked and you gave me clothing, I was sick and you took care of me, I was in prison and you visited me.'[7]

There is something immediate and accessible about this, the 'religion of Jesus', and which formed the basis of the enormous authority of Jesus as a moral teacher. Combined with his gifts as a healer, we must believe that he was one of those rare and charismatic 'saints', rather like Francis of Assisi in the Middle Ages or Mother Teresa in our own day, who captured people's imaginations, filled them with the love of God. The historian comes to this conclusion not for reasons of sentimentality but because it is inconceivable that a movement could have grown up in Jesus's name had Jesus himself not been a person of remarkable virtue, eloquence and personal magnetism.

But then there is a third thing, and here we enter the area of pure mystery in the popular modern sense of that word. For the third reason that Jesus was revered was the manner of his death and the

[4] Mark 1:22.
[5] A clear account of what might be truthfully recovered is to be found in Geza Vermes, *The Religion of Jesus the Jew*.
[6] Vermes, *op. cit.*, p. 202, likens it to the writings of Rabbi Hama, son of R. Hanina: 'Blessed be the name of the Lord of the world who taught us his right ways. He taught us to clothe the naked by his clothing of Adam and Eve. He taught us to join the bridegrooms and brides by joining Eve to Adam. He taught us to visit the sick by revealing himself in a vision of the Word to Abraham when he was sick. He taught us to comfort mourners by revealing himself again to Jacob on his return from Padan at the place where his mother had died. He taught us to feed the poor by causing bread to descend from heaven for the children of Israel . . .', etc.
[7] Matthew 25:35–6.

circumstances associated with his death. This man, of unquestioned spiritual power and extraordinary goodness and unselfishness, who by his simple teaching had made his followers believe that they understood the Love of God itself, was put to death as a Roman criminal. Luke recalls the two followers, after the death of Jesus, walking along in dismay and grief for one 'who was a prophet mighty in deed and word before God and all the people, and how our chief priests and leaders handed him over to be condemned to death and crucified him. But we had hoped that he was the one to redeem Israel.'[8] Within twenty years, we find evidence in the Jesus Hymn of this 'hope', transformed and still alive. Among his followers, the belief in his Rising Up, his resurrection, his conquest of death. This belief is so strong that it transforms and overshadows the two earlier reasons for Jesus's popularity. The memories of Jesus as a healer and Jesus as a teacher will be preserved; but the life of Jesus is now viewed in terms of the death of Jesus. And the death of Jesus is seen in terms of the resurrection of Jesus. And this is the point where knowledge and ignorance are both silent and must choose whether or not to pass into faith.

All that we know of Jesus comes to us through the writings of the early church: there is no contemporary evidence. There is not even any incontrovertibly authentic evidence about the beliefs of the so-called 'Jerusalem church'. Did James and the other surviving brothers of Jesus believe that God had given to their brother 'a name that is above every name, so that at the name of Jesus every knee should bend'? These questions depend on faith and on that comparable and related quality, imagination. The hymn from which the words of this Hellenistic Jesus-worship come probably derives from Syrian Antioch.

Leaders of the Antioch community included a Cypriot Jew named Barnabas, Simeon who was called Niger, Lucius of Cyrene, Manaen. Quite possibly, Simeon Niger was the man who, according to later Gospel legend, had been taken out of the crowd by the Roman soldiers and made to carry the cross of Jesus. It is in this place that Paul's ideas concerning the Crucifixion grow and develop. The Cross, and the Crucifixion, are at the very centre of this religious vision, not as an airy concept or a metaphor, but as a bloody death actually recollected. The central question develops from the Cross – how could God have chosen this man, Jesus, as the Messiah if he had died in such abject

[8] Luke 24:19–21.

defeat? What does it tell us about God? about Jesus? about the Jews who allowed it to happen, by handing Jesus over to the Roman authorities for execution?

Paul, to whom these matters were of such urgent concern, attached himself to the Hellenists of Antioch, rather than to the Jerusalem Church, not long after his 'revelation' of the risen Jesus.

Trade, in all likelihood, first drew him to this the third largest city in the Roman world, which was surpassed in population only by Rome and Alexandria. Like every other Greek city, it was a centre of games.[9] They attached enormous importance to their athletics stadia. Paul, who speaks of athletics in one of his letters,[10] would have seen the crowds accumulating for the athletic contests even if he did not attend them himself. He would have seen the extraordinary aqueduct which supplied the city with water, starting forty-five miles to the south-east of the city in a steppe to the east of the great river Orontes.[11] If he ever went to the public baths he would have seen that the Antiochenes were fascinated by the figures of Greek mythology, and he would have seen statues and reliefs of Theseus and the Minotaur, Apollo, Olympos, Scythes and Marsyas – all playing flutes, for Antioch was a great musical centre. At the theatre there was a sacred 'synod' or association of actors who were devoted to Dionysus. One of the most famous actors in Antioch, Iulius Paris, did mimes or ballets from the Greek mythology.[12] He would no doubt have enacted the myth of Dionysus himself. (We have already seen how Luke, himself a native of Antioch,[13] used the language of the Dionysian mysteries when he came to describe the 'conversion' of Paul.)

Greek culture, Greek gods, Greek ideas and Greek pastimes had all been transmitted on a popular level to the populace and it was in this place that Paul first came to prominence as a Christian leader. It is unthinkable that Luke is wrong to place Paul among the notable 'Christians' of Antioch.[14] According to Acts, the Holy Spirit spoke to the prophets and teachers of Antioch and said, 'Set apart for me Barnabas and Saul for the work to which I have called them.' The

[9] 'It is impossible to exaggerate the significance of the athletic and other contests which were so important a part of the collective life of Greek cities in this period.' Fergus Millar, *The Roman Near East, 31 BC–AD 337*, p. 259.
[10] 1 Corinthians 9:24.
[11] Millar, *op. cit.*, p. 262.
[12] *ibid.*
[13] F. F. Bruce, *Paul: Apostle of the Free Spirit*, p. 133.
[14] Acts 13:1.

other brothers laid hands on them, and, after a period of prayer and fasting, the two set off. Both men would seem to have come from a similar background. Barnabas, as has been said, came from Cyprus, Paul from Cilicia; both were of Jewish parentage. Barnabas – meaning 'son of encouragement' – had been a nickname given to him by the Jerusalem brothers when he sold up his real-estate in the city and gave the money to the new cause.[15] Some traditions identify him with that Barsabbas who 'stood for election' as a member of the Twelve after the suicide of Judas Iscariot, losing the poll to Matthias.[16] If that is the case, then his Jewish name was Joseph, and we can conclude that he was very close to the original followers of the Way. According to Acts, members of the Jerusalem 'Church' were in financial difficulties, in, say, 46, and the Son of Encouragement was called upon once again for his help. This seems to have been the occasion of Paul's second visit to the church in Jerusalem, of which he writes in Galatians, and if this is the case, then it was Barnabas who introduced Paul to the Twelve. After they had taken 'famine relief' to the poorer brothers and sisters in Jerusalem, Paul and Barnabas brought a young man named John Mark to Antioch, and they were ready for what pious history calls the 'first missionary journey' of the Apostle Paul.

The scholars never want us to forget that Luke wrote Acts with a purpose: that is, to reconcile the two factions in early Christianity – Jerusalem and Antioch, those who thought that the Jesus-movement was always to be contained within the parent of Judaism, and those who believed that the Gentile believers were the new Israel, that 'Judaism' had been supplanted by 'Christianity'. It is clear as day to us that this division was going to happen, but even at the date when Luke was writing – let us say AD 80? – it was still a possibility that the two 'Ways' could be reconciled. No such division of the Ways had occurred when, in let us say 47–8, two Jews called Saul and Joseph sailed to Cyprus and 'proclaimed the word of God' in the synagogue at Salamis.[17] The next few chapters of Acts have to be read gingerly, for the reasons we have reiterated. They are propaganda, designed to make us think that 'the early Church' was always 'Christian' – whereas in fact, of course, it belonged to an era when the very word 'Christian' was simply a nickname for a sect within Judaism. Nevertheless, it

[15] Acts 4:36.
[16] Acts 1:23.
[17] Acts 13:4–5.

– 119 –

seems unduly sceptical to dismiss the accounts of this 'missionary journey' as pure fiction, and they repay study.

First, we discover that the Jewish 'missionaries' saw themselves as a superior type of magician. Having preached to the Jews of Salamis, on the east coast of Cyprus, they crossed to Paphos in the west, where they encountered the governor, Sergius Paulus. Their first clash is with another Jewish magician called Bar-Jesus, a Jewish mage – probably the same as the man Josephus calls Atomos.[18] (Luke calls him Elymas, a derivation from the Arabic word for *wise*, in some texts, Hetoimas in others.) Pliny and Lucian both take it for granted that sorcery was a traditional Jewish skill, in spite of the fact that the Jewish Scriptures forbid it.[19] When Atomos denounced Paul and Barnabas, they demonstrated that their magic was superior. Paul looked at the court sorcerer and said, 'You son of the devil, you enemy of all righteousness.' And Atomos – like Paul himself when he had defied Jesus – is sent blind. The author of Acts does not tell us whether the false Cypriot magician ever regained his sight, or indeed whether he became so enlightened as to follow the Way, but when the proconsul Sergius Paullus saw it, he was deeply impressed and became a follower of the Way. If so, he was quite a catch. He is very likely the Lucius Sergius Paullus referred to in the Latin Inscriptions as one of the curators of the Tiber during the reign of Claudius. It is possible that this family was one of the first of the rich and powerful converts made by the Church.[20]

If that is one story used by Luke from his sources, another is the one which immediately follows, namely Paul's speech allegedly delivered to the Jews of Pisidian Antioch, when they had left Cyprus and sailed to Perga in Pamphylia and so to the Pisidian capital.

The speech is a 'set piece', comparable to the sermons of Peter and of the Hellenist martyr Stephen in the earlier chapter of Luke's book. Its theme is that the Israelites have persistently mistaken God's purposes for them and failed to understand his messengers, of whom the last was their Saviour, Jesus. 'And we bring you the good news that what God promised to our ancestors he has fulfilled for us, their children, by raising Jesus.'[21] This apparently eirenical speech is followed – it will

[18] F. F. Bruce, *The Acts of the Apostles*, p. 257.
[19] HN, XXX, 11; *Podagra* 173, quoted by James Parkes, *The Conflict of the Church and the Synagogue*, p. 118.
[20] Bruce, *Acts*, p. 256, quoting Ramsay, *Bearing of Recent Discovery* believes that the daughter of this proconsul, Sergia Palla, was a Christian, together with her son, C. Caristanius Fronto; a prominent family in Pisidian Antioch.
[21] Acts 13:32–3.

be a familiar pattern to Luke's readers – by the 'conversion' of many Jews and of the Gentile god-fearers who heard Paul's words; it is also received with fury by 'the Jews', who were 'filled with jealousy; and blaspheming, they contradicted what was spoken by Paul'.[22] Such was the bad feeling stirred up by 'the Jews' that they incite the leading men of the city to 'persecute' Paul and Barnabas and drive them out. The same thing happens again in Iconium – an attempt to spread 'the word', frustrated by 'the Jews'.

We need to remember that the actual quarrel was taking place in some year such as 46, 47 or 48 among real Jews, not among the fantasy Jews of a later Christian imagination, which had built up a caricature in its mind of what Judaism was like and what Jews believed. Why does Paul stir up such fury and resentment in the synagogues? Why is his companion ('St Barnabas' the Christian missionary in the Christian view of things; actually a Jew called Joseph) destined to part company from Paul after this 'missionary journey'? The synagogues of the Diaspora had been founded and kept going by the 6,000 or so Pharisees in the world. These Pharisees had not persecuted or killed Jesus, still less had they been friends of Pontius Pilate, who was their most ruthless persecutor. Nor did they object to the Gentiles hearing the word of God. They taught that the Teaching (Torah) which came from Almighty God – while itself being holy and unchangeable – was of universal application. It was addressed to all mankind, to Gentiles as well as to Jews, and it was therefore necessary in every age and in every place to interpret the Torah for those willing or able to listen to it. On Israel had been laid the responsibility of 'being witnesses for God to mankind and of making known the truth concerning him, proclaiming the religion which had only the One and only God for the object of its worship'.[23] This was the Pharisaic teaching in which Paul says he was brought up, and Barnabas no doubt believed that it was to preach this word that they had first set out from Syria.

Paul, however, as we know from his writings, replaced the Torah with the mystical Christ who had been revealed to him in his éclaircissement, his apocalypse, his epiphany, his 'conversion'. All the teachings, all the prophecies, all the history of Israel preserved in the sacred writings of the Jews pointed to one divine event, the coming into the world of a Saviour. 'Let it be known to you therefore, my

[22] Acts 13: 45.
[23] R. Travers Herford, *Judaism in the New Testament Period*, p. 103.

brothers, that through this man forgiveness of sins is proclaimed to you; by this Jesus everyone who believes is set free from all those sins from which you could not be freed by the law of Moses.'[24] This is the beginning of the Christian religion, the beginning of what makes it distinctive. There have been many Jewish 'heresies', but this inspired misreading of the idea of Torah, this treating of Torah as a rigid condemnation of the inner human being's struggle for union with God, lies at the heart of Paul's brilliantly tormented view of the human condition.

Why should any person need a Saviour? The Pharisees, and indeed the generality of Jews, would consider the idea to be veering on the blasphemous, just as for the Stoics it would have seemed superfluous, unnecessary. The hysteric crowds in Tarsus could call out for their Saviour Herakles as the great statue was carried through the streets each year. Coming from a tradition in which religion and morality were entirely separate, such 'pagans' could, in all their confusion and sinfulness, hope to be washed from their sins by the blood of Mithras or rescued by the Man-God who went down into the underworld to rescue human souls from death.

For a Jew, however, the Scriptures make it apparent again and again that God is a God of mercy, who forgives sins. 'He does not deal with us according to our sins, nor repay us according to our iniquities. For as the heavens are high above the earth, so great is his steadfast love toward those who fear him; as far as the east is from the west, so far he removes our transgressions from us.'[25] Jesus himself, in the fragments of his teaching which survive in the Gospels, would seem to have been a completely mainstream Jew in his teaching about divine forgiveness. With the Pharisees, of whom he was probably one, he believed that anyone who turned to God in penitence and faith would be forgiven.

In Judaism, there is the idea of the *yetzer*, the two impulses. Everyone has two impulses, to good or to evil. The authentic Jewish idea survives in the New Testament in the letter of James: 'one is tempted by one's own desire'.[26] It is our own selfishness which creates evil. To do good, we must turn to God's will.

This is genial, even uplifting, but to the restless and almost

[24] Acts 13:38–9.
[25] Psalms 103:10–12.
[26] James 1:14.

Nietzschean mind of Paul, it leaves unanswered and untouched the two most troubling elements in the observed universe; namely, its apparently blameless suffering and its boundless wickedness. Any metaphysic which blandly assumed that it was possible for evil to be 'forgiven' simply by the assertion that God was good could not answer the intense isolation of the human soul in the grip of sin or psychological nightmare; nor could it really correspond to the world as it was actually observed – a world as Paul would conceive it, where demonic powers were at work, filling the minds of the mad with evil nightmares and the bodies of the weak with sickness and disease, a world out of joint, a universe groaning and travailing towards some violent consummation. Let the Pharisees and the Stoics, who apparently found the practice of virtue easy, continue to live in their moralistic isolation. Their good, even generous and abstemious, lives could shine as lights, but could not change the world; their willingness to give money to the poor, to abstain from excess, to be sober and vigilant, even their piety surreally ignored the urge towards cruelty, madness, wickedness and lust which possessed so high a proportion of the human race; ignored the 'nasty, brutish and short' lives they led; ignored the fundamental questions which such evil and such suffering raised about the very 'righteousness' of God himself. Imagine the court of Caligula as described by Suetonius. Imagine, even, the atmosphere of the barrack room at the Antonia Fortress in Jerusalem, where soldiers played dice and swore and talked of sex and superstition. Paul would have heard them, met them, known them if he was a temple guard. How pallid the moral essays of Seneca or the Jewish Book of Wisdom would have seemed in such a mad, Dostoevskian world crying aloud for vengeance or redemption!

Into such a world, Paul, with an inspired and completely original vision of Jesus, believed that a unique figure had stepped; one who was both a Prometheus, whose own weakness defied the strength of the Allfather; whose innocent folly overcame the wisdom of his ancestors; whose lawlessness – dying the death of a criminal – overcame the law; and whose pure and unflinching agape, charity or love overshadowed the malice which all discerning people might have felt or guessed to be at the heart of the First Cause, if there were a First Cause. Both a Prometheus, then, and a Saviour to whom human beings could look for rescue and salvation; human beings who were too tired or too drunk or too weak or too stupid to be able to rise to the concept of virtue and good behaviour practised by Pharisees and Stoics.

The majority of good people in the world, and the majority of religious people, have always been Stoics or Pharisees. (The great monotheistic creeds of Judaism and Islam owe their appeal to this fact.) They believe that there is a God, who has revealed how human beings should behave. It is our function to follow the precepts of chastity, generosity towards those less fortunate to ourselves and piety. That is the whole requirement of the Torah.

But Paul who was a religious revolutionary, really had a much more developed sense of the difficulties of this position than any Jew since the author of the Book of Job. As a Hellenist who had absorbed as much 'Greek' wisdom as Jewish, he rejected the Jewish idea of *yetzer*, two impulses, and believed that flesh and spirit were fundamentally opposed: a completely unJewish idea. 'For what the flesh desires is opposed to the Spirit, and what the Spirit desires is opposed to the flesh; for these are opposed to each other, to prevent you from doing what you want.'[27]

The human position, once this idea has been grasped imaginatively, becomes intolerable. Paul really had thought himself into one of those extreme positions of metaphysical isolation which we would associate with the nineteenth-century spiritual exiles Nietzsche or Kierkegaard. He was Jewish enough and had enough common sense to know that a purely 'spiritual' way of life was impossible for most human beings. No Pythagorean vegetarian he, no advocate of Platonist celibacy, though he was celibate himself. Human souls were, for him, self-contradictory devices imprisoned in flesh which was always, through weakness and desire, going to lead them into disaster. Nor does this simply refer to sexual desire. Good teachings, whether we call them the Holy Koran, or the Tao or the Torah, serve only to heighten the difference between the good after which we aspire and the sheer folly of our actions, the wickedness of our cruelty and dissipation as a race of humanity. Viewed in this light, the Torah was not a blessing at all, but a curse. 'Law came in, with the result that the trespass multiplied.'[28] Anyone who has attended a synagogue and observed the reverence with which the scrolls of the Torah are treated will see why Paul's ideas produced such anger, such outright rejection and fury, in the synagogues of Pisidian Antioch and Iconium. What Paul had to say, far from being in the mainstream of Judaism, struck at the very roots

[27] Galatians 5:17.
[28] Romans 5:20.

not just of Judaism but of 'natural theology'. If there had been, in the past, a Revealed Religion, given to Moses and through Moses to the People of God on Mount Sinai, there was now a New Revelation and a New Covenant. This time, the covenant had been vouchsafed not to Moses but to Paul. 'Paul's claim for immunity from criticism was based on the possession of a divine gift of the Spirit, which was nothing less than the mind of the Lord.'[29]

[29] Wilfrid Knox, *St Paul and the Church of the Gentiles*, p. 117.

VIII

ANTIOCH v. JERUSALEM

PLATO, AS IS notorious, banished the poets from his *Republic*. One of his objections to Homer was the ancient poet's view that the gods themselves travel around human habitations disguised as men.[1] ('The gods in the guise of strangers from afar put on all manner of shapes, and visit the cities, beholding the violence and righteousness of men.')[2] We find a curious parallel to this Homeric notion in the odyssey of Paul's life, known as Acts.

In the year 49, Paul and Barnabas entered the city of Lystra, some miles south of Iconium, where Paul had tried to speak in the synagogue, and been threatened with stoning. Coming upon a lame man in Lystra, Paul performed a faith healing. The man, who according to Luke had never been able to walk in his life, leapt to his feet on the Apostle's instruction. Perceiving the miracle, the crowds began to cry out, 'The gods are come down to us in human form.' Inspired by such a show of popular devotion, the priest of Zeus brought oxen and garlands to the gates of the city, and prepared to offer sacrifice in honour of Paul and Barnabas, who were imagined to be Zeus and Hermes. (Interestingly, they regarded Paul, whom we should think of as the more likely divine messenger, as Zeus and Barnabas as the Mercury-figure). Paul and Barnabas managed to dissuade them by crying out, 'Friends, why are you doing this? We are mortals just like you, and we bring you good news, that you should turn from these worthless things to the living God, who made the heaven and the earth and the sea and all that is in them. In past generations he allowed all the nations to follow their own ways.'[3] No sooner had this disturbance been quelled than Jews arrived from Iconium and Pisidian Antioch who, according to Acts, persuaded the multitude to stone Paul. He was dragged out

[1] *The Republic*, 381d.
[2] *Odyssey*, 17, 485–6.
[3] Acts 14:15–16.

of the city and left for dead, rescued by his disciples and taken to recover in Derbe, a town midway between Lystra and Tarsus.

In this strange vignette (presumably semi-fictionalized) we find the second half of the Acts of the Apostles in miniature. The whole story is here: Paul attempting, with a mixture of success, to confront the Gentile world with the falsity of their own gods and to tell them about the true, the Living God of Israel. The Jews resenting him, persecuting him and just failing to kill him.

The incident took place towards the end of what tradition paints as Paul's first missionary journey, those travels in modern-day Turkey which Paul undertook between perhaps 47 and 49. At the beginning of this period, Acts presents a world scarcely evangelized and a faith whose centre was Jerusalem. The Way was still not so much a branch of Judaism or a movement within it as a debate about the nature of Judaism, whose truth and necessity no one within the group questioned. By the end of this 'missionary journey', Paul and his friends have established 'churches' all over Asia Minor.

There can be no way of guessing the numbers of Paul's converts in Iconium or Lystra or Derbe, but it would be astonishing if they were numbered in hundreds rather than dozens. The world itself – the world of legions and magistrates, temples and market-places – went on unaware and unaffected by Paul's 'missionary' activities. The fact that subsequent generations can tick off on the map these names of towns in Asia Minor as territory conquered for Christianity is an anachronism – an anachronism which exists more in our minds, even, than it does on Luke's page.

One of the most puzzling events in Luke's narrative occurs when Paul went back to Lystra and met the young man who was destined to be, if this title belongs to any single individual, his successor as the Apostle to the Gentiles, Timothy. As Luke tells the tale, it would seem as though Paul's decision to take Timothy with him on his subsequent journeys was an impulsive one, but there was a difficulty. Timothy, though the son of a Jewess and therefore by some standards a Jew, had not been circumcised. His father was a Greek. Luke tells us that in order to avoid further quarrels with the synagogues as they continued in their missionary activity, Paul 'took him and had him circumcised'.[4] This is one of the details which above all others casts doubt on Luke's credibility as a historian. In Paul's letter to the Galatians, written in all

[4] Acts 16:3.

likelihood within a few years of meeting Timothy (conceivably in the very year itself), Paul inveighs against those who insist that Gentile converts should undergo this rite of passage. 'Listen! I, Paul, am telling you that if you let yourselves be circumcised, Christ will be of no benefit to you. Once again I testify to every man who lets himself be circumcised that he is obliged to obey the entire law. You who want to be justified by the law have cut yourselves off from Christ; you have fallen away from grace . . . For in Christ Jesus neither circumcision nor uncircumcision counts for anything; the only thing that counts is faith working through love.'[5]

The story of Paul going to the trouble of having his friend circumcised must, therefore, be one of those passages in Acts which are pure fiction. Famous as Paul is for inconsistencies, and for changing his mind – he is the most famous convert in ancient history – it is not possible to believe that he could write so eloquent a denunciation of circumcising the Gentiles and then consent to the operation being performed on his most trusted lieutenant simply in order to pacify 'the Jews'. His own letters bristle with a desire to antagonise 'the Jews'.

Luke, by contrast, is a man who wants to pour oil in old wounds, to pass over differences, or to heal them. While Paul in his letters has no shame about presenting himself as a bullish, impulsive visionary who does not care how many people he offends, Luke represents him as a tolerant, sensible man who is prepared to go against his principles, when necessary, for the sake of making peace with the original Jewish believers. In this way Luke can represent Paul and Christianity to the Romans as an essentially peace-loving movement, one which is not the group of troublemakers described by Suetonius. The story is useful for Christian teaching, too, as well as for political propaganda. For Luke's second- or even third-generation Christian readership, Acts can represent the early days of the Faith as ones in which compromises were forged. Ebionites and Gentile Christians alike can read Acts and believe that their Church was founded on compromise. And so we read of the circumcision of Timothy.

To some Gentile readers, this circumcision debate might seem peripheral. Some men are circumcised, others not – so what? In order to see the revolution that Paul was effecting within Jewish circles (or satellites) we turn to the old rabbinic texts. The rabbis considered

[5] Galatians 5:2–6.

circumcision so important that they declared[6] that were it not for the blood of the covenant – that is to say, the blood which flowed from Abraham's penis when, at God's insistence, he circumcised himself – heaven and earth *would not exist*. The teaching of Judaism was that a child must still shed the blood of a covenant (*hattafat dam berit*) even if he is born without a foreskin, and even if for some medical or other reason he is circumcised before the mystical eighth day. Even the angels are circumcised. In the Book of Jubilees we read, 'all the angels of the presence and of the Glorification have been so, from the day of their creation, and God's anger will be kindled against the children of the covenant if they make the members of their body appear like those of the Gentiles and they will be expelled and exterminated from the earth.'[7]

Converts to Judaism in the Roman period had to undergo circumcision. 'The Sabbath keepers who are not circumcised are intruders and deserve punishment,' we read.[8] Strangely enough, in Palestine rules were more liberal than in the Diaspora, and there were Proselytes of the Gate, as they were known, who were allowed to 'become Jews' without circumcision. But such was not the general rule. It was widely believed that the admission of uncircumcised men into Jewish religious worship 'impeded the arrival of the Messiah'.[9] While 'semi-converts' were allowed, those who observed the Sabbath and the dietary laws, they were to be regarded as heathens if after a twelve-month period they had not undergone circumcision.[10] These stringent rules did not deter converts. Titus Flavius Clemens, a nephew of the emperors Titus and Domitian, was converted with his wife Drusilla, and was punished by death by the Roman authorities for undergoing circumcision. The rite was sufficiently popular for Hadrian to ban the circumcision of Gentiles, and it was the cause of the Bar Kokhba rebellion in the early second century. People, in other words, were prepared to go to war for this issue, just as, in the Maccabean period, in the century before Jesus, Jewish mothers were prepared to be martyred rather than neglect the circumcision of their sons. When a Roman official asked Rabbi Oshaya why God had not made man as he wanted him, the rabbi replied that 'it was in order that man should perfect himself

[6] Shabbat, 137 BC (Rabbinic text, quoted *Encyclopaedia Judaica*).
[7] Book of Jubilees, 3:190–2.
[8] Deuteronomy Rabban, i.
[9] Abodah Zarah, 3b.
[10] Rabbi Johanan, *ibid*.
[11] Genesis Rabban, ii. 6.

– 130 –

by the fulfilment of a divine command'.[11] The very thing here symbolised, self-improvement or self-perfection, was inimical to the principles of Paul's religious idea – namely that the agent in any improvement of self is God Himself, without whom all human efforts to be good are worthless.

By Roman times, circumcision was done with a metal knife, and, if we believe that Paul did insist on Timothy undergoing circumcision, it is perhaps worth reminding ourselves of the three essential parts of the ritual, without which it is not complete. The first part is *milah*, the cutting away of the outer part of the foreskin. This is done with one sweep of the knife. The second part, *periah*, is the tearing of the inner lining of the foreskin which still adheres to the gland, so as to lay it wholly bare. This was (and is) done by the operator – the *mohel*, the professional circumciser – with his thumb-nail and index finger. The third and essential part of the ritual is *mesisah*, the sucking of blood from the wound. Since the nineteenth century, it has been permissible to finish this part of the ritual with a swab, but in all preceding centuries and certainly in the time of Paul it was necessary for the *mohel* to clean the wound by taking the penis into his mouth. In the case of a young adult male such as Timothy the bleeding would have been copious.[12] We can easily imagine why Paul's Gentile converts were unwilling to undergo the ritual; and, given the more liberal attitudes towards the Torah which had already begun to emerge among the Hellenists of Syrian Antioch, it is not surprising that the custom of circumcision should have started to wane. It took the extremism of Paul to think that the knife of circumcision would actually 'cut you . . . off from Christ'. But could any greater contrast be imagined between this belief and the traditional Jewish view that those who did not wield that knife delayed the coming of the Messiah?

Luke could not get around the fact that the differences between Paul and the 'Jewish Christians' – for want of a better term – were very deep. The story of Timothy's circumcision was not sufficient on its own to suggest to any Gentile reader that a compromise had been reached, so in the fifteenth chapter of Acts, which precedes the story of Timothy's circumcision, we read of the first Church Council being held in Jerusalem.

---

[12] For circumcision, see *Encyclopaedia Judaica*, vol. 5, 1984; *The Encyclopaedia of Religion*, vol. 3, 512; George A. Barton, 'Circumcision', in *Encyclopaedia of Religion and Ethics*, ed. James Hastings, vol. 3, pp. 679–80. See also Julian Morgenstern, *Rites of Birth, Marriage and Death and Kindred Occasions among the Semites*.

Almost all the modern accounts of this Council speak of it as a debate about whether 'Christianity' would break away from 'Judaism.' That is because we know that the followers of Peter and James – Jewish Christians, Ebionites, Judaisers, call them what you will – eventually lost the argument with the Paul-ites, the Gentiles for whom the word Christ was synonymous not with the Anointed Jewish Deliverer of Israel, so much as with an inner known God, a hidden Saviour, a Blessed Sacrament called Jesus.

When Paul and Barnabas returned from their travels in Asia Minor they went back to Syrian Antioch, and it was there that they met Peter and had the stupendous quarrel with him to which we have already alluded. We have already discovered that the 'Church' at Antioch had developed, *faute de mieux*, a liberal attitude towards diet. Peter, visiting the Christians of Antioch, took a kindly view of this at first and was inclined to turn the blind eye to the fact that the food at table, all bought at the market in Antioch, was unlikely to answer the strictest dietary requirements of the Law. Then, some friends of James came to Antioch from Jerusalem and Peter became self-conscious. Rather than eating with the Gentiles, as he had done before, he 'kept himself separate for fear of the circumcision faction'.[13] Paul's account of the quarrel, written soon after the event, shows that he did not mince his words when he 'opposed' Peter to 'his face'. He made it clear that those who insisted on 'mutilation' – he would not even call it circumcision – deserved themselves to castrated.[14]

The matter needed to be resolved. Who was right, Peter or Paul? Clearly, there were those, such as Barnabas himself, who could not resolve the matter in their minds. Once the Jews and Gentiles had separated themselves over this matter at Antioch, Barnabas went to eat with the Jews – Barnabas who had been Paul's travelling companion and friend. 'Even Barnabas was led astray by their hypocrisy' is how Paul describes it,[15] though we can see that it could all be described rather differently. Barnabas as a believing Jew simply could not envisage being disloyal to his religion and abandoning the dietary customs which separated Jews from Gentiles. The various followers of the Way – Peter and his followers, and the Hellenists of Antioch, and Paul and his friends – agreed to meet up with James and the Twelve in Jerusalem.

[13] Galatians 2:12.
[14] Galatians 5:12.
[15] Galatians 2:13.

Paul, who describes the quarrel so vividly, does not tell the Galatians anything about it being resolved in a Council at Jerusalem. Paul tells us that he went to Jerusalem in response to a revelation, and not because of any concensus being reached by the fledgling Church. That some consensus was sought, and possibly achieved, entirely depends on which point of view you took of the original quarrel. In all likelihood, Luke's account of it in Acts 15 does represent the 'moderate Jewish' (if we can call it that) outlook on Paul and his missionary activities. This tells us that the elders and leaders of the Jerusalem church received Paul and Barnabas and thanked them that they had 'risked their lives for the sake of our Lord Jesus Christ'. They then issued what could be regarded as the first Encyclical of the Christian Church: 'For it has seemed good to the Holy Spirit and to us to impose on you no further burden than these essentials: that you abstain from what has been sacrificed to idols and from blood and from what is strangled and from fornication. If you keep yourselves from these, you will do well.'[16]

The problem of what to do if you sat down to dinner and found that you were being offered meat which had previously been sacrificed to an idol was scarcely one that was likely to occur in Jerusalem. It is something which represented a difficulty for Jews of the Diaspora and for Christians. That some such formula of practice was worked out we can not doubt, since Paul advises his Gentile converts on dietary matters along precisely similar lines in his later career, but that is in Corinth, not in Jerusalem. Such a rule continued to be followed by Christians for several centuries. We know that the prohibition against eating blood was taken seriously by later generations of the Church, since Tertullian (who lived c. 160–c. 225) claims that pagans used to test Christians by trying to tempt them into eating black pudding.[17]

But the formula does not mention the most contentious point at issue: circumcision. It is not an area which admits compromise. Either you are circumcised or you are not; either you think it is important or you do not. However dispassionate the Christian scholars think they are being, they find it impossible not to fudge this question.

'The outcome of the apostolic assembly is important for theology, for the history of the church, and for world history alike. It shows that the church's unity had not fallen in pieces. The danger that the mother church would harden into a sect of Judaism and that Hellenistic

---

[16] Acts 15:28–9.
[17] *Apologeticum*, 9, 13–14.

Christianity would dissolve into a welter of non-historical mystery cults had been averted.'[18]

It was in 1831 that the Tübingen scholar F. C. Baur[19] first advanced the theory that, from the very beginning, there was not one Christian gospel, but two. One propounded by the Jerusalem church, by Jesus's brother and his friend Peter, held it was necessary even for Gentile converts to embrace the whole Jewish obedience, including circumcision, the dietary laws and the marriage laws, before joining the Jesus-movement. The other, Paul's church, preached the 'gospel of Christ' in which the Old Law had passed away and the initiates, let free into the glorious liberty of the children of God, could discard circumcision and the requirements of the dietary laws. Other scholars, developing Baur's theory while not necessarily sharing his ideas in detail, have tried to work out how the two 'churches' differed in their teachings and practice.[20]

The truth is that however much scholars strain towards an exact reconstruction of what the first Christians believed, there is only enough evidence to paint a very generalised picture. We do know, however, from the letter Paul himself wrote to the Galatians that there was an absolute division of the ways over the question of Gentile converts and their reception into the Jewish community. When Peter came to Antioch to visit the followers of the Way, it would seem that in a spirit of friendliness he had eaten with the Gentile converts; but when 'certain persons came from James' in Jerusalem, Peter, and even Barnabas, withdrew and would no longer eat with the Gentile converts. 'I said to Cephas' (i.e. Peter) wrote Paul, ' "If you, though a Jew, live like a Gentile and not like a Jew, how can you compel the Gentiles to live like Jews?" '

The practicalities of following the Way in a Gentile city such as Antioch were quite different from those governing life in Jerusalem. In the Jewish capital, the followers of the Way would probably have eaten meat only at festival times, collecting their lamb-joints from the temple when they had been killed in the kosher manner. The Gentiles of Antioch, when they bought a chicken in the local market, would have no way of knowing whether the bird had been killed by the butcher or killed in a pagan temple.

[18] G. Bornkamm, *Paul*, p. 42.
[19] Founder of the Tübingen school, as it came to be known, the earliest scholars in history to approach the New Testament with the impartial rigour which would be applied to secular texts.
[20] The liveliest recent approach is to be found in Michael Goulder, *A Tale of Two Missions*.

But from a very early stage, the division was inspired by something much deeper than the question of whether some newly-converted follower of the Way in Antioch still felt an inclination to eat forbidden food such as prawns or hare. Even Luke is unable to disguise the fact that Paul and Barnabas quarrelled after the Jerusalem Council and went their separate ways. Barnabas wanted to take John Mark with them, but Paul did not want to take with them someone who had deserted them in Pamphylia. Perhaps the quarrel had been a purely personal one – Acts does not make this clear; but if it is serious enough to mention in a short book, it was surely much more likely that the differences between Paul and his former companions were ideological rather than temperamental.

Paul, it would seem, has now been through two distinct phases. In the first, we see him as a persecutor of the Way, and an employee of the high priests. In the second, we find him the ally of the Hellenists. In both, as in his somewhat confusing claim to have been raised a Pharisee, we see him definitely within the body of Judaism.

But though Acts and subsequent Christianity speak of a compromise after the Jerusalem Council, Paul says nothing about any such agreement. Compromise is not a word in his vocabulary.

Acts represents Paul, after the Jerusalem Council, meeting up with Timothy, the son of a Greek, with a Jew called Silvanus or Silas, and making his way up through Syria, back through Asia Minor and through the regions of Phrygia and Galatia, and up through Mysia, where they attempted to enter Bithynia – 'but the Spirit of Jesus did not allow them'.[21]

Jesus was leading them in a very different direction, a direction which would ultimately have the most profound implications and results. At Troas, Paul had another of his visions. There was a man saying to him, 'Come over to Macedonia and help us.'[22] In mileage this was no great distance and they took a boat to Samothrace. The following day they reached Neapolis, and thence to Philippi, a Roman colony and the leading city of Macedonia. We don't know, and never will know, how many different versions of the Way there were in 48. Judaism's tendency to fragment, and yet to retain a cohesion, a unity, is mirrored in the fragmentary nature of early Christianity. But a division of the ways had occurred and once it had been articulated by

[21] Acts 16:7.
[22] Acts 16:9.

Paul in his letter to Galatia there was really no turning back.

He turned now towards the world of the Empire, the world of Nero and not of James. He turned his back on Palestinian Judaism. And the extraordinary thing from the point of view of world history is that he now turned away from Asia and towards Europe.

IX

PAUL IN EUROPE

EVEN IF WE do not subscribe to the old view that 'the Faith is Europe, and Europe is the Faith',[1] the very idea of European civilisation is impossible to extricate from the story of Christendom. Would the writings of Plato have survived to us if they had not first been filtered through the Fathers of the Greek Church? If the monks of Benedict had not preserved manuscripts in their libraries, how much of classical literature would have survived in the West? Even if we posit that there would have been other powerhouses of 'civilisation' during the 'dark ages', it is still unimaginable because what history *in fact* provided was a Christian civilisation. Europe without Benedict, Europe without Dante, Europe without the cathedrals, Europe without the mediaeval universities, Europe without the fifteenth-century humanists, Europe without the Reformation; Europe without the Crusades, the Inquisitions, the Religious Wars. No Ambrose, no Augustine, no Aquinas, no Marsilius, no Duns Scotus. No Hume, Marx or Voltaire reacting against them. No Bach, no Michelangelo, no Shakespeare. No Kant, no Schopenhauer, no Wagner creating other imaginative worlds. Of course, if the Faith had not been European, and Europe had not adopted the Faith, there would have been some other story. But it would not have been our story. The moment, therefore, when the Apostle reaches European soil is bound to excite strange feelings.

The more so, when he comes to Philippi in Macedonia, a city which, so far as we know, had no significant Jewish community. The archaeologists have discovered no synagogue in this magnificent place. We, whether Christians or not, inevitably think of Paul's arrival in Europe as the harbinger of a new dawn, when the first seeds of Christian civilisation are sown in pagan soil, or, if we take a Gibbonian view of things, when Europe detected the first glimmering symptoms of the virus which would eventually undermine all that was good

[1] Hilaire Belloc, *Europe and Faith* (1920).

about the Graeco-Roman world. We have Paul's writings from about
this date and we know that this was not how he viewed matters at all.
He did not think of himself as founding a universal church, or preparing
the Western Empire for a new religious dispensation. In his belief, the
Day of the Lord was imminent, and he was hurrying to tell this Good
News to as many god-fearing Gentiles as would hear him. And in this
place, Paul, with his friends Luke,[2] Silas and Timothy (we know almost
nothing about them), arrive at the summons of a dream.

You need a quorum of ten male Jews to start a synagogue – what
is called a *minyan*. Paul and his three friends did, however, go to a
meeting of god-fearers, who assembled not at a synagogue but at a
'place of prayer' – a *proseuche* in the Greek – by the side of the river
Gangites. Whether the *proseuche* was a building used by these god-
fearers for their Shabbat meeting, or whether it was simply a spot by
the river in the open air, we can not guess.

If the group was not led by a woman, then the least we can say is
that it was a woman who is mentioned as the most significant member
of the party praying by the riverbank. Lydia, the woman in question,
came from the city of Thyatira, where there were Jews, and it was
presumably there that she had become a god-fearer. Since women
were unaffected by the circumcision question, it is not surprising that
there were more female converts than male to Judaism. There is some
evidence, moreover, to suppose that the position of women in
Macedonia was freer than in Achaia. Lydia was a woman of some
substance. She was the head of her household, which makes us suppose
that she was probably a widow. She was running an extremely
prosperous business and the household was large enough, after her
encounter with Paul and his friends, to invite them to come and live
with her. She received baptism at Paul's hands and insisted that her
slaves and dependants did the same. 'A woman progresses from being
a marginal member of a Jewish circle in which she could never receive
the covenantal sign, to being a central figure in the local Christian
church and the first baptised convert in Europe.'[3]

Thyatira is famous as a centre of dyers.[4] Purple, *porphyra*, the most
luxurious of the dyes, was obtained from the murex shellfish; but it is
possible that Lydia, who is described by Luke as a seller of purple, was

[2] This is the point in Acts when the narrator starts to use the source written in the first
person plural. Acts 16:11, 'We set sail from Troas' etc.
[3] Ben Witherington, *Women in the Earliest Churches*.
[4] *Inscriptiones Graecae* ad res Rom, part IV, nos 1213, 1250, 1265.

in Philippi to make use of their local, slightly cheaper, purple vegetable dye. Purple, either way, is a luxury item. We have left behind not only the Judaism of the Jerusalem church but also the homely Galilean traditions of holy poverty that were practised by Jesus. Lydia is a Greek-speaking merchant who has settled in Philippi, alongside the Italian agrarian colonists, and she is clearly occupying a position of wealth, even if she is in some senses an outsider from society.[5] Her substantial house now becomes 'the church'. It is the first 'house church' mentioned in Acts and it will set the pattern for the rest of Paul's journeys.

Lydia, as a widow, might have been in the fortunate position of being in charge of her own destiny. The property, and the business, must have been hers – so we assume either that the laws and customs of Philippi were liberal towards women, or that the comparatively exacting requirements of Roman law did not apply in Lydia's case. No woman in the Roman Empire served in the armed forces, none could vote, nor appear as witnesses in a lawcourt. There was therefore no 'rite of passage' for a woman to correspond to the adoption of the toga by a Roman boy or the barmitzvah for a Jewish boy to show that she had passed from childhood to adulthood. In some important respects many women in the ancient world never did become adults in the modern sense of the word. A woman would remain in the control, the *manus* of her father even after marriage, which was in any event a much less formalised matter than in modern Western society, often involving no signed contract or formality or ceremony. On some occasions, the woman when she married would pass from the *manus* of her father to that of her husband, but in the event of a divorce, she would revert to her father's *manus*. If she became a widow and inherited her husband's property, then she might well come into the *manus* of her husband's family, who would in turn exercise the right to forbid her from marrying again.[6]

The modestly prosperous *bourgeoise* such as Lydia might therefore be freer in some senses than a more nobly-born or rich woman, who might remain, technically at least, the chattel of her husband or her father for all her days. It is surely only fair to remember this background when approaching Paul's attitude to women in his writings.

[5] Wayne A. Meeks, *The First Urban Christians: The Social World of the Apostle Paul*, p. 63.
[6] See for instance Susan Treggiari, 'Divorce Roman Style: How Easy and Frequent Was It?' in, *Marriage, Divorce and Children in Ancient Rome* ed. Beryl Rawson, p. 31.

The misogyny of the Christian tradition could claim its origins in the writings of the New Testament. 'Woman! You are the gateway of the devil. You persuaded him whom the devil dared not attack directly. Because of you the Son of God had to die. You should always go dressed in mourning and rags' wrote Tertullian (end of second century), whose definition of a woman was 'a temple built over a sewer'. Augustine's disgusting commingling of the sexual and excretory organs – *inter faeces et urinam nascimur* – sets the pattern of Christian attitudes towards sex, women, the human body and relations between the sexes for a thousand years.

But is any of the blame for this to be laid at the feet of Paul? True, in his letters Paul introduces the idea (his invention?) of the Fall of Man: 'as all die in Adam, so all will be made alive in Christ'.[7] The conclusion drawn by the later fathers of the church is that the blame for Adam's death must be attributed to Eve, but this is not something which Paul ever seems to have thought of for himself.

His writings do not suggest misogyny. True, he thought that the woman is the glory (*doxa*) of the man.[8] But it is hard to know what that means. He believed in the Jewish myth that women were created from Adam's spare rib and that women were created for the sake of men. This is not what most people think in the late twentieth century, but it does not mean you were misogynistic if you thought it during the reign of Claudius or Nero. In those days you would have been hard put to find anyone who believed in 'sexual equality' in the modern sense, and the person who comes closest to it is, strangely enough, Paul.

Again, we have to admit that he was horrified by lesbianism, but so he was by male homosexuality. This is not something which would endear him to many modern Europeans and Americans who, after generations of prejudice against homosexuals, have decided that it is wicked to 'discriminate against gays'. Such language and thought-processes belong to the late twentieth century. Paul's views of homosexuality are well known: 'God gave them up to degrading passions. Their women exchanged natural intercourse for unnatural, and in the same way also the men, giving up natural intercourse with women, were consumed with passion for one another. Men committed shameless acts with men and received in their own persons the due

[7] I Corinthians 15:22.
[8] I Corinthians 11:7.

penalty for their error."[9] Certainly, Plato, had he lived to read these words, would have found them rather surprising. His myth, put into the mouth of Aristophanes in the *Symposium*, was that the human race used to consist of three four-legged sexes: the all-males, the all-females and the hermaphrodites. To keep them in their place, the gods chopped the people in half, so that the individual halves would spend their lives looking around for their partners. The half-all-males would go in search of male partners; the half-all-females would go in search of lesbian lovers; and the half-hermaphrodites would be what we call heterosexual. The idea that the gods would be angry with a man for loving boys would have struck any of Paul's Greek or Roman contemporaries as laughable. (The emperor Claudius was regarded as very eccentric for only liking women.) Gays no doubt feel entitled to hate Paul for introducing this strand of puritanical Jewish thinking into Europe and making it part of 'civilisation'. Many Christian homosexuals have perhaps been made unhappy by it, but in his defence it should be remembered that Paul was not laying down the ground rules for the Christian centuries, but getting ready for an imminent End. Though the consequences of his stringent condemnation of gay sex might have been widespread, they were not consequences which he could have foreseen himself.

His attitude to marriage, likewise, was largely coloured by his belief that the Day of the Lord was about to happen. It was entirely with the Day in mind that he urged his friends:'He who marries his fiancée does well; and he who refrains from marriage will do better.'[10] Again, later generations have distorted this'text'to make it into a justification for Christian monasticism; but Paul lived before there was in any recognisable sense a Christian 'Church', and he would certainly have regarded monasticism as ridiculous. His belief that women should be veiled when uttering their prophecies strikes the modern reader as quaint, rather than offensive, and comes in a passage in which he is denouncing the male custom of wearing hair long. It is a passage fixed in its own time: hair fashions for men in the reigns of Claudius and Nero were short; long hair would have been worn by Orientals, as would beards. In telling the Corinthians to get their hair cut, Paul might be seen as following urban, Roman fashion as against the exotic customs either of the Jews or of other oriental cults. Roman women

[9] Romans 1:26-7.
[10] 1 Corinthians 7:38.

of the period, likewise, have long hair. Older women, matrons, bound it up in a pyramidal knot, a *tutulus*, on the top of their head. In the grander of such matrons, whose statues survive, we can see that their *coiffure* was elaborate. For such women as Paul's widow-friend Lydia, we must assume that the style was simpler, but it would have been similar, with, perhaps, the chief characteristic of female hairstyles of this time, a club of hair falling down the back of the neck. If one had to draw a conclusion from Paul's views on hairstyles, it would be that Gentiles can continue to be Gentiles and do not have to pretend to be Jews. But as far as a modern reader is concerned, this passage really does not have any general application, and one can not blame Paul for subsequent Christian misogyny merely on the grounds that he believed that angels were hovering over the heads of those who prayed.

More notoriously, in the same letter, occurs the sentence 'women should be silent in the churches'.[11] This sentence seems wholly in line with sentences which we can find in a group of other letters, which are very different in style, flavour and content from the authentic letters of Paul.

In I Timothy we read, 'I permit no woman to teach or to have authority over a man; she is to keep silent.' We also learn from the same author that women can be saved through childbearing; that the womanly virtues are all submissive ones, that women should be 'self-controlled, chaste, good managers of the household, kind . . . submissive to their husbands so that the word of God may not be discredited'.[12]

There are many reasons to suppose that the letters in which these sentences occur belong to a period later than Paul's, and that they were written in a so-called school of Paul, perhaps by one of his converts. The world which these letters reflect is not the one seen through Paul's frantic eyes, a world about to dissolve, as Christ appears in glory in the clouds. On the contrary, the later New Testament writings seem to have settled down to the discovery that Christ will not be returning quite as soon as the Apostle predicted. They set up a 'Church', with fixed officers (elders, deacons, bishops), and lay down the rules for a dull and virtuous life in which women know their place. To such a world, surely, belongs the sentence in I Corinthians in which we read that 'women should be silent in the churches'. In short, the sentence is an interpolation.

[11] I Corinthians 14:34.
[12] I Timothy 2:12, 15 etc.

In the world of Paul himself, we know that the women were far from silent. Only a little earlier in the same letter, he tells them that they should be veiled as they utter their prophecies. Self-contradictory he might have been, but surely not as self-contradictory as this? If the women were allowed to prophesy in Paul's 'churches', we can assume that they did not do so by sign-language.

Paul's vision of Christ was of one who had transformed everything. The human condition, and all the rules which applied before it, have changed. This is true in the case of the personal encounter with Christ which will be felt by an individual believer: 'if anyone is in Christ, there is a new creation: everything old has passed away.'[13] For that reason, Paul can have a vision of humanity in which 'there is no longer Jew or Greek, there is no longer slave or free, there is no longer male and female; for all of you are one in Christ Jesus'.[14]

I do not believe therefore in a misogynistic Paul, though it is obviously true that the Church which came after him was deeply and incorrigibly misogynistic. Luke depicts a Paul who makes friends with women, who allows Lydia to preside over the house-church at Philippi and who enters into a similar arrangement at Corinth with Priscilla. In those letters of Paul which are unquestionably authentic, we find evidence that Luke's picture was the true one. 'Help these women,' he writes to the Philippians from prison, 'for they have struggled beside me in the work of the gospel.'[15] In Romans, he greets a list of friends who include Mary and Junia (compatriots or relations of Paul's), Tryphaena and Tryphosa, Julia and the sister of Nereus.[16] And it would seem as if Romans, the greatest letter he ever wrote, was borne to the capital of the Empire by a deacon called Phoebe, with the injunction to 'welcome her in the Lord as is fitting for the saints, and help her in whatever she may require from you, for she has been a benefactor of many and of myself as well'.[17] In none of this does one detect the misogyny for which Paul is so unjustly famed.

In so far as he retained the attitudes of his race, Paul was probably by modern standards unenlightened about women. To be unenlightened because one shares the beliefs and attitudes of one's own time and group is not to deserve singling out for vilification. Slavery

[13] 2 Corinthians 5:17.
[14] Galatians 3:28.
[15] Philippians 4:3.
[16] Romans 16.
[17] Romans 16:2.

in modern eyes is an abomination. Do we hate Aristotle because he saw nothing wrong with it? To this day, Orthodox Jewish women, however powerful as personalities in their own home, remain almost without status in a religion which begins its morning liturgy with giving thanks to God that those assembled have not been born as women. Old-fashioned liberal Protestants detected in the Gospels the seeds of modern feminism – *Talitha cumi*, Damsel arise, became the motto of Victorian Christian feminists. The Jesus of the Gospels outraged Jewish opinion by speaking to the woman at the well of Samaria, and by offering forgiveness to the prostitute who, though she had sinned much, had also loved much. Impossible, says such wisdom, to imagine the misogynist puritanical Paul extending such forgiveness, nor being so much at ease with the opposite sex!

I have fallen for such a picture myself in my own book about Jesus, but the longer I think about it, the less convincing it seems. Jesus might or might not have expressed forgiveness to prostitutes, and he might or might not have been friends with women, both strangers and kinswomen. In so far as there is any historical evidence on the subject, we have to conclude that the Twelve, the followers of Jesus said to have been chosen by him, are all men. (A fact trotted out again and again by the opponents of female ordination.) Since the Twelve represent the Twelve tribes of Israel, this is hardly surprising, and it is highly probable that there was such a group, based on the Jewish church of Jerusalem with James as the Head, the replacement as it were of his brother Jesus.

The Jerusalem church, in so far as it remained purely Jewish, excluded women from positions of authority. We do not read of any Lydias or Tryphemas or Phoebes or Priscas in that circle. These names are all the converts of Paul. This is not quite the place to discuss the evolution of the written Gospels; but if it is true, as I believe it is, that the Jesus of the Gospels is an artificial creation, a collective work of art who evolved through the combined consciousness of two generations of Christian worship, then we can decide which is the more likely: that Jesus the Jew did defy his own people by demonstrations of proto-feminism; or that the Gospels themselves grew out of the Gentile Christianity which is largely the inspiration of Paul. Readers can decide, of the two men, which was the more likely to have met prostitutes: a rustic exorcist who limited his sphere of operations almost exclusively to fishing villages on the shores of the sea of Galilee, or a ubiquitous and highly sociable tradesman, whose friends lived in the ports and capitals of the pagan Mediterranean.

Paul believed himself to have been 'shamefully mistreated' at Philippi.[18] Luke tells his readers that one day, when Paul and friends were going to the *proseuche*, they met a slave girl who was hired out as a fortune-teller. She had been making a nuisance of herself by following Paul and crying out, 'These men are slaves of the Most High God.' Paul, who tired of this, eventually turned on her and denounced the evil spirit which was possessing her: 'I order you in the name of Jesus Christ to come out of her.'[19] The exorcism was successful, the wicked demon left the girl, and with it her power of divination. Seeing that their livelihood was thereby destroyed, the girl's owners took Paul and Silas before the magistrates and said, 'These men are disturbing our city; they are Jews, and are advocating customs that are not lawful for us Romans to adopt or observe.' The consequence was that Paul and Silas were flogged and imprisoned.

At midnight, Paul and Silas were praying and singing hymns to God, 'and the other prisoners were listening to them'[20] – with what degree of appreciation, Luke does not say. There was an earthquake, the prison doors burst open, and the gaoler came running. When he saw that the prison had burst open, he prepared to fall on his sword, but Paul prevented him. 'Do not harm yourself, for we are all here.' The gaoler was converted and, together with his entire family, baptised. When the morning came, the magistrates sent word that Paul and Silas should be released; but Paul decided to stand on his dignity and say, 'They have beaten us in public, uncondemned, men who are Roman citizens, and have thrown us into prison; and now are they going to discharge us in secret? Certainly not! Let them come and take us out themselves.'[21] The magistrates therefore came and released Paul and Silas, who departed for Lydia's house. Clearly, Paul's own suggestion that he was disgracefully treated in Philippi could very well refer to some such incident of wrongful arrest. Whether the reader believes in the unclean spirit, the earthquake, the pious gaoler, or even in the Roman citizenship of Paul, will be largely a matter of taste. It is one of those stories in Luke which suggest the situation of the writer himself and the church from which he comes. Whatever the truth of

[18] 1 Thessalonians 2:2.
[19] Acts 16:18.
[20] Acts 16:25.
[21] Acts 16:37.

the original incident in Philippi, Luke writes it up to emphasise that Paul and his friends were Roman citizens, law-abiding and pious.

What then of the suggestion, made by the fortune-teller's pimps – if we may call them that – that Paul has been 'advocating customs that are not lawful for us Romans to adopt or observe'? This is clearly one of those moments in Acts where the historians feel happier than the theologians with the text as it stands. The procedure adopted against Paul and the description of the magistrates in Philippi seem to be authentically rendered. The authorities (*archontes*) are informed. The particular authorities in Philippi are called in Greek the *strategoi*, the generals, a Greek word which was the equivalent of the Roman *praetores*. As in other Roman colonies, the senior magistrates at Philippi would have been known as the *duoviri iure dicundo*, literally the 'two men for saying law'. There was no Greek equivalent of this clumsy Latin phrase, but there can be no doubt that Luke intends us to believe that Paul's activities were brought to the attention of the highest authority in the city. He is charged with affray, or causing a riot, which was, by Luke's account, the result of the fracas with the fortune-teller. And he is charged with unRoman practice.

The scholars differ concerning the plausibility of this. Some have believed that it was a basic principle of Roman law that Romans were not allowed to participate in foreign cults which had not been approved by the Senate. Perhaps this had been true in Italy and at a time when the body of Roman citizens was much smaller than in the 50s; but many have doubted whether such a law could conceivably have been enforced in every corner of the Mediterranean.[22] The point as far as Luke is concerned is that such apparently anti-Roman behaviour is not in fact disturbing to the State. He writes after the Neronian persecution and is trying to appease Roman fears that Christians are troublemakers, anarchists, refuseniks.

Divination and fortune-telling were an obsession with the Romans and a key part of that State religion which Augustus himself had been responsible for reviving. Such superstitions as the consulting of auguries were an essential part of State business in Rome, at a period when magic, astrology and superstition of all kinds had never been more popular. It has been said that the sharpest contrast between the classical period and late antiquity is precisely in this spread of superstition and sorcery during the later period. In the old Greek religious mythology,

[22] See A. N. Sherwin White, *Roman Society and Roman Law in the New Testament*, pp. 78–9.

it is significant that the two most famous witches, Kirke and Medeia, were both foreign women, and that the goddess of witches, Hekate, came from Karia, in the south-west corner of Asia Minor. These figures, who would have been regarded in Plato's generation as foreign absurdities, as quite literally uncivilised, were, by the era of Paul, serious patronesses.[23] Cicero placed enormous value on the auspices and made repeated reference in his letters – in all seriousness – to the usefulness of fortune-telling in elections: 'For the immortal gods have often restrained, by means of the auspices, the unjust impetuosity of the people.'[24] Paul was moving about in a world where absurd superstitions were swallowed wholesale. Some of his own ideas, which would strike a modern as extraordinary – his belief in demons and spirits and his view that human beings could be conveyed from one spiritual 'dimension' to another, rather like a traveller in outer space – would have been perfectly intelligible to his contemporaries. Most modern readers of the Acts of the Apostles, whether or not Christian believers, would have regarded the activities of the slave girl as mumbo-jumbo. In the world of classical antiquity, however, most people would have accepted the powers of the unseen; it was simply a question of which demons or gods were better than another, or, if you were Jewish, which were legitimate. One of the reasons for the Jewish religion being so popular was the widely held belief that the Jews were good fortune-tellers, and, well into the Middle Ages, the Psalms, for example, were used by the rabbis for their astrological significance, as fortune-telling devices. The point at issue in Philippi was not the lawfulness of fortune-telling, still less its efficacy, but who was in charge. Paul was regarded as a threat by the astrologers because he was a threat; he was deliberately posing one. A new commodity had arrived, which Paul was selling hard, and if it took hold and became popular, it would inevitably drive the rival spiritual attractions out of business.

So, Paul and Silas moved the ninety or so miles from Philippi to Thessalonica (the modern port of Salonica). To this day, it is a magnificent harbour, and the city climbs up a steep hillside above it. Being placed on the great Roman road running from the Adriatic to the Black Sea it was prosperous and important commercially. It had

[23] See Martin Persson Nilsson, *Greek Piety*, pp. 117–18.
[24] *De Legibus*, III, 27, quoted by G. E. M. de Ste Croix, *The Class Struggle in the Ancient Greek World*, p. 344.

done well in the Civil War, siding with Octavian, who, when he had become Augustus Caesar, made it a free city with its own internal government.

There is a marked contrast between Luke's account of Paul's visit to Thessalonica and the Apostle's own. Luke says that Paul visited the synagogue at Thessalonica on three successive Sabbaths, proving from the Scriptures that Jesus was the Messiah; and that the Jews became jealous of him and persuaded 'ruffians in the market-place' to start a riot. 'These people who have been turning the world upside down have come here also . . . They are all acting contrary to the decrees of the emperor, saying that there is another king named Jesus.' On this account, according to Acts, Paul and Silas left the city and went to Beroea.[25]

When we turn to Paul's own letter to the Thessalonians, however, a rather different picture emerges. For a start, it is obvious from what he writes that he was in Thessalonica for much longer than three weeks. He alludes to his custom of continuing with his trade while spreading the word. 'You remember our labour and toil, brothers and sisters; we worked night and day so that we might not burden any of you while we proclaimed to you the gospel of God.'[26] He would not have written this about a mere three-week trip. He obviously had made contacts in this great commercial centre and we can assume that he was there several months at least.

More significantly, it is clear from his letter to the Thessalonians that he did not make Jewish converts but Gentile ones. Nor did they turn away from what we might call mainstream Judaism to the worship of Jesus, for we read, 'how you [the Thessalonians] turned to God from idols, to serve a living and true God'.[27] There is no mention of a Thessalonian synagogue in the letter. (Nor incidentally is there any evidence of a Jewish settlement in Thessalonica, though there must have been Jews in a port of this size and level of prosperity.) Luke never wants his Roman readers to think that the Christians are indeed anarchists who want to turn the world upside down by worshipping 'another King'. So, wherever there is trouble, he blames the Jews, and if there is a memory of Paul causing a civil disturbance – as evidently there was in Thessalonica – he invents the idea that the Jews were behind it.

[25] Acts 17:6–7; 10.
[26] I Thessalonians 2:9.
[27] I Thessalonians 1:9.

Paul in fact has broken new ground in Thessalonica; planted the divine seed in virgin soil. 'The word of the Lord has sounded forth from you not only in Macedonia and Achaia, but in every place.'[28] There is no suggestion that the divine Word depends on the presence of Jews, nor on the inspiration of Scripture. The times are too short and too urgent for that. God is choosing his own, and at any minute, the Day of Christ will dawn. We know exactly the Gospel which Paul had proclaimed to the Thessalonians. These Macedonian believers must, once they have heard the Word, wait quietly for the Day, which will not be long in coming. Evidently, when a few months passed and some of the first converts died, they were anxious that these dead Macedonians might have missed their chance of seeing the coming Christ, Paul however, was able to reassure them:

> But we do not want you to be uninformed, brothers and sisters, about those who have died, so that you may not grieve as others do who have no hope. For since we believe that Jesus died and rose again, even so, through Jesus, God will bring with him those who have died. For this we declare to you by the word of the Lord, that we who are alive, who are left until the coming of the Lord, will by no means precede those who have died. For the Lord himself, with a cry of command, with the archangel's call and with the sound of God's trumpet, will descend from heaven, and the dead in Christ will rise first. Then we who are alive, who are left, will be caught up in the clouds together with them to meet the Lord in the air; and so we will be with the Lord forever. Therefore encourage one another with these words.[29]

Paul wrote his letter to the Thessalonian Christians from a later stage of his journey, probably from Corinth in perhaps 51.

Since Paul's letters have been mentioned so often in this narrative, it is perhaps worth pausing to ask what we mean by them. They are, after all, our primary source for writing about Paul and his world, far more important than the secondary source of Luke's histories. Letters in the ancient world fell into two broad categories. There were formal compositions which were really treatises or lectures cast in an epistolary form; some of Cicero's letters (but not all) come into this category, as do many of Seneca's. Secondly, there were real letters – documents

---

[28] I Thessalonians 1:8.
[29] 1 Thessalonians 4:13–18.

written to real people on actual occasions. Such letters could rise – again, Cicero demonstrates this, as does Pliny the Elder – to a high art form. All Paul's letters fall into this second category. They are all, or very nearly all, written with a particular purpose. All, or nearly all, are written in response to particular requests from some Christian group or another. That said, of course, Paul's letters would not have formed the basis of Christian literature, would not have been copied and recopied and edited and imitated, and preserved for hundreds of years, if they had been no more than purely localised scribblings. He used the occasions of the letters he wrote to expound what he called (did he coin the word?) his Gospel, his Good News of Jesus Christ. In the course of these writings, he makes allusions to himself, allusions to his friends, allusions to the quarrels and friendships in which they have been engaged. We, as historians, have tried to reconstruct from these allusions, what was going on in his world.

Paul dictated his letters and they must sometimes have been written down by one of his companions, perhaps Silas or Timothy. Sometimes he added messages of his own in his own large handwriting. The letters were written on papyrus. Once written, the letters would have been dispatched by a private messenger service. Christianity could never have spread as rapidly as it did throughout the Mediterranean world without the Roman roads and the Roman trade routes. Interestingly enough, the Empire did not invent a postal service in the modern sense. The government of Augustus generated, as we should expect from the Widmerpool of the ancient world, a vast amount of correspondence. Provincial governors were given their own *tabellarii* for sending memos. A few slaves and freedmen would be given the right to convey government documents – *speculatores* (scouts) and *frumentarii* (supply-officers). Letters would often be sent by supply-ship. Such couriers of information were not at the disposal of ordinary citizens, still less of non-citizens.

Presumably, Paul was able to send letters with the help of his trade contacts, just as it was trade, we can infer, which enabled him to keep up such a rapid progress from place to place when he fell foul of a particular civil or religious authority. Clearly, he had encountered opposition in Thessalonica, and whether it was from Jews, Gnostics (did such a group exist at this date?) or others[30] we shall never know. He moved on, hoping to return to his friends in Thessalonica. This was not to be. 'Satan blocked our way.'[31]

It is possible that Paul considered at this juncture setting out for

Rome. (He told the Roman Christians that he had 'often intended' to go to the capital of the Empire.)[32] If this were the case, Paul and his companions would have been travelling from east to west along the Via Egnatia, planning to follow the road to Dyrrhachium (Dubrovnik), and then taking the sea-crossing from the Adriatic to Italy. Instead, however, he left the main road and headed for Beroea (modern Karaferria), 57 miles south-west of Thessalonica, a pleasantly situated town on the slope of the Bermios range in the valley of the Haliacmon. Here he found a synagogue of Jews who were more sympathetic to his ideas, perhaps because there were some upper-class Greek god-fearers, male and female, who formed part of the congregation.[33] Or so Luke believed. We know the names of some of his converts in Beroea. Sopater, son of Pyrrhus, was to accompany Paul to Jerusalem seven years later;[34] if he was the same as Sosipater whom Paul mentions in Romans then he was a Jew.[35]

But when Paul was arriving in Beroea something was happening in Rome which was to have a fundamental influence on the development of Paul's life for the next few years. In 49/50,[36] Claudius expelled the Jews from Rome.

The expulsion was seen by Suetonius and Dio Cassius as part of general xenophobia and paranoia on Claudius's part, rather than as a result of a particularised antisemitic impulse. Tacitus reminds us that all the borders of the Empire at this date were in turmoil – savage hordes making trouble for the Roman fleet on the Danube and British warriors carrying into its ninth bloody year their resistance to the Roman invasions. From Gaul to Scythia, Rome was not finding it easy to establish its monolithic rule upon the world. Claudius, intensely superstitious and philhellenic as he was, wanted Italy was to be the centre of everything. Those foreigners who came to the capital and behaved themselves, such as the Parthian and Armenian envoys who were granted seats with the Senators in the orchestra at the Theatre,

---

[30] For a summary of the arguments and an account of the literature, which is vast, see Ernest Best, *A Commentary on the First and Second Epistles to the Thessalonians* (Black's New Testament Commentaries, 1972), pp. 16–22.
[31] I Thessalonians 2:18.
[32] Romans 1:13; 15:22ff.
[33] Acts 17:12.
[34] Acts 20:4.
[35] Romans 16:21.
[36] See W. M. Ramsay, *St Paul the Traveller and the Roman Citizen*, p. 254, for reasons why 50 is a more probable date.

were rewarded. Those, such as the Lycians, who made trouble were ruthlessly suppressed, and their national sovereignty and rights to self-government removed.[37]

There were too many Jews in Rome for Claudius to have expelled them all, but he evidently made an example of a few of them, including a married couple called Aquila and Priscilla, tentmakers like Paul himself, and soon to become some of his closest friends. Between Suetonius's 'disturbance at the instigation of Chrestus' and Tacitus's Nero making torches of the Christians as scapegoats for the fire, there is a gap of fourteen years. These are the crucial fourteen years of the early history of Christianity, and he and his friends play a vital role in them. In that period, relations between the Romans and the Palestinian Jews deteriorated. While Paul and his congregations were engaged in comparatively esoteric discussions about the admissibility or otherwise of Gentile converts who remained uncircumcised, the Empire was becoming more autocratic, the Jewish population of Palestine more restless, the tension between the two more explosive. In the middle of it all, there was this tiny sect, gradually evolving from the parent stem of Judaism. All these elements in the story feed upon each other. Without the political struggle between Rome and the Jews, it is questionable whether the differences between church and synagogue would have led to a break. The Jews and Romans would have had less motive – perhaps no political motive at all – in wishing to isolate the Christians and make them different from the Jews in political terms. Equally, had the relations between Rome and Jerusalem been equable, then the Christians would have had no motive for establishing, in the eyes of the Romans, their complete difference from and independence of the synagogue. In 50, it was still possible for the Romans to think that a 'disturbance at the instigation of Chrestus' took place among, simply, 'the Jews'. Chrestus is just an unheard-of Jew. The Jews and the Christians are interchangeable.

Paul turned not to Rome now, but to Athens.

Therefore, when we could bear it no longer, we decided to be left alone in Athens.[38]

The Athens entered by the Apostle Paul circa AD 50 was a very different

---

[37] Tacitus, *Annales*, XII, 25–39; Suetonius, *Claudius*, xxv.
[38] 1 Thessalonians 3:1.

place from the prosperous, populous and politically powerful city-state of the fifth and fourth centuries BC. In 88–7 BC it had been involved in a war against Rome. The Roman general Sulla besieged it in 86 BC and imposed on it a constitution. Nevertheless, as the life of Cicero reminds us (he spent six months studying there in 79 BC), Athens retained its status as the philosophical centre of the universe, even though there was probably no single individual living there who was worthy to hold a candle to Pericles or Plato or Aristotle.

Plato had established his school there a mile from the city gates in 387 BC. Since the site was dedicated to the hero Academus, to whom it had once belonged, it became known as the Academy. The gymnasium in Plato's time was planted with plane and olive trees – hence the 'grove of Academeia'. Sulla cut down the grove in 87 BC to build siege engines. The Academy was still open in the first century AD, though bore no more resemblance to the school of Plato's day than twentieth-century Eton bears to the grammar school for poor scholars founded on the site near Windsor by Henry VI. By about the third century BC the Academy seems to have abandoned the teachings of Plato in favour of a more sceptical school of thought. The revived Platonism of the first century AD can best be appreciated in the writings of the Jewish Alexandrian Philo, who made Moses's encounters with the Deity compatible with the quest for the Good in Plato's dialogues. Ammonius was the head of the Academy at Athens in Paul's day, and he was also an exponent of what could be termed the Platonist revival.

We have no evidence that Paul ever read Plato, though by focusing on the use made by both writers of certain words and concepts, we can make up our own minds about the degree to which the Apostle had absorbed the philosopher. Four hundred years after *The Republic* was written, Paul would in any event not have been exposed to undiluted Platonism so much as to Plato filtered through recent writers – perhaps through his contemporary Seneca or through Cicero. Central to their idea of goodness is the notion that virtue is its own reward and that righteousness (*dikaiosune*) is a human quality. It is even a craft in Plato, a *techne*, which can be mastered. Socrates in *The Republic* attempts to demonstrate by analogy and argument that 'morality' (the way that a modern translator would probably render *dikaiosune*) is beneficial to rulers, that it profits them more than its opposite. (Hence Jowett's rendering of the word as *justice*.) Thrasymachus attempts to argue that brutal and even immoral behaviour does in fact pay. He singles out political tyranny: 'You see, Socrates, immorality if practised on a large enough scale has more power, license and authority than morality.'[39] But even this argument is turned around when it is demonstrated that 'morality is really the advantage of the stronger party'. For Socrates/Plato, the existence of political corruption and human wickedness provides all the more reason for wise men to learn the craft of morality and righteousness, and to bring the practice of it into their public as well as into their private lives. Four hundred years later, under one of the most oppressive tyrannies which the human race has ever endured, Paul's perspective was very different. Paul is patron saint of toadies and high Tories because of his apparent acceptance, expressed in the letter to the Romans, of Thrasymachus's notion that governments decide what is 'right': 'Let every person be subject to the governing authorities.'[40] But Paul took this further. In his world-view, righteousness was unattainable for the human race. *Dikaiosune* was not in fact a human quality at all, it was a divine quality which can be dispensed to the human race only by celestial decree. Indeed what Plato called righteousness could in most cases be translated into what Paul calls The Law (*Ho Nomos*). Merely to contemplate it is to reflect upon the huge gulf between our perception of what is good and our capacity to attain to it. 'For I do not do what I want, but I do the very thing I hate':[41] words to be understood not as a tormented personal confession so much as an analysis of the human condition. Plato (Cicero, Seneca) posits the optimistic possibility that righteousness, law, politics, personal morality might all be one. For Paul they are all at odds. The world is gone awry. All souls must submit to the higher powers. The good they want to do, they don't do. Men such as Caligula, Claudius and Nero are the emissaries of God. None can do good except by God's grace. Socrates, and still more the Roman Stoics, exasperate us by their lofty refusal to see the world as it is, just as they inspire us by their courageous holding-fast to that which is good. Paul took the madness, the chaos as the starting point. He was not one of those thinkers with a desire to upset and make us question contemporary orthodoxy. He is not indulging in paradox for its own sake. But by the time he comes to contemplate it, the applecart is already upset. God's promises to Israel have not been fulfilled as anyone could understand or expect. The condemned criminal, the crucified

[39] *The Republic*, 344c.
[40] Romans 13:1.
[41] Romans 7:15.

− 154 −

anarchist comes back to haunt Paul, not only as the saviour of Israel but as the redeemer of the ruined Kosmos. Moving from Chapter One of *The Republic* to Paul's letter to the Romans is like moving from a civilised atrium where the only noise is that of human voices raised in passionate debate, but debate punctuated by laughter, to a crazed scene painted by Hieronymus Bosch in which the human race, given over to every kind of vice and immorality, is pitchforked by demons and by the Almighty himself into a predestined perdition and where righteousness rains down only in sacrificial blood. For the crucial difference between Plato and Paul is that Paul believes God is responsible for everything, whereas Plato believes that God is merely responsible for the good things (*me panto aition tonTheon alla ton agathon*). Plato, as far as the civilisedWest is concerned, invented the concept of monotheism. His concept of God bequeathed many problems, intellectual and religious, to those who accepted his first premises – not least, how God could be good and have any responsibility for a universe so manifestly squealling with misery and steeped in sin. The Platonist tendency was to posit an impassible God who could not move, and who was, like an airily ineffectual headmaster of a chaotic private school, not strictly speaking responsible for anything. Much confusion has resulted from this view, just as much misery has resulted from Paul's determinist view that God is responsible for everything.

From the beginning, the Academy attracted students from outside Athens. The image of the Apostle in Rome excites an exaggerated sense of political paradox, a confrontation between Caesar and Christ, in which the powerless tentmaker is laying the foundations for a European religio-civilisation. Knowing as we do that the emperor Constantine, nearly three centuries after Christ, is destined to pick up the Cross and turn it into a sword, our thoughts of Paul in Rome are focused on the political dimensions of Christendom.

In Athens it is otherwise. Christianity is destined for an intellectual history which is, to say the least, eclectic and which will owe as much to Plato as it does to Moses. If in Rome, we think of images of conquest: a succession of emperors persecuting the Church, and then a reversal of power in which the Church is triumphant, and the Bishop of Rome becomes the Pontifex Maximus. In Athens we think of the strange history of Christian Dogma, the sheer oddity of the fact that Plato and Aristotle come to the modern world, historically speaking, filtered through Christian monasticism; that Christianity itself, as a doctrinal entity with all its esoteric formulations about the nature of the Deity, and of the soul, and of the self (divine and human) of Christ, and the heavens and the earth, derives largely from the late Platonism.

We know that Paul went to Athens, since he says so himself in the Thessalonian letter; and that having arrived here with Timothy and others he sent them away, back to confirm the converts in Macedonia while he remained in Athens. Luke represents Paul as wandering about the city and finding the place full of 'idols' which were little to his taste. Then we find him preaching Christianity in the market-place and indulging in philosophical debates with Epicurean and Stoic philosophers. Then comes the famous speech which he makes on the Areopagus,[42] his allusion to an altar to the Unknown God which he has seen on his peregrinations about the city and his revealing of the identity of this unknown deity. Finally, he proclaimed the resurrection of the 'appointed man'. 'When they heard of the resurrection of the dead, some scoffed; but others said, "We will hear you again about this." 'We are told that he made a few converts, a woman called Damaris and Dionysius the Areopagite – known to history as St Denis.[43]

Like most of Luke's stories, this one fills the head of the reader with some puzzlement. Since we know from I Thessalonians the sort of teaching which Paul was peddling at this period, how are we to account for the apparent volte-face before the Athenian philosophers? The 'commonplaces by which Hellenistic Judaism sought to establish the unity of God' were 'totally inconsistent with the belief that the world could come to an end'.[44] True, Paul's sermon on the Hill of Mars does mention a day of reckoning, but the hectic apocalyptic tone of Thessalonians is entirely lacking. One can't really believe that *our man* can be indulging in these really rather boring thoughts about God, with their careful quotations from Epimenides and Aratus.

Aratus was a Stoic and you could say that Stoicism was the 'received wisdom' of the governing and thinking classes of that period, rather as liberalism is in Europe and the United States today.'The Stoic teaching, indeed, was nothing more than a corroboration and theoretical defence of certain traditional values of the governing class in an aristocratic

---

[42] A spur, jutting out from the western end of the Acropolis, and used, time out of mind, as a place for legal processes and debates. The legend had it that Mars here cleared himself of the murder of Hallirhothius, son of Neptune, hence its other name of the Hill of Mars.
[43] Acts 17:34.
[44] Wilfrid L. Knox, *St Paul and the Church of the Gentiles*, pp. 1ff.

and republican state.'[45] Stoicism takes its name from the *Stoa poikile*, the painted stoa, or colonnade, a porch-like structure which was erected along the north side of the agora in Athens in the fifth century BC. (The '*poikile*' refers to the huge paintings, the Athenian equivalent of the Soviet *plakat*, in which giant representations of Athenian military heroes were displayed.)

Wilfrid Knox, one of the most imaginative scholars who has ever written about the subject, was an intelligent Cambridge classicist who was also an Anglo-Catholic priest. Without realising that he has done so, we sense that he has created a St Paul who read Classics and Moral Sciences at Cambridge before the Second World War, and who, moreover, has a spiritual history remarkably like Knox's own. At Athens Paul discarded the Judaic apocalyptic of Palestine and embraced the purer air of Hellenism, just as at Cambridge Knox abandoned the heavy evangelical religion of his father and became, roughly, an Anglo-Catholic modernist. If so scrupulous a scholar as Knox can be said to have echoed his own spiritual story while attempting to tell the story of the Apostle Paul, what hope for the rest of us who have tried to treat of the same material with the right blend of engagement, curiosity and detachment?

The truth is that Knox's view is acceptable only if we are trying to reconcile Acts with Paul's letters. If we do that, we must suppose that Paul abandoned his faith in Jewish apocalyptic after his visit to Athens, and the evidence of his great letters – Corinthians and Romans were certainly written after his visit to Athens – is that he never lost hope in the Day of Christ coming as a thief in the night. As soon as we make the leap, which a clergyman of Knox's generation could not do, we can admit that much of Luke is fiction and that the contents of the speech are 'a first-rate witness to post-apostolic preaching and theology, but not up to the historical Paul.'[46] One could go further and say that the speech that Paul is supposed to have delivered to the Athenians is the strongest possible indication of the fact that Acts is a late work, belonging to a period of Christianity which post-dates Paul and his world by as much as a quarter of a century. Post-apostolic Christianity (and you could miss the adjective post-apostolic out of that phrase) is mild stuff beside the pure pungent mixture of Paul's preaching. 'For Jews demand

[45] Ronald Syme, *The Roman Revolution*, p. 57.
[46] G. Bornkamm, *Paul*, p. 65.

signs and Greeks desire wisdom, but we proclaim Christ crucified, a stumbling block to Jews and foolishness to Gentiles, but to those who are called, both Jews and Greeks, Christ the power of God and the wisdom of God.'[47]

[47] 1 Corinthians 1:22–4.

X

CORINTH

That Asian seaboard where Greeks and Orientals live side by side in crowded
magnificent cities.

Euripides, *The Bacchae*

Corinth, once the second city of Greece though today a ruin, is easily
approached by the modern sea-traveller because of the canal which
links the Adriatic to the Aegean. When this canal was finally dug in
1893, evidence of Roman shafts and channels revealed that as much
as one fifth of the canal had actually been dug during the reign of
Nero, who dreamed of renaming the Peloponnesus the Neronnesus.[1]
Such a canal, had it been built, would have enormously facilitated the
communications between the eastern and the western Mediterranean.
Nero failed to complete the project which was so dear to his heart.
(Vespasian tried again with 6,000 captives from the Jewish war, but
still failed to cut through the solid rock.) Since the sixth century BC a
causeway (*diolkos*), four miles long, had been erected that enabled
ships to be dragged across the Isthmus, but this would only have been
possible for those ships which carried a considerable number of slaves.
Others would have to continue to sail around the Peloponnese.[2] Paul
would have made the short journey down the Aegean coast from
Piraeus (the port for Athens) to the Corinthian port of Cenchreae,
which stood on the eastern side of the Isthmus. Here stood the temple
to Poseidon, the god of the Mediterranean itself, whose capricious
anger kept Odysseus so long from returning to Ithaca from the Trojan
wars. Many travellers must have arrived, queasy and frightened by
storms, to give thanks to this stern god (who in benign mood had
taught the human race the art of managing horses, and who offered
his patronage to horse-races) for their delivery from shipwreck and

[1] Susan E. Alcock, 'Nero at Play?', in Elsner and Masters (eds), *Reflections of Nero*, pp. 102–3.
[2] Fik Meijer, *A History of Seafaring in the Classical World*, pp. 30, 83.

PAUL

their safe arrival on dry land. The monotheistic Paul perhaps cast a
disdainful eye at the stupendous fane and gave little attention to the
shady pine groves in the temple grounds where the Corinthians, famed
throughout antiquity for their naval prowess, held the celebrated
Isthmian games. These happened biennially and attracted huge crowds
from all over the Hellenic world. We know them to have been popular
during the Roman period.[3] Nero, the most philhellenic of all the
emperors, was to attend the games there on 28 November 66. He
proclaimed freedom to all the Greeks in a speech which is still preserved
in the Acraephilae. 'Other men', it was said, 'have given freedom to
individual cities, Nero alone has freed a whole province.'[4]

Lifting his eyes, Paul could have seen Corinth itself, perched over
1,800 feet above the harbour on the mountain known as the
Acrocorinth. The city at this date divided between the upper town
and the lower, near the harbour. Corinth was to be Paul's home, on
and off, for two years, between 50 and 52. It was in effect a Roman
city. All but destroyed in 146 BC by the Romans, it had become one
of Julius Caesar's favourite colonies, renamed Laus Julius Corinthus.

It was in Corinth that the 'blushful Hippocrene' sprang up when
Pegasus, the winged horse, struck it with his hoof. The idols in Corinth
would have been of a particularly choice variety. When Caesar rebuilt
the city he excavated many superb bas-reliefs, bronze vessels and statues
from the Greek period. Corinth was a centre of painting and
modelling[5] and many of its finest treasures were taken as spoils by the
Romans to adorn the capital of the Empire – for example, the paintings
by Aristeides of Dionysus were used to adorn the temple of Ceres in
Rome. Many treasures remained, however. The verb to ornament
comes from the river Orneae which flows past Corinth, watering the
temple of Priapus. It is safe to say that had they only survived, the
Corinthian treasures which would most delight the eye of the aesthete
would be the very objects which most offended Paul and his friends.
In particular, unless one shares the monotheistic obsession with idolatry,
Paul's anxiety on this account would be puzzling to any twentieth-
century reader except Jews, Muslims and extreme Protestants.

Few of the great cities of the world at this time had by modern
standards large populations. Corinth had probably only 130,000 people.
But it might have felt as crowded as Hong Kong or Manhattan, with

[3] Victor Paul Furnish, *II Corinthians* (New York, 1984), p. 15.
[4] Arnaldo Momigliano, in *The Cambridge Ancient History* (1934), vol. 10, 21, p. 735.
[5] *ibid.*, VIII, vi, 23.

much of life lived on the street – even more than is the case in Mediterranean cities today.[6] This was a city where much was for sale and much was visible. Little had changed about its character since Herodotus said that traders were held in low esteem, except in Corinth.[7] It was a trading town and, so far as we know, it was trade which drew Paul there.

It was a place of proverbial wickedness, energy, riches, noise. The verb 'to Corinth' (i.e. *Korinthiazesthai*) in popular Greek meant to fornicate; *Korinthiastes*, the title of one of Philetaerus's plays, means 'the whoremonger'. Corinth, 'the sacred hill-city of Aphrodite',[8] as Euripides called it, was a great centre of the worship of the goddess of love, whose temple, the Acrocorinthus, crowned the high mountain on which the city stood. The temple was staffed by a thousand female slaves, which according to Strabo was the reason for the great popularity of the place. Sea-captains were known to frequent the temple when they put in to shore at Cenchreae or Lechaeum (the western port). Once, when one of the whores was accused by a female visitor to the temple with being lazy, the visitor received the reply: 'Yet, such as I am, in this short time I've brought down three big ship's masts.'[9]

Was it a place and a period in which sexual licence was particularly widespread? Seneca says in one of his essays that unchastity was the greatest evil of the age, but in another he contradicts himself and says, 'You are wrong, Lucilius, if you think that our age is peculiar for vice, luxury and the desertion of moral standards, and all the other things which everyone imputes to his own time. These are the faults of mankind, not just of any age.'[10] He wrote in Italy, however, and not in Corinth.

Certainly Paul's letters to Corinth, more than the rest of his surviving work placed together, dwell most conspicuously on questions of marriage and sexual morality. Shortly after Paul left the place, the followers of Christ in Corinth became involved in a sexual scandal. One of the church members had an affair with his stepmother. As a man who entirely accepted the monogamous traditions of Judaism, Paul was scandalised, exclaiming that such behaviour was not so much

[6] See Wayne A. Meeks, *The First Urban Christians: The Social World of the Apostle Paul*, p. 28.
[7] Herodotus, *Historia*, II, 167.
[8] *Fragment* 1084.
[9] Strabo, *Geographia*, VIII, vi, 20–3; Pausanias, *Description of Greece*, II, i, 1–5.2.
[10] *Ad Helviam* 16, 3 and *Epistle* 97.

as spoken about among the Gentiles.[11] Paul is making the primary point that if the guilty couple intended to marry, they would be breaking Roman law.[12] Although the Romans had fairly lax marriage rules, they did have a code of practice relating to the spouses of parents. Men were not allowed to steal their father's women. Strange to say, the Jewish view of this question (because the Jews were concerned less with property-rights and more with inner or personal sexual morality?) was more relaxed. Jewish proselytes were allowed to marry their stepmothers, though not, obviously, their mothers. For those born Jews, it was forbidden to marry their stepmothers.[13]

Paul, like his contemporary Seneca, was suspicious of carnal relations, though he was less puritanical than the Stoic philosopher.[14] Seneca said, 'You and I who are still far from wise, must not commit the error of falling into a stormy passion which enslaves us to someone else.'[15] There were those in Corinth who took this view; they boasted that they had 'handed over' their bodies so as to lead a 'spiritual life'. All right if you can manage it, was Paul's view, but for those with normal sexual appetites it was asking for trouble. Better to marry than to be on fire with lust.

Paul's apparently grudging attitude to marriage provided celibate fanatics in later Christian generations with plenty of ammunition to support their body-hating, women-hating philosophies, their monkish despairs, their flagellations, their hairshirts, their cells and their vows. The monks' attitudes to sex derive as much from Plato as they do from the Jewish tradition, and from the Greek conception that matter itself, the very world of the physical, is evil; that God is by definition spiritual.

Paul preferred, he said, to remain single so as to have more time for the Lord's work. ('The unmarried man is anxious about the affairs of the Lord, how to please the Lord; but the married man is anxious

---

[11] 1 Corinthians 5:1. AV: 'such fornication as is not so much as named among the Gentiles' is the accurate rendering. Modern translations which translate *tois ethnesi* as 'the pagans' miss the point of what Paul is writing.

[12] We are speaking of marriage. Incest was probably as common in the first Imperial Age as at any other period of history, though perhaps few would have gone as far as Nero, who had incestuous relations with his stepbrother Britannicus and his mother Agrippina before having them murdered.

[13] The relevant texts are Leviticus 18:8; 20:11. Talmud Sanhedrin 57b f.

[14] And less of a humbug; Seneca who inveighed so often against unchastity and who told his wife, while he was committing suicide, that the greatest reward he could leave her was the memory of his virtuous life, was a known and habitual pederast.

[15] *Epistolae morales ad Lucilium*, 116. 5ff.

about the affairs of the world, how to please his wife.')[16] He disapproved of fornication and he believed that married couples should lead decent lives. Equally, he told the Corinthians not to abstain from sex – certainly partners should not 'deprive one another'.[17] But all this was to be understood against the background of an imminent End. 'If you marry, you do not sin, and if a virgin marries, she does not sin. Yet those who marry will experience distress in this life, and I would spare you that. I mean, brothers and sisters, the appointed time has grown short; from now on, let even those who have wives be as though they had none, and those who mourn as though they were not mourning, and those who rejoice as though they were not rejoicing, and those who buy as though they had no possessions, and those who deal with the world as though they had no dealings with it. For the present form of the world is passing away.'[18]

More than any other surviving documents, Paul's letters to the Corinthians provide us with an invaluable insight into the social world of his converts and the problems they encountered when they embraced his beliefs. These letters also tell us more vividly than any other New Testament documents what it must have been like to attend Early Christian religious meetings.

Paul started the church at Corinth, but he had the good fortune, when he arrived, to meet up with two business associates, leather[19] tentmakers like himself, called Priscilla and Aquila. Just as the foundation of the first church in Europe owed everything to Paul's friendship with a rich businesswoman named Lydia, so in Corinth we again encounter a tradeswoman. Clubs, or voluntary associations of tradespeople, were one of the distinctive social units of this period. Well-heeled leather-traders would have belonged to just such an association, with shared property and an agreed share of their market, so that when Paul arrived at a place such as Corinth he could have joined up at once with others who were similarly engaged. Comparable social units would be the Freemasons' lodge, which served the double function of providing business contacts and support as well as a shared social fellowship. The words club, association, ecclesia or church are

[16] 1 Corinthians 7:32. Paul is not asking the question, Which man is the less selfish? It is obvious that, judged by such standards, single people have only themselves to please.
[17] 1 Corinthians 7:5.
[18] 1 Corinthians 7:28–31.
[19] *Skenopoios*, translated tentmaker in nearly all English versions of Acts, generally means 'leatherworker'.

all the same in Greek. We do not unfortunately know enough about the 'church' of Corinth in Paul's time, but it is probably no exaggeration to say that it started as a business club among the leatherworkers and tentmakers, just as in Philippi it had started with Lydia and the clothworkers. These clubs were especially advantageous to women who could trade in their own right with the support of like-minded trading communities. Juvenal blamed much of the immorality and superstition of the age on the fact that women had found emancipation through these clubs. In Pompeii we read of Eumachia, who made her money as a brick manufacturer and paid for one of the biggest buildings in the town, donating it to the workman's association. Priscilla belonged to just the same social stratification. She was married to a man called Eagle, or Aquila. Luke says they were Jews. Whether they moved directly from 'mainstream' Judaism to Paul's persuasion, or whether Paul converted them from an Ebionite, Petrine point of view to his own ideas, we can not know. Nor do we know whether it was in their house, or in the house of some other rich person, that the first Christians in Corinth were accustomed to gather together for religious worship.

They were to become some of Paul's best friends: 'Prisca [he prefers the shorter, more formal nomenclature] and Aquila, who work with me in Christ Jesus, and who risked their necks for my life, to whom not only I give thanks, but also all the churches of the Gentiles', he wrote in Romans, having known them for a number of years.[20] After staying with Aquila and Priscilla for a while, Paul moved to the house of a Gentile god-fearer named Titius Justus, who, perhaps significantly, lived next door to the synagogue.[21] It is probable that the synagogue stood in the Lechaeum Road, although the fragmentary archaeological remains – a white marble lintel inscribed SYNAGOGE HEBRAION and an impost decorated with the seven-branched candlesticks – probably date from 300 years after Paul's time. Other notables in Corinth who were converted to Paul's way of seeing things included a householder called Stephanas, Fortunatus and Achaicus. Paul had to remind the Corinthians, when he had left them for Ephesus, that it was such rich men who kept the community alive and provided them with a meeting place. (In subsequent generations, the house of such a benefactor might become the 'church' to which the Christian community congregated.

[20] Romans 16:3–4.
[21] Acts 18:7.

The earliest Christian building identified by archaeologists is a third-century house in the Roman garrison town Dura Europos – remodelled over the generations from domestic to liturgical use. The Mithraeum at Dura and the synagogue went through similar transformations, starting life as private houses.)[22]

As well as a meeting place, the householder would provide financial protection to his fellow-believers. If we were to revisit first-century Corinth and go to the house of Aquila and Priscilla, or that of Titius Justus, what would we find was happening there when the Christians gathered on the first day of the week?

No doubt, there would have been a celebration of the Lord's Supper, the *kuriakon deipnon*. The very phrase, borrowed from the Mithraic mysteries, takes us far from the Palestinian world of Jesus, even though Paul believed that he had received instructions from Jesus himself about the institution of this great Christian sacrament. 'For I received from the Lord what I first handed on to you, that the Lord Jesus on the night when he was betrayed took a loaf of bread, and when he had given thanks, he broke it and said, "This is my body that is for you. Do this in remembrance of me." In the same way he took the cup also, after supper, saying, "This cup is the new covenant in my blood. Do this, as often as you drink it, in remembrance of me." For as often as you eat this bread and drink this cup, you proclaim the Lord's death until he comes.'[23]

There is not even the suggestion by Paul that this tradition derives from anyone who was actually with Jesus on the night before he died. And the idea that a pious Jew such as Jesus would have spent his last evening on earth asking his disciples to drink a cup of blood, even symbolically, is unthinkable. It is possible that when the Jewish followers of the Way met together, they broke bread in remembrance of Jesus; it is even possible that his Last Supper with his disciples was a Passover meal. But it took the genius of Paul to put all these facts together and to focus religious attention on the Blessed Sacrament. 'For our paschal lamb, Christ, has been sacrificed. Therefore, let us celebrate the festival.'[24] Paul's fertile brain makes Christ available to the believer in a variety of imaginative gestures, images, rituals. 'Christ' becomes that source of spiritual nourishment which all religious believers seek. He

[22] Wayne Meeks, *The Moral World of the First Christians*, p. 111.
[23] 1 Corinthians 11:23–6.
[24] 1 Corinthians 5:7.

is, or was, the rock in the wilderness, from which gushed water to feed the children of Israel who followed Moses. In other words, Christ is the presence of God in the world, and not just the figure of the historical Jesus. He is a force, or a presence, within the believer. He is, once again, a sacrament.

Paul's letters are a feast of imaginative discovery about Christ, who rises like a new star in his sky. We are not for one second accusing the Apostle of chicanery when we say that so many of these images derive from his imagination. Quite the reverse. Without Paul, what would the Christian Eucharist have been? As far as we can judge from Acts, it was not practised at all by the Jerusalem 'church'. Christianity without it is hard to imagine. Of all the great Christian *things* – books, church structures, hierarchies, religious orders, buildings – the Eucharist is surely the central mystery, the thread of continuity which stretches through all lands and all times back to the origins of the Church itself. The pious will always link it with the Last Supper, and thereby enter into Paul's understanding of the sacrificial nature of the death of Jesus. Paul's invention of the Christian Eucharist, as an addition to the 'agape meal' or love-feast practised by all Christians, is of a piece with his understanding of the sacrificial nature of Christ's death, which he saw in the same light that the followers of Mithras saw the death of the sacrificial bull. This would have had a powerful appeal to the pagans of Corinth, though it would have been meaningless, and highly distasteful, to the Jews. But who can deny that the existence of the Eucharist, the Mass, the Lord's Supper has been of stupendous imaginative importance in the history of civilisation? The liturgies of East, and West; the cathedrals and basilicas which were built to enshrine them; the music which was composed for their setting. All this we must say that we owe to Paul. For even if you can believe that Jesus 'instituted the Eucharist' in any meaningful sense of that phrase, it is hard to see how the Gentiles could ever have heard of it, given the intransigent attitude of Jesus's Jewish followers and friends – the Peter church. 'Do this in remembrance of me.' In any town in the world, more or less, the Christian Eucharist can now be found, even in Communist China. We do not have to believe in it, or to attend it, still less to know what we understand of it, to be impressed by this extraordinary link in an historical chain. When the traveller, perhaps in a hotel, perhaps walking down a street in some unChristian country, sees evidence that once again the Christian mysteries are to be celebrated, he can not fail to be impressed. Of all Christian things it is the one which most deeply reinforces the truth of John Cowper Powys's words: 'It is possible, I suppose, that some religious system, more or less akin to Christianity might have risen round the memory of Jesus of Nazareth if St Paul had never been converted, but it is hard to believe it would have lasted down to our own age, or been the Christianity, whether Catholic or Protestant, that we of the West confess, whether we like it or not, in the veins of our psychological consciousness.'[25]

In those early days, when the number of Christians was small enough to be accommodated in one room, it was obviously possible for the Christian mysteries to be performed in a reasonably seemly manner. But shortly after he left Corinth, Paul heard that the assemblies had descended into mere anarchy, with divisions among the believers. These were not like the disputes between church and synagogue. They were a division among the Christians themselves along the lines of social class.

Clearly the *kuriakon deipnon*, the Eucharistic ritual sharing of the symbolic Body and Blood of Christ, happened within the context of a social meal. Probably, like the Palestinian Jesus-movement, the Gentile churches kept up the tradition, which survived throughout the patristic age,[26] of an agape-meal preceding the mysteries. For reasons of space, the believers had to assemble in the house of the richest member of their group. And it was evident that the criterion of division was according to wealth.[27] In the ancient world, there was no feeling of shyness about riches. The ancients shared Samuel Johnson's view that 'in civilized society, external advantages make us more respected'.[28] If you were rich, you flaunted it. In the triclinium or dining-room of Priscilla's house, or Stephanas's or Fortunatus's, or whoever it was, there would have been room only for a few of

[25] J. C. Powys, *The Pleasures of Literature*, p. 170.
[26] It certainly happened until the time of Tertullian in tandem with the Eucharist. By Cyprian's (d. 258) time the custom had developed of fasting before Communion. The Eucharist was therefore celebrated in the morning and the agape meal was eaten in the evening. 'The agape seems to have become more and more a charity supper and is described as such by St Augustine.' F. L. Cross (ed.), *The Oxford Dictionary of the Christian Church*, p. 23.
[27] This is the real meaning of 1 Corinthians 11:19. '*Hoi dokimoi phaneroi geontai en humin*' does not mean as in RSV 'for only so will it become clear who among you are genuine' but 'who among you are rich or notable'.
[28] James Boswell, *Life of Johnson* (Oxford, 1980), p. 311 (20 July 1763).

the richer persons to loll about on their couches. The plebs would have had to wait outside in the atrium for the rich to finish eating. They might well have come along after work, since these meetings happened in the evening of the first day of the week,[29] the supposed day on which the Lord Christ had risen from the tomb. 'I partly believe there are divisions among you so that it can be made clear who is richer than the others.' That is something Paul takes for granted. Unlike Jesus, he never expressed a sentimental belief in the virtue of poverty. He had discovered the necessity of earning money in order to maintain his independence in the world. 'I have worked like a slave in order to maintain my independence in relation to all.'[30] By the time the rich in the triclinium had finished their meal, the rabble of plebs waiting in the hallway outside had often become drunk. 'What!' Paul asked them crossly, 'do you not have homes to eat and drink in?'[31] Very likely not, if the poorer members of the flock had come straight from a day's work in the docks. Some would have brought food, others not. By the time the bread and wine were offered up by the Eucharistic president, and the Body and Blood of Christ were passed out to the people, some of them would have been rather the worse for wear.

The vignette which Paul offers must often have troubled modern European or American Christians who (excepting for the cases of midnight Mass at Christmas in city churches) will not be used to the sight of drunkenness at the Lord's Supper.

In addition to drunkenness, there would have been various religious effusions among the Corinthian faithful which could easily have been mistaken for the effects of alcohol – as was the case with the first descent of the Holy Spirit on the disciples at Jerusalem (see p. 62).[32] Evidently at some stage, perhaps before Paul had even arrived on the scene, there were some in Corinth who believed themselves to have been possessed by the spirit. They called themselves the Spiritual Ones, the *Pneumatikoi*. One of the signs that they had been possessed by the spirit was that they would speak with tongues. Paul thought that the strange sight and sound of a Spiritual One gibbering incomprehensibly might convert the unbelievers, but it soon became clear that these

[29] The ancients did not observe the Sabbath; one of the reasons why Cicero despised the Jews was their habit, in his view a lazy one, of resting on one day of each week.
[30] 1 Corinthians 9:19 (author's translation).
[31] 1 Corinthians 11:22.
[32] Acts 2:13.

Spiritual Ones were threatening to take over the Corinthian church. Paul believed that anyone who came in from outside and saw them moaning and mumbling would consider that he had walked into an assembly of lunatics.[33] In addition to the ability to speak in tongues, some Corinthians were privileged with the gift of prophecy. Many of them did not wait until the last prophet had finished uttering before hastening to communicate his or her prophecy to the rest of the faithful, so that the meetings degenerated into a cacophony of sound with no one listening to one another. 'God is a God not of disorder but of peace',[34] Paul urged them. His words were doomed to fall on deaf ears. The gifts of the Spirit were, naturally enough, deeply divisive. Those who could speak with tongues scorned those who could not. Those who could prophesy did not bother to listen to those who could merely teach. We discover from Paul's letters to Corinth that it was not long before the 'church' there had broken up into factions. An Alexandrian Jew named Apollos brought them the religion of 'the Baptism of John'. A delegation from Jerusalem, the so-called party of Cephas, were perhaps the same as, perhaps different from, a little group who thought that, having received the spirit, they could behave as they wished. Others believed in the necessity of celibacy. The historian who looks for a unified 'Church of Corinth' must reject it, if by 'church' is meant a single organised unit, rather than a rabble of very different, very unintellectual and very disorganised people who happened to meet together in one another's houses for religious meetings. Paul, however, felt protective towards his flock and rejected the idea that there could be a 'Paul' party or an Apollos party or a Cephas party. All are one in Christ! He resorted to metaphor to make his case. 'No one can lay any foundation other than the one that has been laid; that foundation is Jesus Christ.'[35] He saw the Corinthians as a building of which Jesus Christ is the chief cornerstone. He saw them as a temple. He saw them as a body of many different constituent parts but all, in essence, one. 'If the foot would say, "Because I am not a hand, I do not belong to the body" that would not make it any less a part of the body. . . If the whole body were an eye, where would the hearing be?' . . . and so on.[36] 'Now you are the body of Christ

[33] 1 Corinthians 14:23.
[34] 1 Corinthians 14:33.
[35] 1 Corinthians 3:11.
[36] 1 Corinthians 12:14ff.

and individually members of it.'[37] Christ, in the thought of Paul, is an almost indefinable concept. He is, of course, Jesus, the Crucified Saviour. He is also the Holy bread, broken for his people and shared in the blood of his chalice. He is the presence of God in the world, and he has always been in the world. For even as the people of God followed Moses through the wilderness and received water from the rock, 'the rock was Christ'.[38] And Christ is both the sacrificial victim who saves his people, and the people themselves. They are fed by his body but, also, they *are* his body. Paul tells the Corinthians that he and others did actually know Jesus in his lifetime, but that is no longer what they mean by the word Christ. 'Even though we once knew Christ from a human point of view, we know him no longer in that way. So if anyone is in Christ, there is a new creation: everything old has passed away; see, everything has become new! All this is from God, who reconciled us to himself through Christ and has given us the ministry of reconciliation; that is, in Christ God was reconciling the world to himself, not counting their trespasses against them, and entrusting the message of reconciliation to us.'[39]

Out of the sheer chaos of the Corinthian church, Paul found, or yearned to find, a union in Christ. Whether it could be said to have existed in fact, his surviving words have remained – to the Christian Church a self-defining basis of its theology; to countless individuals a source of extraordinary inspiration.

What of the rest of the week? How were the new Christians to conduct themselves? We are far from Syrian Antioch, where delegations of Jews might arrive from Jerusalem and suggest that Gentile and Jewish believers eat at separate tables. Though there are Jews aplenty in Corinth, the church which Paul established seems to have been primarily of Gentile composition. There are unlikely to have been many founder members who had the Judaic life-habits in their blood – a natural repugnance, for example, for non-kosher food. They had, rather, to learn their own rules, and to a large extent devise their own rules. Should Christians, for example, be vegetarian? This was the simplest way of avoiding eating food which had been sacrificed to idols. In most cities of the ancient world, the butchers were the

[37] 1 Corinthians 12:27.
[38] 1 Corinthians 10:4.
[39] 2 Corinthians 5:16–19.

priests and the priests were the butchers.[40] Temples were places where animals were killed, and it was to temples that your cook would have gone to buy the meat when he was preparing a dinner party.

So, Titius Justus, a god-fearer, who under the influence of Paul has given his heart to the Lord Christ, goes out to eat with his friend down the road, who is neither a Jew nor a Christian. And it is a good dinner, and in comes the sumptuous joint of roast lamb! He knows full well where his host's slave acquired this delicious feast. He knows that the animal has been sacrificed to Poseidon or to Aphrodite. The early Christians did not believe, as modern Christians might do, that the gods were mere symbols, or figments of the collective imagination, or hangovers from a primitive animist past. All the teaching of the Christian churches for the first few centuries agreed that the ancient gods were devils. We know that Paul believed this, just as much as any other of the ancients. In this matter, however, he took the same attitude as the more genial rabbis in later ages. For although the demons and devils and 'powers' were all hovering about the world, and even worshipped as if they were gods, he never lost the idea that there was an infinity of difference between the gods and God. An outsider might believe that Yahweh, whose temple was to be found in Jerusalem, was a Jewish God, just as Poseidon was a Greek God, or Thor a Northern God. But the whole essence of Judaism was that there was only one God; that the word, the unmentionable Tetragrammaton, the ineffable mystery, the unsayable word, applied only to One. That is why Paul, in common with the more sensible rabbis in the Mishnah, took such a relaxed and common-sense – as we should think – view of the question of meats sacrificed to idols. Clearly, with Paul's libertarian views of diet, it was impossible for meat to be defiled merely because a butcher-priest in the local temple had muttered some mumbo-jumbo while slitting the neck of a goat. Some of the believers in Corinth, however, decided to become vegetarians, rather than appear to participate in idol-worship. Others were frightened of the effect it would have on non-believers if they saw a Christian eating such meat – does it imply a belief in the idol? For Paul, the important thing is that Christ has made us free. So long as 'this liberty of yours does not somehow become a stumbling block to the weak', he is happy that the Corinthians should do as they like about this matter. But: 'if food is a cause of their falling, I will never eat meat, so that I may not cause one of them to fall. Am

[40] Wayne A. Meeks, *The Moral World of the First Christians*, p. 112.

I not free? Am I not an apostle? Have I not seen Jesus our Lord?'[41]

Many modern people, even Christians, regard Paul as a restrictive or puritanical presence in the Christian tradition. They blame him for taking what they suppose to have been the simple religion of Jesus and institutionalising it, or theologising it, or somehow making it more 'restrictive'. A reading of the few surviving authentic writings of Paul – Romans, Galatians, the two Corinthian letters, Philippians – absolutely contradicts such a view. Paul is the great libertarian of religious history. Though a Jew of Jews – by his own account – he had the most cavalier view even of the written word of God. It sometimes amuses me to note modern evangelical Christians poring over the works of Paul as if they were Holy Writ. Over some of the questions which preoccupy the modern church, such as the admissibility of women to orders, or the allowability of homosexual practices, these good evangelicals will produce phrases of Paul's to enforce their arguments one way or another, as if Paul's letters were 'Scripture' in the sense of the Torah being 'Scripture'. This is what Paul's letters were destined to become in later ages of Christendom, in fact, remarkably soon after his death. But when he wrote his letters, they were all occasional pieces, in response to particular needs and queries which had arisen among his friends and converts. One of the reasons that Paul must have made his own Jewish contemporaries so angry, and one of the reasons they must have wanted to beat him with the thirty-nine strokes and drive him out of the synagogues, was that he was an outright non-believer in such 'evangelical' readings of the Bible. He was far more like Swedenborg or Blake than he was like Luther.

Indeed, like the Quakers at some periods of their history, or like the Doukhobors, Paul believed that human beings were the temples of the Holy Spirit. The Holy Spirit flows through us, and Christ lives in us. In order to find out the mind of Christ you need to look in your own heart, not to consult a work of historical reference, even one as venerable as the Holy Bible. For people of the book, such as the Jews, there is no more shocking heresy imaginable. Yet this is what Paul told his friends in Corinth. 'Are we beginning to commend ourselves again? Surely we do not need, as some do, letters of recommendation to you or from you, do we? You yourselves are our letter, written on our hearts, to be known and read by all; and you show that you are a letter of Christ, prepared by us, written not with ink

[41] 1 Corinthians 8:13–9:1.

but with the Spirit of the living God, not on tablets of stone, but on tablets of human hearts.'[42]

The essence, the end and the beginning of God's work in Christ, is love. The self-giving love which Paul saw when he contemplated the figure of Jesus of Nazareth dying on the Cross became for him the emblem and sign of God's love poured out for us. This was the subject of his most famous hymn, words which, if he had written nothing else, would have guaranteed that subsequent generations would have revered Paul, seeing him as one of the most stupendous religious poets and visionaries whom the world has ever known.

If I speak in the tongues of mortals and of angels, but do not have love, I am a noisy gong or a clanging cymbal. And if I have prophetic powers, and understand all mysteries and all knowledge, and if I have all faith, so as to remove mountains, but do not have love, I am nothing. If I give away all my possessions, and if I hand over my body so that I may boast, but do not have love, I gain nothing.

Love is patient; love is kind; love is not envious or boastful or arrogant or rude. It does not insist on its own way; it is not irritable or resentful; it does not rejoice in wrongdoing, but rejoices in the truth. It bears all things, believes all things, hopes all things, endures all things.

Love never ends. But as for prophecies, they will come to an end; as for tongues, they will cease; as for knowledge, it will come to an end. For we know only in part, and we prophesy only in part; but when the complete comes, the partial will come to an end. When I was a child, I spoke like a child, I thought like a child, I reasoned like a child; when I became an adult, I put an end to childish ways. For now we see in a mirror, dimly, but then we will see face to face. Now I know only in part; then I will know fully, even as I have been fully known. And now, faith, hope, and love abide, these three; and the greatest of these is love.[43]

Modern readers must sometimes have been puzzled by the image of the mirror at the end of this famous poem. On the wall of one of the Pompeiian villas is represented a scene in which a young satyr is gazing

[42] 2 Corinthians 3:1–3.
[43] 1 Corinthians 13.

intently into a bowl which is being held out for him by old Silenus. It is a representation of a Dionysiac initiation. Bowls were used as mirrors in the ancient world, as Pliny tells us.[44] The initiate would see a mere reflexion. Then he would look up and see reality. It is a metaphor comparable to Plato's cave myth in which, having gazed at shadows cast by the fire, the seeker after truth can turn back to the mouth of the cave and see the true source of light itself, the sun. The so-called mystery religions offered many such stages of enlightenment in a ritualised form. No need to imagine that Paul had attended such rites himself, though in his language about the inner life of the Christian he often borrows mystery-terminology. He describes the life in Christ as a mystery. In baptism, the Christian has passed from death into life. In Eucharist, the Christian drinks the blood of the Lord. These are all rituals and fashions of speech which would have been recognisable to Paul's contemporaries as mystery-talk. And similarly, the mirror into which the Corinthians gazed. They would have known that mirrors or bowl-mirrors were actually used in magical rites. Paul is not a magician. But he uses, with a boldness lacking in the other New Testament writers, tropes and figures from paganism. He made the converts feel at home. They had brought the old pagan luggage into their new abode.[45]

Priscilla and her husband Aquila were refugees from Rome. Dio Cassius tells us that Claudius tried to expel the Jews from Rome, but was unable to do so because there were so many of them.[46] If Suetonius is right when he says that Claudius planned a mass expulsion of Jews, it is odd that Tacitus, who chronicles the same period in his *Annales*, makes no mention of it. Much likelier, Claudius merely expelled the troublemakers, among whom, we must take it, he numbered the prosperous petit-bourgeois Aquila and Priscilla – just the sort of class, incidentally, who were responsible for the French revolution and who were the founding fathers of English and American radicalism in the eighteenth century. It was as troublemakers, again, that the Christians of Corinth came before the Roman magistrate, and, as it happens, we here confront the only incident in the New Testament to which it is possible to assign a date: Paul up before the magistrate's bench in

[44] HN, XXXIII, 129.
[45] See Richard Seaford, '1 Corinthians 13:12', in *JTS*, 35 (1984), pp. 117–20; and N. Hugédé, *La Métaphore du Miroir dans les Epîtres de Saint Paul aux Corinthiens*, pp. 38–44.
[46] Dio Cassius, *History of Rome*, 40.60.6,6.

Corinth. For most years of New Testament scholarship, no one had any idea whether this story was true or false. There was no other evidence that Gallio, Seneca's brother, was ever the governor of Corinth. Then, in 1905, an inscription was found in Delphi (dated 1 August AD 52) which confirmed the plausibility of Luke's history in this one particular. Gallio's year as proconsul would have fallen between the latter end of 51 and the early part of 52, so that Paul's arrival, eighteen months before he appeared in front of Gallio,[47] could be dated to late 49 or early 50.

In Luke's story, we find the Roman magistrate sitting on the raised platform (*bema*). The author of Acts has given us a completely accurate account of judicial procedure in a Roman province. An aggrieved group of people, in this case Jews, have brought before their magistrate a man – Paul – whom they accuse of 'inducing people to worship God in ways that are against the law'. It is hard to imagine why 'the Jews', whoever they were, considered this an appropriate matter to be decided by the Roman proconsul, unless we remember two things. First, a breach of the peace was involved, and Sosthenes, described as having some official position in the synagogue, is given a public beating in front of the proconsul.

Secondly, the Jews had lately been expelled from Rome by the Emperor Claudius for just such a breach of the peace as was being witnessed in Corinth by the proconsul Gallio. Prisca and Aquila and Paul were sufficiently irritating to their neighbours at the synagogue for it to be possible to describe them as rioting 'at the instigation of Chrestus'.

Much more exciting than the fact we can put a date to this incident, is the fact that the Acts of the Apostles here bring us face to face with an identifiable secular figure! Paul and his friends belong to the real world of history and not to mythology. Their actions, even their beliefs, if we are patient enough and imaginative enough to see them in their true historical context, do not belong to our 'Christian Bibles' but to that brightly sunny Mediterranean world in which Gallio and Paul found themselves face to face. The year is 51 or 52. By counting backwards we can estimate that it is some eighteen years since Paul's conversion. By his own account, Paul had spent nearly all this time as a spiritual outcast. He had not been mixing with the disciples of Jesus. To his converts in Corinth he was to speak of an adventurous life:

[47] Acts 18:11.

'five times I have received from the Jews the forty lashes minus one. Three times I was beaten with rods. Once I received a stoning. Three times I was shipwrecked; for a night and a day I was adrift at sea; on frequent journeys, in danger from rivers, danger from bandits, danger from my own people, danger from Gentiles, danger in the city, danger in the wilderness, danger at sea, danger from false brothers and sisters.'[48] Some of these experiences belonged, in all likelihood, to his years of obscurity and 'retreat'. For, whatever the Jews thought of him, Paul continued to believe himself to be a Jew. To a benign outside observer, such as Gallio, the quarrels between the 'church' of Paul and the synagogue looked merely like 'bickering' among coreligionists; and so it would look to us if we read the pages of Paul's letters and the Acts of the Apostles without our modern Christian baggage, and without the urge to read back into the text our knowledge of Christian history. Modern translations of the Bible do not help us much in this respect. The New English Bible, for example, loves to intrude the word 'Christian' into Paul's writings, even though it never once appears in anything he wrote![49]

At some stage while he was in Corinth, he wrote to those whom he had persuaded of the rightness of this view, in the large seaport of Thessalonica. It is his earliest letter and it contains views which he never seems to have modified in any of his other surviving writings. 'From Thessalonica the word of the Lord rang out', he writes, in a revealing sentence. Those Jews who might have expected the word of the Lord to ring out from the temple at Jerusalem, or from the Torah, or from the acknowledged experts in the Scriptural schools stand corrected by Paul's demotic outcry. The word comes not from the wise, not from the well-born, not from the educated, but from a rough seaport in Macedonia. The Thessalonians, and Paul himself, have been undergoing what he calls 'persecution' and 'enmities'.[50] He

---

[48] 2 Corinthians 11:24–6.
[49] Some examples: 'I say the truth in Christ' (Romans 9:1) becomes in NEB, 'I am speaking the truth as a Christian' – a different concept altogether. 'I know and am persuaded by the Lord Jesus' (Romans 14:14) becomes, 'I am absolutely convinced as a Christian'. 'If any brother hath a wife that believeth not' (1 Corinthians 7:12) becomes, 'if a Christian has a heathen wife'! The 'false-brethren' in Galatians 2:4 become 'sham Christians' in NEB – hardly the same thing. There are scores of examples. The most intrusive comes in the NEB's translation of Ephesians 5:8: *Ete gar pote skotos, nun de phos en kurio*, which AV renders with terse accuracy: 'For ye were sometimes darkness, but now are ye light in the Lord'; NEB has, 'Now as Christians you are light'. Why?
[50] 1 Thessalonians 1:6; 2:16.

tells the Thessalonians that the 'Jews' have been persecuting those who think as they do in Judaea. The letter breathes discontent and disagreement with the mainstream of Jewry. Reading it today, after nearly 2,000 years of Christian history, we take it for granted that this is Christian discontent with Jewry; and that the Thessalonians are already a 'different denomination' (as we should say) from their former friends in the synagogue. But this is a completely anachronistic way of reading the letter. Paul is urgently continuing his dialogue with 'the Jews'. And that is because he believes not merely that he is a Jew, but that the messianic promises will find their fulfilment when all mankind will worship the God of Israel.

Paul's utterances seem bizarre enough within the context of Jewish hopes. Outside that context they are simply gibberish. It disturbs us that a sublime religious genius could entertain such primitive and limited ideas, but that is our man. On the one hand he has seen, since his apocalypse, that human beings, regardless of their race and regardless of their religious allegiances, are the children of God. He has seen that in the revolution which the Messiah has brought to pass the human race can praise its maker, 'Jews or Greeks, slaves or free'.[51] But he is certainly not preparing succeeding generations for a long and harmoniously ecumenical future in which, as in some Anglican missionary society, the 'best' can be taken from the 'Jewish tradition' while leaving behind the demands of dietary purity and circumcision. Paul's message, written at about the time when he was being dragged before Gallio by the angry synagogue officials, was that within a very short time, the world was coming to an end. This is the most fundamental of all Paul's beliefs. All his actions and words take their place behind the fact that he felt the time to be short. Quoting from the fund of the Gospel tradition – whether this is something Paul had read, or heard spoken of we do not know – 'the day of the Lord will come like a thief in the night'.[52] Within the lifetime of his friends in Thessalonica, Jesus, who had been crucified some twenty years previous, would return on the clouds, like the Son of Man in Daniel. A trumpet would sound and the dead 'in Christ' – presumably those who had believed in the Messiahship of Jesus – will be the first to be gathered up into the clouds. Then, without undergoing a physical

---

[51] I Corinthians 12:13.
[52] I Thessalonians 5:1.

death, the other followers of Jesus will be gathered up into the clouds, 'to meet the Lord in the air'.[53]

It is important to remember that though Paul does use allegory and flights of 'poetic' language in his letters, as with his mirror allegory, or his belief that 'the rock was Christ', he evidently expected the End of Time as a completely literal eventuality within his own lifetime. This fact should put us on our guard against supposing that he, any more than Jesus before him, wished to start a new religion, or an alternative to Judaism. It simply was not like that. Paul believed that he had cracked the 'secret' – to use his word – of what Judaism was. He thought that it was a series of promises which had been fulfilled with the arrival of the Lord's anointed. He thought that the life, suffering, death, resurrection and rising into heaven of Jesus were the preludes to the End of History. And he thought that he had a unique part to play in that drama.

Such ideas are hardly calculated to appeal to the most erudite, sane, or comfortable citizens in society. And, though they are all derived from the Jewish Scriptures (and even though variations of such doomsday beliefs were being entertained throughout Palestinian Jewry at the time), it is not difficult to imagine how such talk would appeal to the more balanced and erudite synagogue-leaders throughout the Diaspora.

Corinth, with its eclectic racial mixture of Greeks and Jews, Levantines, North Africans, Asians and Europeans, its sailors and its dockers, its traders in spice, leather, cloth, its artists, its carvers, its sculptors, its builders, its entrepreneurs, its spivs, its weirdos, its crackpot religionists, its fortune-tellers, its quacks, its prostitutes, was ripe for the picking. The Marseilles or the Miami of its time, it did not appeal to the fastidious. Nero loved it and so did Paul. Not so, the Old Etonian Gallio, who, when he became ill during his year's exile in Achaia, went on board ship 'exclaiming that it was not the sickness of his body but of the place'.[54] We can just imagine what Gallio (described by all his Roman acquaintances as a bright popular affectionate man – 'sweet Gallio') made of these brawling Jews when they were brought before his tribunal. Paul felt, after his two years among the strange people who were his earliest converts, that 'God chose what is foolish in the world to shame the wise; God chose what is weak in the world

[53] 1 Thessalonians 4:17.
[54] Seneca, *Epistolae* 104, 1.

to shame the strong; God chose what is low and despised in the world, things that are not, to reduce to nothing things that are.'[55] If he spoke in this way to Gallio, would it not have sounded very like sedition?

The case, however, in Luke's narrative was a non-case and it was immediately dismissed by Gallio. We are told that the Roman was 'quite unconcerned' by the disturbance.[56] Do we believe this? We know that this is what Luke wants his Roman readers to think in matters where Christians come up before the magistrates, and that by describing Paul's appearance before a famous magistrate, Luke is providing a *locus classicus* for lesser Christians and lesser magistrates in a subsequent generation. Luke places in Gallio's mouth the judgment which he would like other magistrates to pronounce over his own contemporaries. At the time, it might have been very different. Perhaps Gallio in reality did make such a genial judgment: 'If it were a matter of crime or serious villainy, I would be justified in accepting the complaint of you Jews; but since it is a matter of questions about words and names and your own law, see to it yourselves.'[57] But the Jews had only lately been expelled from Rome for making just such disturbances in the capital. Acts is surely right to attribute to Gallio an absolute indifference to religious squabbles among the Jews and their hangers-on. But no Roman magistrate was ever indifferent to disputes which caused a breach of the peace. If the authorities really cared as little as Luke would have us believe about these disturbances, why did Paul keep moving on? One could provide 'innocent' answers to that question. We can believe that he needed to make a business trip; and we can believe that he felt impelled to take the message of Christ into new territory. We read that he took the boat from Cenchreae. For once, Poseidon did not cast Paul's ship upon the rocks or hurl his diminutive body into the brine. The boat headed eastward towards another of the great cities of the ancient world, Ephesus, where different gods and demons were preparing to torment him, and where other riots, at the instigation either of Chrestus or of his most vociferous representative on earth, were waiting to happen.

[55] I Corinthians 1:27–8.
[56] Acts 18:17 (NEB).
[57] Acts 18:14–15.

XI

EPHESUS

To the angel of the church in Ephesus write:
'... I know your works, your toil, and your patient endurance ...'
Revelation 2:1–2

FROM THE EVIDENCE of surviving milestones, we know that in Asia
Minor at this period they measured distances from the *caput viae* in
Ephesus.[1] All roads led from Ephesus, the commercial centre of this
region, which was in reality, much more than Palestine, the birthplace
or nursery of Christianity. That is to say, it was in Ephesus and its
satellite cities – Colossae, Laodicea and Hierapolis to the east, Smyrna
to the north; all connected by the so-called Royal Road which the
Romans built between Mount Timolus and Sardis – that Christianity
as a new and distinct faith began to emerge. In Asia Minor, there
were still disputes – as in Jerusalem, Macedonia, and Rome – with
the synagogue. But it was here that Christ was first tested not against
the other Messiahs or prophets of Judaism but against the gods, demons
and powers of popular religion. This is the region that a convert Jew
called John, who saw the world in terms of his own nation's apocalyptic
tradition, was to depict as the centre of a cosmic struggle between
the Lamb who sat upon the throne and Satan. This was the region in
which the small remnant of the saved would be plucked from the
generality of misguided humanity to sing their hymns of redemption
around the heavenly throne. For, as one of Paul's followers was to
write later in the century, 'our struggle is not against enemies of blood
and flesh, but against the rulers, against the authorities, against the
cosmic powers of this present darkness, against the spiritual forces of
evil in the heavenly places.'[2]

[1] D. H. French, 'The Roman Road System of Asia Minor', in *Aufstieg und Niedergang der
romischen Welt*, 7, 2 (Berlin, 1983), pp. 698–729.
[2] Ephesians 6:12.

PAUL

These 'rulers' and 'authorities' and 'powers' were familiar words of popular magic and religion to describe the heavenly forces which controlled human destiny. A power (*dunamis*) is, in the language of magic, a heavenly agent. The hundreds of magical papyri which have survived to us – formularies used for almost every eventuality in life, from improving your sex life and curing migraine to sending your enemies mad or interpreting dreams – provide evidence of the universal use of magic at this time.[3] Ephesus was a great centre of magic and magicians, and, above all, its presiding deity, Artemis, had the most powerful magic of all and power over the 'powers'. 'O great Artemis of the Ephesians, help!' says one of the surviving prayers.[4] 'Display your power (*dunamin*) upon this young man who has died. For all the Ephesians know, both men and women, that all things are governed by you, and that the great powers (*dunameis megalai*) come to us through you. Give now to your servant what you are able to do in this regard. Raise up your servant Domnos.'

The temple of Artemis at Ephesus was regarded as one of the Seven Wonders of the World. Artemis, or Diana, as the Romans called her, was more widely worshipped than any other deity known to the Greek traveller Pausanias. There were Artemisian festivals, not just in Ephesus, but in all the other towns of Lycia and Phrygia. One month of each year was devoted to her worship. There were Artemisian missionaries spreading her cult throughout Asia Minor. It was therefore, among other things, big business: 'The religion of Artemis became an indispensable pillar in the cultural structures and life of Asia.' And Ephesian Artemis was a patroness of magic. In the magical papyri, she is often interchangeable with Hekate.[5] Pliny tells us that a statue of Hekate stood within the very precinct of the temple of Artemis at Ephesus.[6] Small wonder that in subsequent Christian generations, Artemis should have been seen as a demon, a magician, a wicked sorceress.[7]

[3] See Hans Dieter Betz (ed.), *The Greek Magical Papyri in Translation*.
[4] Quoted by Clinton E. Arnold, *Ephesians: Power and Magic*, p. 22.
[5] Hans Dieter Betz (ed.), *op. cit.*, p. 332. Originally a Thracian divinity and a Titan, Hekate came to be regarded as one of the supreme deities of the underworld, who, when night fell, sent out from the underworld demons and phantoms; the goddess of witchcraft and sorcery, she accompanied the disembodied spirits of the dead, whining and howling like a dog. It was customary therefore to sacrifice dogs to her, as well as black sheep and honey.
[6] HN, XXXVI, 4, 32.
[7] In such apocryphal works as the *Acts of Andrew* and the *Acts of John*, quoted Arnold, *op. cit.*, p. 27.

Those of us who are accustomed to Artemis or Diana as she appears in the visual arts of the Renaissance or the Greek and Roman statues of antiquity – the virgin huntress with her slight, boyish hips, her quiver and her bow – will be surprised when we have our first sighting of an image from antiquity of the Ephesian Artemis. The two goddesses were in fact totally distinct, the Ephesian Artemis having nothing to do with the virginal sister of Apollo. Ephesian Artemis is an Asian fertility goddess. The statue of her which stood in the temple at Ephesus, and its many imitations, are as unvirginal as any image you could find, her chest festooned with a multitude of 'breasts' (*polumastos*). The many breasts of Artemis had a 'magical character';[8] suppliants could derive magical power from her dugs. Not merely her devotees, but also later Christian interpreters took this view. Hieronymus in his commentary on the Epistle to the Ephesians says that these breasts symbolised 'nourishing power'. The priests of Artemis were eunuchs. When the region eventually adopted Christianity, it is unsurprising that the cult of the goddess transferred to that of Christ's Mother. The temple eunuchs, now turned Christian celibates, had no shortage of folk-tales with which to interest the credulous – stories of St John or Luke escorting the Blessed Virgin from Jerusalem to this city in Asia Minor. Pope Paul VI visited Ephesus in 1967 and celebrated Mass in the ruins of the Double Basilica, which had been built in the fifth century to commemorate the Virgin Mary. Even as late as the nineteenth century, it was possible to discover, thanks to the visions of a German nun, the very house in the rugged mountains outside Ephesus where Mary had lived before her Glorious Assumption.

Around the skirts of the sculpted image of Artemis of Ephesus were seen animals, terrifying mythological beasts who symbolise delivery from fear; Artemis had, among her other titles, 'deliverer from fear'. But the great Ephesian Artemis was not alone in holding out this promise. Paul, or so we are informed, was the instrument of extra-ordinary divine miracles. It was not even necessary for him to lay hands upon the sick or the demented. 'When the handkerchiefs or aprons that had touched his skin were brought to the sick, their diseases left them, and the evil spirits came out of them.'[9] It is interesting that Luke should mention these powers of Paul's after his arrival in the

[8] Clinton E. Arnold, *op. cit.*, quoting Elisabeth Lichteneker, 'Die kultbilder der Artemis von Ephesos' (doctoral thesis from the University of Tübingen, 1952).
[9] Acts 19:12.

city of Ephesus, the city of magic, of demons, of the goddess. The post-Enlightenment sophisticate who reads of Paul's miraculous gift will wish to distinguish, perhaps, between Paul's 'faith healing' – the result of 'pure religion and undefiled' – and the superstitions of the 'pagan' Ephesians. Luke seems to make no such distinction.

Significantly, he tells us that Paul, having attempted to argue his point of view in the Ephesian synagogue, left it behind and spent two years arguing daily in the lecture hall of Tyrannus, from eleven o'clock each morning until four in the afternoon, that is when Tyrannus was not lecturing himself.[10] We do not know who Tyrannus was, beyond being able to draw the inference that he was a Gentile. The *schole* or lecture hall where he taught was presumably open to the public for educational purposes. As a result of Paul's lectures, over this two-year period, 'all the residents of Asia [the Roman province of Western Turkey], both Jews and Greeks, heard the word of the Lord'.[11] Perhaps this is written from the perspective of a historian who knew that, in the generation after Paul's, Christianity had spread like wild fire through the Lycus valley and that Ephesus was one of the most vigorous centres – perhaps the most vigorous centre – of the cult. Even allowing for Luke's exaggeration, however, there can be no doubt that Paul's presence in Ephesus caused a major agitation.

He did not limit himself to preaching the word. We read that 'God did extraordinary miracles through Paul'.[12] Although Jesus was the Christ raised up by God, it should not be forgotten that Paul regarded himself as a figure in whom the Christ was now active and alive. If he had been living in a Hindu or Buddhist culture, Paul might well have regarded himself as an avatar. In his own body, he bore the wounds of Jesus;[13] he had the mind of Christ;[14] as a 'person in Christ' he had, like Jesus, ascended into heaven and come down again.[15] It is not to be wondered at that he possessed miraculous or, if this is to make a distinction, magical powers.

Medicine, for most of its history, was a branch, rather than a rival, of magic. Pliny, in his *Natural History*, provides the closest thing to what moderns would regard as a 'common sense' or purely physical

[10] Acts 19:9.
[11] Acts 19:10.
[12] Acts 19:11.
[13] Galatians 6:17.
[14] 1 Corinthians 2:16; Philippians 2:5.
[15] 2 Corinthians 12:2.

explanation for bodily ailments with his belief that there are herbal cures for many of the ills of humankind. In expounding this opinion, he takes many a swipe at the medical charlatans of history, and of his own day, from the priests of Asklepios to the chicanery of Hippocrates.[16] He tells us of a villain named Asclepiades who came from Bithynia to Rome in the late first century; a professor of rhetoric with no medical training, Asclepiades was able to persuade 'almost the whole human race . . . just as if he were an apostle from heaven' that he had healing powers. Pliny, by denouncing magic as 'detestable, vain and idle', is one of the most eloquent witnesses we have of its popularity. Philo, likewise, tells us of the healing powers of the Therapeutae of Alexandria and the Essenes of Palestine, and Josephus writes as if any intelligent reader would share his belief that illness was caused by demons.[17] Virtually everyone believed in demons.[18] Superstition was by no means limited to the Jews, the god-fearers or the Christians. Paul was able to heal the sick and to drive out demons merely by touch, and the name of Jesus therefore came to be used by other magicians.

Some wandering exorcists, seven sons of a Jewish high priest called Sceva, tried to conduct an exorcism and said over their victim, 'I adjure you by the Jesus whom Paul proclaims'. The evil spirit replied, 'Jesus I know, and Paul I know, but who are you?' The poor lunatic who was possessed of the demon overpowered his exorcists and ran through the crowd. Gradually it became known that the name of Jesus was the most powerful 'magic' of all, and Paul's followers organised a huge public burning of magical books. The value of the books destroyed was 50,000 silver coins.

It was fairly obvious that Paul's missionary activity was making serious inroads into the profits of the resident religious and magical leaders in Ephesus. A silversmith named Demetrius, who must have employed a substantial number of people in his workshop manu-facturing religious souvenirs and *bondieuserie* (silver 'shrines' to the Ephesian Artemis), reacted as a modern tradesman would do in Lourdes or Knock if an itinerant evangelist had persuaded the tourists not to buy statues of Mary and Bernadette. 'Men, you know that we get our wealth from this business.'[19] Evidently something of a demagogue,

[16] HN, XXIX, 5, 6–8 and *passim*.
[17] Howard Clark Kee, *Medicine, Miracle and Magic in New Testament Times*, pp. 23ff.
[18] E. R. Dodds, *Pagan and Christian in the Age of Anxiety*, p. 38.
[19] Acts 19:25.

Demetrius persuaded the mob (perhaps not unreasonably) that if Paul's work continued the temple of Artemis itself would be scorned and the goddess 'would be deprived of her majesty that brought all Asia and the world to worship her'. This exclamation had the effect that such rhetoric will always have on religiously excitable crowds. Imagine an insult to the Holy Prophet in a market-place in Isfahan or disobliging words about the Pope in certain saloon bars of Belfast. The crowd managed to get hold of two of Paul's companions, some Macedonians called Gaius and Aristarchus, and to drag them to the vast amphitheatre.

When we read about it in Acts, particularly when we read it in a modern translation, we might suppose that what took place was a public riot. Some of the crowd wanted to hear a speech from one Alexander, 'whom the Jews had put forward', but as soon as the mob saw that he was a Jew they began to heckle and bellow and the row continued for two hours. Eventually, the town clerk arrives and quietens down the row with a speech of sweet reason, pointing out that Paul and his friends 'are neither temple robbers nor blasphemers of our goddess'.

There are, however, indications that Luke has faithfully reproduced a source within his text without completely understanding it. He uses, for instance, the term usually translated as 'town clerk' (*grammateus*) as the name of the chief magistrate in Ephesus. A meeting of the kind summoned by Demetrius was just the sort frowned upon by Roman magistrates as likely to cause a disturbance – as happened in this case. We read in the letters of Pliny the Younger, governor of Bithynia-Pontus *circa* 110–12, the fear that 'such a gathering would be used to form crowds and unlawful assemblies', when a proconsul's edict has allowed an assembly or *syllogos*.

The angry crowd in Ephesus went to the amphitheatre because, as in many Greek cities, the open-air theatre would be the largest structure with seating – hence the most suitable place for an assembly of citizens. When we are told in this story that Paul wanted to appear before the people (*demos*) it would probably be more accurate to say that he wanted to appear before an assembly. He is dissuaded, not by any old friends, but by 'officials of the province of Asia', 'asiarchs'. Luke, once again, wishes to give the impression that Paul is beloved by magistrates and bigwigs and officialdom. The scholarly commentators believe that what is being described here are judicial procedures, assizes, before which citizens can bring their fellows if

they believe them to be guilty of an offence. The chief indigenous
magistrate, the Ephesian town clerk, reminds his hearers that any issues
which troubled Demetrius and his friends could be dealt with in this,
the correct and legal procedure. 'We are in danger of being charged
with rioting today', is how he concludes his speech; 'we', note. He is
reminding them that Ephesus is now a Roman colony. The Indian
official of the maharajah is begging his fellow-countrymen not to
allow this matter to pass into the hands of the British ICS or
government official or magistrate. The Roman proconsul, or even
the emperor himself, might hear of this riot and decide to punish the
entire city. We know from an inscribed edict from Ephesus about
some bakers who caused a riot, the kind of response which the town
clerk was dreading. We know how the proconsul of Bithynia-Pontus
circa 100 responded to anarchy — he banned the local parliament or
assembly from meeting: 'Those charged with taking part in such
disturbances should already have paid the penalty. But since one must
count the interest of the city as more important than retaliation against
these men, I have considered it necessary to bring them to their senses
by an edict. Wherefore I forbid the bakers to assemble as a club or to
take the lead in insolence; instead I order them to obey completely
those made responsible for the public interest and to supply the city
without fail with the necessary output of bread. Whenever any of
them may be caught hereafter either assembling contrary to the ban
or starting some hubbub and riot, he shall be charged and be punished
with the appropriate retaliation.'[20] The *grammateus tou demou*, the clerk
of the people, did not want such an edict to be served on himself or
on Demetrius. Luke describes him as dismissing the very idea that
Paul or his friends have done anything wrong. Piecing the evidence
together from the letters, however, many scholars believe that Paul
spent a period in prison in Ephesus, perhaps as long as two years.

Luke tells a tale which seems at best inconsequential, and at worst
unlikely. Surely the only interest of the riot, in the context of his
story, is if it has something to do with Paul? There are in fact strong
reasons for supposing that Paul was imprisoned in Ephesus, and by far
the likeliest reason for this is that Paul provoked public riots. If the
narrative of Acts started life as a defence document prepared for Paul's
trial in Rome, it would not do much for his chances before the
Imperial court if he is shown to have been stirring up an affray of the

[20] Quoted by Richard Wallace and Wynne Williams, *The Acts of the Apostles*, pp. 109–10.

kind described in Ephesus. Nor would it do much for the reputation of Christians in the second generation – when the present draft of Acts was written – if their most distinguished founding father was seen to be a seditious agitator. So Luke, having recorded with great vividness and evident accuracy a riot in the amphitheatre, adds the unconvincing disclaimer that Paul, though trying to get to the theatre to defend himself, was in fact nowhere near the scene of the crime. On the advice of his grand friends the asiarchs, he stayed away.[21]

Asia Minor was not merely the centre of the goddesses of magic, Artemis and Hekate. Smyrna boasted of the first temple to Roma (the deification of the Roman people) as early as 195 BC. There was one in Pergamum in 29 BC; this time, a joint dedication to Roma and Augustus, the first recorded instance of a temple being dedicated to the divine Caesar. In the reign of Tiberias, the cities of Asia sycophantically competed with one another to become the centre of the Imperial cult. Deputations were received by the Roman senate. There was a suggestion from Ilium/Troas that since Roma was the new Troy, they should have the temple of Tiberias. In the event, it was voted to allow Pergamum to build a temple of Tiberias. The Ephesian delegates were turned away on the grounds that they were 'fully occupied with their state cult of Diana'.[22] Religion was handed down by the state; Plato would have approved. There was no great Imperial temple in Ephesus, because in the Roman view of things the cult of Artemis served the same purpose of instilling social cohesion and civil obedience into the populace; for this reason there was an annexe to the Artemision containing a temple jointly worshipping Roma and the memory of Augustus. 'For Greeks such cults were political and diplomatic acts . . . As is the custom in politics and diplomacy . . . the cult of Roma covered the entire range of political emotion: enthusiastic affection, servile flattery, gratitude, suspicion, naked fear. It was a cult based on political, rather than religious, experience.'[23] Another way of putting it is that the emperors, like the National Socialists, knew how to harness religious emotions for political purposes. The purist, anarchist, stance of later Christianity to the worship of the emperor, deriving from Jewish fears of idolatry, is not

[21] Acts 19:31.
[22] Tacitus, *Annales*, IV, 56.
[23] Ronald Mellor, *Thea Rome* [sic]: *The Worship of the Goddess Roma in the Greek World*, p. 16.

what we find in the writings of Paul when he addresses the matter of state-worship. *Exousia*, authority, is a divine attribute, as any Jew would agree. Hence the Jewish distrust of monarchies throughout the ages, the distrust embodied in their folk-tales of the ejection of the people by God when they asked Samuel to give them a king, and the misfortunes which befell King Saul when he disobeyed the word of the Lord. Paul, as ever, is eclectic about this matter, difficult to categorise or to pin down. If Jesus really said 'Render to Caesar the things that are Caesar's, and to God the things that are God's', Paul turned the saying surprisingly on its head. While the Jesus-religion taken to its extreme form (the devotion to Another King) might see anarchism as an obligation – pacifism and non-involvement in the socio-political order – the Paulist would say, with Marsilius of Padua or Aquinas, that the state enshrined the things of God; that this was one of the mysteries of the Incarnation. Anyone who resists the *exousia* resists what God has appointed. It is the duty of the devout therefore not merely to accept the emperor, not merely to keep his nose clean, but to revere authority which is God-given. The Roman emperor (probably Nero by the time Paul wrote the words) is 'God's servant for your good'.[24] This is a contemporary debate within Judaism. Within a decade of Paul writing those words, the debate would have become a war. On the one side are those Jews who agreed with Paul and (coming at it from a completely different angle) Josephus that the Roman power is not irresistible by accident – it is decreed by God. On the other hand there are those who take the Maccabean view that God's kingdom can not come until the blasphemous presence of the Romans be driven out of the Holy Land. Paul's old employers the high priests in Jerusalem would have approved when he said that Higher Powers deserved the absolute submission of their Jewish subjects. Jesus and the Pharisees and the Zealots would surely not have agreed. This strand of Paul's thinking has been most faithfully understood by eastern Orthodoxy, which canonised Constantine and saw the divine presence as working through the existent political order. It is anathema to those for whom Jesus, rather than Paul or his Christ, is the focus of devotion. Tolstoy, for instance, took it as axiomatic that Christians should defy emperors, which was one of the reasons for his excommunication at the hands of the Orthodox Church. The Paul/Jesus dichotomy is never more sharply shown than in its political

[24] Romans 13:4.

implications; nor is it a Catholic/Protestant divide. On the whole, the more Paulist the Christian, the more likely to support the political *status quo*: Luther shored up the German princes and Cranmer baptised not merely the Tudor *realpolitik* but the English idea of themselves as an independent entity at the birth of the nation state in Europe. Ignatius of Loyola, by contrast, served a theocracy of which he believed Jesus to be king, and saw nothing wrong with undermining and spying against sovereign states. Paul would have been amazed by the idea of Jesuits; Simon the Zealot would have understood them. The United States was founded by Protestant Jesus-worshippers, even by free-thinking Jesus-worshippers such as Jefferson, who rewrote the New Testament to exclude all its miraculous elements. The Soviet Union, for all its Stalinist desire to suppress belief in God, inherited the Paulinist idea of '*dunamis*' – the very word for government in Russian is *vlast*, which means the same. The Cold War was between the heirs of Jesus-worshippers, idealists and libertarians in the West, and those who believed that resistance to the higher power was not so much pointless as irrelevant to the central business of human life, which was to cherish the Christ within and await the arrival of Christ from without.

Paul's eclecticism, however, makes it difficult to extrapolate from his writings a purely orthodox or Thomist view of political duty. His belief that the world order was coming to an end sits oddly beside his idea that his followers should revere the existing powers. If the Day of Christ was soon to sweep away emperor, senate, lawcourts, armies, is that not in itself as seditious an idea as could be imagined? And if the state-allowed or state-authorised religions are overthrown, is that not, too, seditious? Tacitus was right to call the cult of Ephesian Artemis a 'state cult'. The enraged citizens quoted by Luke more or less use the same terminology.

It is generally agreed by Christian scholars that Paul spent quite some time in Ephesian prisons and it is overwhelmingly likely that he wrote some of his letters from here.[25] His own way of viewing the matter was that he had fought with beasts at Ephesus.[26] When he wrote that famous phrase, he was not boasting to his Corinthian friends that he had actually been thrown into an arena for the entertainment of the Ephesian crowds to wrestle with lions, as would happen to subsequent generations of Christians. The wild animals in his mind

---

[25] See, for example, G. Bornkamm, *Paul*, chapter 9.
[26] 1 Corinthians 15:32.

were synagogue officials, magistrates, local shopkeepers and guild-leaders, and the hostile mob. No wonder Christianity was persecuted, no wonder the Christians, particularly those of Paul's persuasion, continued to feel that such persecution was unfair. Riots were inevitable wherever the ideas of Paul were propagated; and yet, by a curious paradox, he believed that the institutions of this world would continue in their divinely ordered and unaltered form until the Day of Christ. He believed – how very Jewish of him – that the political institutions, the senates, the courts, the emperor himself, could be revered by those who did not worship them as false gods. He believed that the institution of marriage and the family could continue likewise. By the same token, he wished to smash the household gods and overthrow the civic deities.

You might derive the view from Acts – certainly from subsequent Christian readings of Acts – that Paul, by his activities, had 'converted' Ephesus. Although, as we have said, it was destined to be one of the most important centres of Christianity, no such momentous development took place, and the great temple of Artemis and her bizarre cult flourished for another two and a half centuries, until new times and a new dispensation brought about the conquest of the goddess by Christ.

Luke writes as if Paul had a comparatively peaceful time in Ephesus until the entirely unjustifiable riot. From the evidence of his letters, however, we should infer that Paul's Ephesian sojourns were full of worry and agitation. The Day of the Lord still bafflingly refused to arrive, and no sooner had Paul made converts than he discovered that they had not properly understood his message. The Corinthian letters, written during this period and from Ephesus, reflect turmoil and conflict and confusion about sexual morality, about the relationship between the Way and the synagogue, about the gifts of the spirit. In Galatia, meanwhile, Paul's converts had been 'debriefed' by more conservative followers of the Way who told them that it was not possible to be a disciple of Jesus without submitting to the precepts of the Torah. (As later generations would imagine it, 'reverting to Judaism' – but this is the wrong reading of Galatians.) The Corinthian letters as printed in the New Testament are not quite as Paul wrote them. Textual scholarship reveals that there is at least one lost Corinthian letter and that the second letter in fact contains the text of two letters, cobbled by a later redactor. What the letters themselves reveal is a perpetual mismatch between Paul's vision and the intractable human nature with whom he shared it.

Between the years 50 and 55, Paul's life was one of inner excitement and outer restlessness. Some time around 50, he founded the church at Corinth. A year or so later, in 51, we find him up before Gallio and moving on with Aquila and Priscilla. Over the next two years, Timothy, his lieutenant, is dispatched on several missions to the churches of Macedonia to deal with disciplinary problems (the man who married his stepmother) and doctrinal muddles. The letter we know as 1 Corinthians was probably written in October 54; and in 55 Paul went back to Corinth (his 'sorrowful' visit) to attempt to sort out the mess – the divisions among the Christians, some of whom said they were for Apollos, some for Cephas, some for Paul, some for Christ; the sexual laxity; the intellectual confusion. Some time after that he was imprisoned in Ephesus, presumably as a result of the riots, and in 55–6 he was released from gaol and made his way back to Macedonia. In 56, he returned to Corinth for his third visit, and it was during the last part of that winter that he heard that there was another famine in Palestine and that the church in Jerusalem needed relief. It was in the spring of 57 that he made his final journey to Jerusalem, with such momentous consequences.

There could be no more eloquent reminder of the essential paradoxes of Paul's vision of things than the fact that at just about this time he wrote his greatest work, addressed not to the believers in Jerusalem, but to those in Rome. The letter to the Romans ends with a catalogue of names – twenty-eight persons to whom the Apostle wishes to extend his greetings. They are obviously people Paul knows. Some are Jews. Some are Greeks. Some come from Corinth. Some are people he met on his travels. Some, perhaps, were Christians before they met Paul, some are his converts. The list is hardly long compared with the length of the current Roman telephone directory, in which most of the names, presumably, belong to the Roman Church. Nevertheless, the list is a sign of how far the Gospel had spread, and among what a variety of people, with its Hebrew, Greek and Latin names. It is also patently informal and affectionate, a sign that Paul had many friends and was much loved.

The letter reflects a yearning by Paul to visit the capital of the Empire. He had always made it his custom not to 'poach' on the territory of other missionaries. 'His' churches in Corinth and Galatia were founded by him. The church of Rome was already in existence, before he had visited it. The opening words of the letter suggest that the church of Rome was not of apostolic foundation. Paul announces that he is 'called to be an apostle, set apart for the gospel of God'. He seems to say that while he does not trespass where others have founded churches, the Roman situation is a little different, since they do not yet have an 'apostle'.[27]

> Thus I make it my ambition to proclaim the good news, not where Christ has already been named, so that I do not build on someone else's foundation, but as it is written,
> 'Those who have never been told of him shall see,
> and those who have never heard of him shall understand.'
> This is the reason that I have so often been hindered from coming to you. But now, with no further place for me in these regions, I desire, as I have for many years, to come to you when I go to Spain.

Yes, Spain. Paul wanted to preach Christ Crucified to the ends of the known world. And then, perhaps, Christ would come!

> For I do hope to see you on my journey and to be sent on by you once I have enjoyed your company for a little while. At present, however, I am going to Jerusalem in a ministry to the saints; for Macedonia and Achaia have been pleased to share their resources with the poor among the saints at Jerusalem . . . So when I have completed this, and delivered to them what has been collected, I will set out by way of you to Spain.[28]

The Corinthian letters are full of problems. The Corinthians almost treated Paul as an agony uncle – what can they do about this apostate? what happens when they are given meat sacrificed to idols? or when a marriage breaks down? or when one partner believes and the other doesn't? It was while wrestling with these specific and often vexing difficulties that Paul was able to formulate the closest thing we possess to a general synthesis of his religious position: Romans has been called the Gospel According to Paul.

It is one of those books, such as Rousseau's *Contrat Sociale* or the *Communist Manifesto* or *The Origin of Species*, which are perceived to

---

[27] Those who believe that the Apostle Peter founded the church of Rome would of course interpret this phrase otherwise.
[28] Romans 15:20–9.

have changed the way the human race regards itself. It is the quarry to which the great Christian originals and originators have returned again and again – Marcion, Augustine, Wycliffe, Luther, Calvin, Wesley – to renew the idea of what it was to have Life in Christ. In so doing, they very often redefined other things in the process – the political life of nations, the fabric of church and state. Romans, deemed by Coleridge to be the 'most profound book ever written', is the inspiration of Milton and the progenitor of the Romantic movement in literature. And then again, in the nineteenth century, when Christianity, intellectually speaking, imploded upon itself, it was to Romans that so many of the new critics of the Tübingen school and the historians of doctrine and reinventors of Christianity turned once again. If Renan and Tolstoy were classically Jesus-worshippers, then G. F. Strauss and Harnack, and Heidegger and Bultmann were Romans -men; as also, paradoxically, were those twentieth-century Christians who rediscovered the possibilities of a much more 'realist' orthodox faith – the followers of Karl Barth against whom Bultmann and his school rebelled. And the reason that Romans is so important is that, unlike any of the Gospels, it sails straight into the heart of the deepest metaphysical questions: what is God like? Why was a Christ necessary? How does it make any difference to life – to the individual human life and to human history – whether you believe in Christ or not? What is religion itself and why has it led the human race into deeper depravity and fouler wickedness than no religion at all? How can God be worshipped in a world so full of pain and darkness and muddle? What is the role of 'revelation' – are we really to suppose that God 'revealed' himself on Mount Sinai when he gave the Ten Command-ments to Moses and then left it to the Jews to interpret the Divine Law for the rest of history? If not, how can God be known? Romans, one should emphasise, is not a work of philosophy. It is more like a poem than it is like a work of logic, but it touches upon the deepest metaphysical questions which any of us could ask, and it posits some truly revolutionary and extraordinary answers. That is one of the reasons why it continues to exercise a fascination upon anyone who is interested in religious questions. That is why, if you go to a theological library, you will discover shelf upon shelf covered with commentaries on Romans. For it is the most interesting, as well as the most impenetrably difficult, book about 'religion' ever written.

In fact, of course, it is not about 'religion' at all, if by 'religion' we mean Judaism or Islam or Taoism or Seventh Day Adventism or

Roman Catholicism. Romans is one of the most devastating pamphlet attacks on 'religion' ever penned. No one who read it and absorbed its profound messages could feel happy with membership of 'a religion' ever again. Jesus might or might not have gone into the temple in Jerusalem and said that he would pull it down and build it up again in three days. The letter to the Romans pulls down the temple at Jerusalem and the temple at Ephesus and the temple at Piraeus and the altars of Athens and every other altar and temple ever built by human hand. 'St Paul understood what most Christians never realise, namely, that the Gospel of Christ is not *a* religion, but religion itself, in its most universal and deepest significance.'[29]

If Romans could be summarised in a few paragraphs, or even in a few pages, then there would have been no need for all the voluminous literature about it, which human beings have been writing almost continuously since the first century AD. Any attempt to summarise it would distort it; any attempt to draw it to its logical conclusions will get it wrong. It does not have any logical conclusions, but that is not to say that it is wholly illogical. The author of a book of the kind you are now holding in your hand can only urge the reader to sit down with a good modern translation of Romans and read it through slowly, absorbing its extraordinary intellectual passion, its spiritual ardour, its clashing contradictions and paradoxes. Read in the wrong mood, read in haste, read with a determination to strike common-sense attitudes, Romans can seem little better than gibberish. Read with patience, it is visibly an attempt to come to grips with the human condition itself; and it is a measure of its genius and profundity that, given the extraordinary differences between Paul and ourselves, the world of Nero's Empire and our own, this short work can still absorb and disturb us, still convince us that it is talking about things which are of fundamental importance to us. An Anglican bishop, driving me in his car, once opined that Paul's letter to the Romans was 'all balls'. At the time I did not see how appropriate this judgement was, since Paul would certainly have returned the compliment and taken a low view of the 'thoughts' buzzing about in this man's head. Anglicanism, an attempt to 'make sense' of things, or to do them decently and in order, but somehow to find a place for God in the world, would probably, had Paul lived to see it, have been for him the ultimate absurdity – more ridiculous than any of the other forms

[29] W. R. Inge, *Outspoken Essays*, p. 229.

of 'Christianity' which would have filled him with despair.

Human beings, with what Paul calls their 'senseless minds',[30] believe that they can keep out the dark beyond their bedroom windows by uttering mantras and inventing gods and rituals and religious mumbo-jumbo; they also think that they can save themselves by some vain appeal to morality. The Judaeo-Christian tradition, and that of Islam, its greatest and most inspired heresy ('back to Plato'), summarises the whole position exactly of what Paul would call 'the law' – the belief that 'God' has revealed his 'law' to the human race and that the only thing we need to do to please 'God' is to be good and follow certain rules.

That any such 'God' would be as earthy, as full of mud and plaster as the idols in a pagan temple does not occur to those who bow down to worship him. It occurred to Paul, however, who saw that, with the world in its present condition of pain, aching sorrow, confusion, bloodiness, dirtiness, and moral anarchy, any God who took responsibility for it would have to be the First Cause of more Evil than Good. Either the Law or Commandments of such a human figment would be completely null – because he could not be a good God who presided over such a chaos as our present universe – or the human race itself was a write-off, impossible to 'save' or to 'justify', since its failure to be good or wise was demonstrated on an hourly basis throughout the world.

So what, then? Is God evil and the human race, in its struggle to be good, like the subservient population of a tyrant, like the good people of Germany or the Soviet Union during the days of their dictators? Or is God all-good, compelled by the logical justice of his laws to condemn us all to perdition for our lustfulness, laziness, murderousness, idolatry, greed and folly? Neither view is endurable. Paul's readers, particularly the cleverest of them such as Marcion or Augustine, have tried to draw a 'logical conclusion' from all this. Marcion, for instance, a shipowner or mariner from Sinope on the borders of the Black Sea, and who lived from c. 85–160, believed that what Romans really taught us was that there were two Gods: a God of Justice, the Old Testament God, who was really incapable of mercy or love, and the Good God, to whom we all respond in the love of our hearts. This Good God, who was made manifest in Jesus, killed the old God, and with him all his bloodcurdling Commandments, his

[30] Romans 1:21.

threats to obliterate his enemies, his thunderbolts, his anger. The God who 'swore in his wrath' that his people should 'not enter into his rest' was killed, in Marcion's theology, by a grand Promethean gesture by Jesus, the embodiment of the Good God, the God of Love.

Though it has often been observed that such thoughts seem to be inherent in Paul's works, they are not exactly what Paul says. Indeed, this 'not exactly' would apply to any reading of Romans, whether the most brilliant, by Marcion, Augustine and Luther, or those of the Orthodox Christians who are so terrified of the letter's implications that they distort Paul's words into being the foundation-stones of Catholic Christianity, seizing a little lamely on the parts of this explosive epistle which speak of the Christian Church as a body with many limbs.[31]

But Romans sets up a chess problem which any player will fail. Either, with most 'religious' people, you believe in the absolute goodness of God – against all the evidence of the suffering universe – and the consequent depravity and wickedness of the poor old human race; or you believe in the decency of the human impulse to be good and you impugn the goodness as well as the justice of God. Instead of writing a *Summa* in dozens of volumes about this dilemma, the visionary Paul speaks to the Romans of their direct experience of the love of God in Christ, which enters the confusion and sorrow of human experience at the very moment when it is most vulnerable, most abject. Abraham becomes the type of man's love affair with God because he has the virtue of trust/faith, and this alone will 'save'. 'God proves his love for us in that while we still were sinners Christ died for us. Much more surely then, now that we have been justified by his blood, we will be saved through him from the wrath of God.'[32] It is Christ who forms the focal point of resolution for these insolubles, the white point of light where the magnifying glass focuses the sun and consumes the leaf. Christ has conquered sin and death; but those who are 'in Christ' know him not as the old worshippers revered their distant God, but as a presence in the midst of all their experiences, all their sins as well as their sorrows. 'For I am convinced that neither death, nor life, nor angels, nor rulers, nor things present, nor things to come, nor powers, nor height, nor depth, nor anything else in all

[31] Romans 12:4ff. I bet my Anglican bishop at the wheel of his car has preached a great deal of 'balls' on this text, interpreting the apostle's reflexions on the coherence of limbs in the body as a platitude about modern life 'in the community'.
[32] Romans 5:8–9.

creation, will be able to separate us from the love of God in Christ Jesus our Lord.'[33] Paul was a poet who could 'mythologise', project into language, not only his own private experience of the risen Christ, but his sense of the significance of Jesus Christ, a significance which stretches beyond the narrow confines of first-century Palestine, beyond Judaism, beyond the Roman Empire. Whether Marcion was right about the two Gods, there will always be two classes of religious person – the one who supposes that the religious need of mankind can be satisfied with 'opium', with an organised religion, whether it is Bible Christianity or Shintoism, and those, a much smaller category, who know that the religious experience and struggle is an intensely personal one, leading to exclamations of despair ('Wretched man that I am! Who will rescue me from this body of death?')[34], to the ecstatic and mystical knowledge that in a human heart of flesh, God's love can be known and experienced. These deep things lie contained within Paul's letter to the Christians of Rome, these and many things more. Beside the arcane claims that the Apostle has discovered 'the mystery that was kept secret for long ages but is now disclosed' is the much more accessible experience of life 'in Christ': 'Let love be genuine; hate what is evil, hold fast to what is good; love one another with mutual affection; outdo one another in showing honour. Do not lag in zeal, be ardent in spirit, serve the Lord. Rejoice in hope, be patient in suffering, persevere in prayer. Contribute to the needs of the saints; extend hospitality to strangers.'[35]

The period when Paul finished the letter was a time of strange portents and prodigies. We do not know if the tentmakers were kept especially busy by the terrifying phenomenon of soldiers' tents being ignited by fire from the sky.[36] A swarm of bees settled on the pediment of the Capitoline temple in Rome. Half-bestial children were born, and a pig with hawk's claws.

The emperor Claudius unwisely allowed it to be known that he intended to discipline his unruly wife Agrippina.[37] The empress, who

[33] Romans 8:38–9.
[34] Romans 7:24.
[35] Romans 12:9–13.
[36] Tacitus, *Annales*, XII, 64.
[37] Agrippina was first married to Domitius Ahenobarbus (AD 28), by whom she had a son, who became the emperor Nero. Next she married Crispus Passienus; thirdly, she married her uncle Claudius.

had her husband's kinswoman Domitia Lepida put to death for practising sorcery against her, decided (if Tacitus is to be believed) to murder Claudius before he was able to make his own son, Britannicus, his heir rather than Agrippina's son.

Lucius Domitius Ahenobarbus, though barely sixteen years old, had already begun to assume the adult garb of the toga and he had been trained from youth, by his tutor Seneca, to consider himself an emperor in waiting.

His great-uncle (and stepfather) Claudius's end was horrible. Tacitus tells us that the divine emperor, having been fed poison by his wife, was purged by the onset of violent diarrhoea. Terrified that he might have voided the poison from his system and that he might live, Agrippina gave orders for a poisoned feather to be held to the emperor's throat, pretending to make him vomit. Even as the lifeless body of Claudius was being wrapped in a blanket in the royal place, prayers were being said by the consuls and priests for the emperor's recovery.

At midday on 11 October the palace gates were thrown open, and Burrus, the commander of the guard, led out the stepson of Claudius to the battalion. When the appropriate donatives had been offered to the soldiers, the youth was put into a litter and conducted to the Guards camp. Once the army had accepted him as their new emperor, the senate followed suit.

He had a carefully prepared speech for the senators, written for him by Seneca. Having declared his uncle divine, the new emperor, who had taken the name of Nero, proceeded to emphasise the need to reform the sorry state into which Claudius had allowed governmental and public life to slide. He would end favouritism. He would declare an amnesty. The new reign, he promised, would be characterised by its enlightened clemency. So, for the first five years, it was. One of the poets who chose to apostraphise and flatter the new emperor, Calpurnius Siculus, praised not only the beauty and the voice of Nero, whom he compared to Apollo himself, but his return to the legal forms and to the freedom of the Senate.[38] The laws of God and Man, which the Christ of Paul had both circumvented and undermined, held out one more illusory hope to their devotees. As they watched the ceremonies of Nero's appointment, and saw the sinister figure of his mother Agrippina take her place beside her seventeen-year-old son on the dais, the Romans were preparing

[38] Miriam T. Griffin, *Nero: The End of a Dynasty*, p. 45.

themselves for the most extraordinary and technicoloured demonstration of the truth of Paul's letter — both its invective against human depravity, and its rueful knowledge that attempts to pursue goodness in such a world often led to the very opposite consequence of the one intended.

XII
=

LAST JOURNEY TO
JERUSALEM

IT IS FROM now onwards that we enter into the dilemma identified by Oscar Wilde: an inability to know how the story ends. Did Luke know? He must have done. The author of the Acts of the Apostles must have known how his hero ended, but he does not tell us. There could be any number of explanations for this, but two simple ones suggest themselves: that the end of the book has been lost; and that the book was written before the story ended.[1]

A third view, to which I incline myself, is that the author *intends us not to know*. Or, if this sounds too cunning, let us say that it suits his purposes very well that we should not know exactly how Paul met his end. In any event, unless we take the eccentric view that the Acts of the Apostles was written *before* any of the events it describes, we must attribute to its author some element of hindsight. Even if he does not know in any precise detail how Paul spent his last days on earth, he knows what happened during Paul's voyage and last visit to Jerusalem. Luke devotes as much space to this 'last phase' as to all the previous missionary endeavours of Paul. Whether it is the equivalent of a Passion narrative, with Paul, like Jesus, being led to an unjust death, or whether it is more like a counsel for the defence, readers may decide for themselves. As we shall see in this chapter, Luke deliberately obfuscates the significance of this journey, turning what was an unmitigated humiliation for Paul into an excuse for defending Christianity to the suspicious eye of some Roman magistrate.

We must assume[2] that Paul's object in visiting Jerusalem in that spring of 57 was to distribute to 'the poor among the saints' the money

---

[1] For further discussion of this, see pp. 246, 248ff.
[2] See p. 192.

which had been raised by his richer friends of Macedonia and Achaia.[3] This is what he himself tells the believers in Rome while he is 'on my way to Jerusalem'. But, while Luke wants us to assume this is the only motive for the journey, the letter itself, in Paul's own words, suggests reasons why there was bound to be trouble once he encountered opposition in the Jewish capital, the 'unbelievers in Judaea'.[4]

To judge from the postscript to that letter, we can guess that he dispatched it from the Aegean port of Corinth, Cenchreae, and that the letter itself was entrusted to Phoebe, one of the church leaders who was evidently on her way to Rome. 'I commend to you our sister Phoebe, a deacon of the church at Cenchreae, so that you may welcome her in the Lord as is fitting for the saints, and help her in whatever she may require from you, for she has been a benefactor of many and of myself as well.'[5]

Paul travelled from Cenchreae in a group, and before heading directly eastwards he goes round in a circle (one which must by now have been very familiar to him), from the tip of Achaia, up to Macedonia, and down to Troas. Presumably, he was collecting the money, and presumably one reason he needed companions was as protection against pirates or robbers. Luke himself is present; Sopater of Beroea, the Thessalonians Aristarchus and Secundus, Gaius the Doberian and Timothy were all there. They sent ahead the Asians Tychichus and Trophimus to wait for them at Troas, while the main party doubled back on their tracks and changed boats at Neapolis, the port for Philippi, setting sail some time after 7 April, when the feast of unleavened bread had begun. The reason for the change of boat was that Paul had got wind of a Jewish plot to assassinate him. There is no possibility, from our perspective, of guessing whether any such plot existed, but we notice the skilful way in which Luke is building up his case, even at this early stage of the journey. Paul, engaged in a purely charitable mission, is threatened with murder by 'the Jews'.[6]

Before he embarked at Troas, Paul addressed the faithful. It is one of those scenes in Acts which seems plausible and realistic. It was Saturday night, the eve of their breaking of bread, which, one can

[3] Romans 15:26.
[4] Romans 15:31.
[5] Romans 16:1. NEB translates 'our sister' as 'a fellow-Christian' – a particularly ripe example of the question-begging use of the word 'Christian' in NEB.
[6] Acts 20:3.

surmise, happened at midnight in commemoration of the resurrection. In many of the scenes in which Luke depicts the Apostle engaged in public speaking, he puts carefully-framed set speeches into his mouth. On this occasion, at Troas, we are not told what Paul said, merely that he went on for a very long time. A youth named Eutychus is sitting in a window of the third-floor room where the oration was happening, and, as the hot lamps flickered in the crowded space, the boy falls asleep.[7] 'Paul went on talking' – a rather happy rendering by the New English Bible. The inevitable happened; the boy fell from the third-floor window and was feared dead. Paul ran downstairs and declared that 'there is still life in him'. Not quite a miracle, even according to Luke, but a vivid illustration for posterity of the fact that to some listeners Paul could be less than enlivening as an orator.

The next day, the group went overland to Assos (modern Behramkale) and took a boat which wove down the coast of western Turkey, putting in at Mytilene (on the east coast of the isle of Lesbos) and then, negotiating the channel between Chios and the Anatolian mainland, to Samos. On the next day they arrived at Miletus, on the south shore of the Latmian gulf. Here the boat harboured for a few days and Paul sent a message to Ephesus (some thirty miles away) asking his friends to come and join him for a reunion.

The speech which Luke writes for him on this occasion makes it reasonably clear that Acts is being written after Paul's death; and that the School of Paul, if one can call it that, will come under repeated pressure after his death to conform to the 'Judaising' tendency. 'I know that after I have gone,' he tells the Ephesians on the shore at Miletus, 'savage wolves will come in among you, not sparing the flock. Some even from your own group will come distorting the truth in order to entice the disciples to follow them.' When Paul had finished speaking, we are told, 'there were loud cries of sorrow... What distressed them most was his saying that they would never see his face again.'[8]

From Miletus, the boat hugged the coast, hopping from the islands of Cos and Rhodes, and then put in at the port of Patara on the south coast of Lycia. They then changed ship once more and, rather than the longer and safer coastal voyage, they took the straight route in a diagonal across the eastern Mediterranean to Tyre. While the ship unloaded cargo and was in harbour for seven days, Paul met some

[7] Acts 20:8ff.
[8] Acts 20:29–30; 38 (NEB).

Christians who warned him that it was not safe to continue his journey to Jerusalem.

This incident suggests to us how well-developed Paul's network of friends had become. It can not have been an accident that the Tyre Christians found Paul and his companions in the harbour when their ship docked. As with any well-developed fifth column, there were 'contacts' for Paul and his friends wherever he went. These Tyre Christians would undoubtedly have been Hellenists of the kind originally driven out of Jerusalem twenty years before. This was where Paul, as it were, 'came in'! Luke tells us that the warning came to them 'by the Spirit', though a secular reader of these words could be forgiven for imagining that someone had tipped them off about the assassination plans which were indeed being prepared. There was – or Luke wants us to think there was – a plot afoot in Jerusalem to kill Paul.

Parting from the Tyre Christians by boat, Paul and his companions went a few miles southwards down the coast to Ptolemais (Akko) and then on to Caesarea, where, once again, he had friends and warnings waiting for him.

The warnings came from an ominous dramatic display at the house of a Hellenist Christian named Philip. A 'prophet' called Agabus, from Judaea, approached Paul, removed his belt, bound his own hands and feet with it and pronounced, 'This is the way the Jews in Jerusalem will bind the man who owns this belt, and hand him over to the Gentiles.'[9]

In case any of Luke's readers could have missed the point, the narrator emphasises that although Paul is doomed to be up for trial before a Roman magistrate, arrested and taken to Rome, it is those troublesome Jews who are to blame. Also, although any Gentile reading the book might be tempted to think that Christianity was nothing better than a Jewish heresy, and therefore that to all intents Christians were indistinguishable from the Jews (with whom, at the time of writing or reading, the Romans are still at war), Luke wishes to emphasise that Paul the Roman citizen is not responsible for the impending trouble: that has all been forced upon him by the Jews, the Jews, the Jews.

Paul bravely disregards the prophet's warning and sets out for

---

[9] Acts 21:11. *Paradosousin* ('they will hand over'), is the Gospel word used for the 'handing over' of Jesus, often translated 'betrayal', by Judas (Matthew 26:15, 16, 21, 23, 25; Mark 14:11, 18; Luke 12:21, 48). *Paradidomi* is the word used by Paul of the surrender of one's body to be burned (1 Corinthians 13:3).

Jerusalem. Accommodation there, for what was clearly a substantial party, had been arranged for them all, not, significantly, with the church 'leadership' but with a Cypriot called Mnason.[10] Called in Greek an '*archaios mathetes*', a 'disciple from the beginning', we can assume that Mnason was one of those Hellenists whose quarrel with the Jewish friends of Jesus had started the whole Christian Way in the first place. It was in this company, with his assembly of Gentile friends, that Paul made the sixty-four-mile journey from Caesarea to Jerusalem by land, presumably with mules or donkeys carrying their possessions.[11]

No book called the Acts of the Jewish Apostles has survived, so we can not guess how Peter or James the brother of the Lord reacted when they were told that Paul, with a substantial group of his own followers, had arrived in Jerusalem. The narrator of Acts does not surprise us by saying that 'the brothers welcomed us warmly'. If there had been food shortages, and Paul with his friends brought substantial donations from the churches of Macedonia and Achaia, there was no doubt some truth in this claim.

It is in the next passage of Acts that we can wonder whether we are being told the whole truth. It would be fascinating to have the account of this incident from the Jewish point of view:

The next day Paul went with us to visit James; and all the elders were present. After greeting them, he related one by one the things that God had done among the Gentiles through his ministry. When they heard it, they praised God. Then they said to him, 'You see, brother, how many thousands of believers there are among the Jews, and they are all zealous for the law. They have been told about you that you teach all the Jews living among the Gentiles to forsake Moses, and that you tell them not to circumcise their children or observe the customs. What then is to be done? They will certainly hear that you have come. So do what we tell you. We have four men who are under a vow. Join these men, go through the rite of purification with them, and pay for the shaving of their heads. Thus all will know that there is nothing in what they have been told about you, but that you yourself observe and guard the law. But as for the Gentiles who have become believers, we have sent a letter with our judgment

[10] Acts 21:16.
[11] W. M. Ramsay, *St Paul the Traveller and the Roman Citizen*, p. 302.

that they should abstain from what has been sacrificed to idols and from blood and from what is strangled and from fornication.' Then Paul took the men, and the next day, having purified himself, he entered the temple with them, making public the completion of the days of purification when the sacrifice would be made for each of them.[12]

Paul, we remember, has just written his great letter to the Romans. We don't know whether 'Luke' ever read this work. He certainly would not have been in a position to know that his own Acts of the Apostles would one day be bound up in a book we call the New Testament, with Paul's letter immediately following Acts. The letter itself, in the safe-keeping of Phoebe, was being carried westwards to Rome. Any readers of the section which we call its fourth chapter would have been able to tell the devout people of Jerusalem that he had indeed told the Jews to 'give up circumcising their children'. The rumours which had reached the holy city concerning this 'troublemaker' were perfectly correct. Luke, though, does not expect his readers to know that. For Paul, in Romans, the promise came to Abraham before he was circumcised: God justifies his chosen because of their faith, and not because they have been circumcised.

As we have been saying throughout this book, the question is a much bigger one than that. Paul believed, and the letter he had written before arriving in Jerusalem makes it perfectly clear, that the messianic prophecies were to be fulfilled through himself and those of his fellow-Christians who shared a belief in 'his Gospel'. 'You know what time it is, how it is now the moment for you to wake from sleep. For salvation is nearer to us now than when we became believers; the night is far gone, the day is near.'[13]

This is urgent talk. Paul is not saying that the Jews have been rejected. Rather, 'Israel failed to obtain what it was seeking. The elect obtained it, but the rest were hardened.'[14] This 'elect', those who share Paul's vision, are the remnant whom God shall save, the brand who will be saved from the burning when the day dawns: and the day is at hand. You can not read Romans without sensing the urgency. So, Paul has not just come to Jerusalem to salute the brethren and deliver some

---

[12] Acts 21:18–26.
[13] Romans 13:11–12.
[14] Romans 11:7.

charity money, as Luke would blandly like us to believe. Luke writes after Paul is dead. He writes in that second era of the Church's history when the Lord has not Appeared, when the Coming has not Come, when life is ticking over much as it ever did, and Christian life, post Jerusalem, post Destruction, has to be led in the Roman world – a world all too eager to persecute the 'elect'. So Luke's perspective is totally different from Paul's.

Paul believes that the end is in sight, not for himself but for the world made by God and redeemed by Jesus Christ. Any orthodox Jew confronted with the Christian idea that Jesus was the Messiah can always answer, 'If you want me to believe Jesus was the Messiah, explain why the prophecies were not fulfilled! When the Messiah comes, the old temple of Solomon will return to replace the new temple of Herod [or its ruins, if you are having this conversation after the Destruction]; the Gentiles will rise up to praise the God of Israel. Then we shall know that the Messiah is come.' Paul, had he heard such objections, would have wished to say that he, by special election and grace, had been appointed to *make these prophecies come true*. He was the instrument. That is why he concludes his letter to the Christians in Rome with the hope that he will visit them on his way to Spain,[15] since Spain was the end of the known world. When Paul had travelled all the way from Jerusalem to Spain, via Rome, the capital of the Empire, then 'the mystery that was kept secret for long ages but is now disclosed'[16] would have been revealed to the human race. Thereafter, God can say to those who have heard the word and not accepted it, 'You have no excuse.'[17] They would all have been warned.

This visit to Jerusalem is therefore full of significance to Paul – a much bigger and a much more religious significance than Luke is prepared to allow. For in Jerusalem he prays that he 'may be rescued from the unbelievers in Judaea, and that my ministry to Jerusalem may be acceptable to the saints'.[18] One last chance. One last chance to persuade the brothers and friends of Jesus that Christ was not so much the man they remembered (though of course he was that) but a presence of divine love in the hearts of believers.

The bland little speech about Gentiles abstaining from fornication and eating kosher meat might well be a repetition of the formula

[15] Romans 15:24.
[16] Romans 16:26.
[17] Romans 2:1.
[18] Romans 15:31.

which, as we know, the Ebionites and the Paulites thrashed out between them at the first Jerusalem Council in 48. But this is ten years later. Luke cannot disguise the fact that those threatening Paul's life are not on this occasion the 'Pharisees', who supposedly quarrelled with Jesus, nor the chief priests, nor the Romans, but the 'thousands' within the Jesus-movement in Jerusalem, who had no conception of the Gospel as it had been expounded in Paul's letter to the Romans.

Luke wants us to believe that an essentially decent Roman citizen is visiting Jerusalem at the time of a feast solely in order to dispense charity. In terms of Paul's own writings, this view does not make any sense. Are we really to suppose, as Luke makes out, that wherever this respectable citizen went in the Empire it was pure coincidence that there was disturbance – in Ephesus, a riot, in other places, scuffles, prison sentences, floggings – all incidents of which Paul himself boasts in his letters, but which the demure author of Acts tries to explain away?

Of course there is conflict and of course there is riot! God is about to revisit and redeem the world. Creation itself is about to be wound up. The righteousness of an angry God is about to be visited on a hopelessly corrupt world. And Paul is the instrument! That is the message of the letters, and no wonder the people of Jerusalem are horrified. Only the year before this last visit of Paul's to Jerusalem, the high priest Ananias had been murdered by a religious fanatic. The situation was, to put it mildly, tense. Not only has this Hebrew of the Hebrews come to Jerusalem to tell the Jews that the Torah has been replaced with the sacrificial love of Christ, but he has also come to tell the members of the Jesus-movement in particular that they have not begun to understand the message – that in Christ there is neither Jew nor Gentile, bond nor free.

One does not wish to diminish the greatness of Paul in the eyes of the reader, but from now onwards there is an element of tragicomedy in the story. Paul is one of the great religious geniuses of history, but, in the predicament which Luke describes, the Apostle becomes something of a Walter Mitty. Presumably it is to diminish the Walter Mitty element of the story that Luke fails to give it an ending.

If we believe that Paul wrote Romans, then we must believe that everything which happens next in the story is a disaster. For the plans of God as they have been specially revealed to Paul just don't work out. Paul thinks that God will be revealed to his chosen few in Jerusalem. The New Israel will thereby be established. It's not going to be the Christian Church, going on for Sunday after Sunday into eternity, with bishops, priests and deacons, and a new Torah. Such an idea would have horrified Paul. That would just be 'religion' all over again, *ho nomos*, the very thing which Christ had overthrown and which could neither give life nor save. God is coming back to his own. First, the veil of the temple, or the wall dividing the Jewish from the Gentile courts, will be rent in twain. Then, the few Jews who have been chosen will praise God in Paul's way, will see the Christ. Then Paul will move off towards the ends of the world in Spain, confirming the churches wherever he goes. And when he gets to Spain, the Lord will come. That is what is supposed to happen. What in fact happened is that Paul was to be arrested by the Romans for causing yet another riot.

By the time Luke writes up the story, perhaps twenty years or more later, it must be obvious that the Lord has not come and that all Paul's immediate prophecies and predictions about the nature of the world and God's purpose for it, have been not just slightly off beam, not open to interpretation, but plumb wrong. Christianity – not a word which Paul ever used – will have to sort out the contradictions of all that. It is Luke's dull task to smooth over the cracks and hide the glaring discrepancies in his story, and to persuade 'dear Theophilus', some Roman magistrate or bigwig, that the Christians are safe, good citizens. As Paul's last visit to Jerusalem shows, he was none of these things.

The next thing to happen is that Paul, who has been spotted during this week in the company of Trophimus the Ephesian, is accused by a mob of angry Jews of taking this Gentile into the temple, an offence, as we have seen, worthy of the death penalty.

We have already said enough about Luke's narrative for it to be obvious that it would be impossible to know exactly what happened next. Josephus tells us of repeated riots provoked by the supposed profanation of the temple by Gentiles between the years 6 and 66.[19] Luke wishes us to believe that Paul was wholly innocent in the matter and that the riot which followed was the result of a mistake. 'All the city was aroused, and the people rushed together',[20] the very situation that Roman governors and army officers most deplored and did their

[19] Richard Wallace and Wynne Williams, *The Acts of the Apostles*, p. 113; Emil Schürer, *History of the Jewish People in the Age of Jesus Christ*, vol. I, pp. 382–6; 455–70.
[20] Acts 21:30.

best to avoid in any of the cities over which they exercised their power. Anarchy was the one weapon the people had against the power of the Roman *lex*. It was a suicidal weapon, but desperation often drove people to use it. Luke depicts the mob dragging Paul out of the temple, where he had been spotted, and clamouring for his death. As happened so often in Roman Palestine, the military were on the spot almost immediately, dispersing the crowds and making arrests. Claudius Lysias, the tribune, had Paul arrested at once, handcuffed and placed between two soldiers, and taken into immediate custody. He was led off to the Antonia fortress, which he must himself have known from his days as a temple guard nearly thirty years before. Things had changed now considerably, and Paul was not recognised. Indeed, the commandant assumed that Paul was 'the Egyptian who recently stirred up a revolt and led the four thousand assassins out into the wilderness'.

It does not suit Luke's purposes to explain why the commandant had leapt to this conclusion, that Paul was a leader of the 'terrorists', as the NEB calls the sicarii, the knifemen who moved about in the crowds at festival time and conducted indiscriminate stabbings.[21] Josephus tells us that in 54, a 'false prophet' from Egypt had won support by the promise that the walls of Jerusalem would collapse at his command. He had disappeared when his followers were routed by the garrison.[22] Luke is able to make his hero correct the mistake at once, demonstrating to the commandant that he speaks perfect Greek and that he is a well-balanced character and, indeed, a Roman citizen. Far from being an Egyptian maniac, he says, 'I am a Jew, from Tarsus in Cilicia, a citizen of an important city.'

No one will ever know exactly what happened. That a riot occurred in the temple area and that it was provoked by Paul seems more likely than not, since Luke evidently feels that he has to explain it. The seemly language with which Paul is made to speak to the crowds is somewhat at variance with the impassioned language of Paul's own letters. We read of him giving one of his three accounts of the 'conversion' on the road to Damascus. When the speech is over, the crowd once more are provoked to frenzies of anger, 'Away with such a fellow from the earth! For he should not be allowed to live', and so on. It is then that Paul is taken back to the Antonia fortress and the

[21] See *BJ*, II, 254–7; *Ant*, XX, vi, 185–7.
[22] *BJ*, II, 261–3; *Ant*, XX, vi, 169–71.

commandant says that Paul should be examined by flogging to find out the reason for the riot.

Only when he has been tied up in preparation for this punishment does Paul ask the centurion in charge whether it is legal to flog a Roman citizen. It provokes an immortal exchange. The tribune came and asked Paul, 'Tell me, are you a Roman citizen?' And he said, 'Yes.' The tribune answered, 'It cost me a large sum of money to get my citizenship.' Paul said, 'But I was born a citizen' – or, as in the better Authorized Version of 1611, 'But I was born free.'

The next day, Paul is brought before the Jewish Sanhedrin. This is another set piece, and, as far as Luke is concerned, it is the last time that the great Christian missionary confronts his former coreligionists, the Jews. Compare it with Paul's apostrophes to the Jews in the letters, and one catches the extent to which Christianity, by the time Luke is writing, has drifted away from its Jewish roots. Though Paul had dreaded 'unbelievers in Judaea' before setting out on this last visit to Jerusalem, he never suggested, in any of his letters, that he (or his Gentile followers) had broken away from 'Judaism'. The quarrel from his point of view was a quarrel within Jewry about the nature of Judaism. He was interested in rescuing worshippers of the true God from the idolatrous habit of treating any worship – even the worship of the true God of Israel – as if it were the idolatrous absurdity of the Athenian shrine or the Ephesian temple. The unbelievers were those who could not see that the messianic promises for the human race were in the process of being fulfilled and that this allowed for the admission of the Gentiles to the fold. 'The Jews were entrusted with the oracles of God. What if some were unfaithful? Will their faithlessness nullify the faithfulness of God? By no means!'[23] By the time Luke is writing, Paul has become the embodiment of a Gentile Christianity which looks upon Jewry, as exampled in this scene of Paul before the Sanhedrin, as stubborn and unenlightened over the Christian doctrine of the resurrection. The high priest strikes Paul over the mouth. Paul rebukes him: 'God will strike you, you whitewashed wall!' Fisticuffs and insults are destined to be the only form of debate between Church and Synagogue for the next 1800 years.

This surely fictitious scene breaks up when Paul has cleverly introduced a reference to the resurrection. The Pharisees, who believe in a resurrection, fall to disputing with the Sadducees, who did not

[23] Romans 3:2–4.

believe in life after death. The following night, 'The Lord stood near him and said, "Keep up your courage! For just as you have testified for me in Jerusalem, so you must bear witness also in Rome." '[24]

According to James in a previous speech[25] and according to Luke's own narrative, there are literally thousands of Jewish believers in Jesus's name in Jerusalem. This seems momentarily to have been forgotten for the rhetorical purposes of allowing the Lord to tell Paul that he can now turn his back on Jerusalem (which had been obliterated from the earth by Roman soldiers by the time Luke came to write) and turn towards Rome.

Paul's sister's son – the first time in the narrative that we are told that Paul had family in Jerusalem – comes to the Antonia to inform his uncle that there is a plot afoot to ambush Paul and assassinate him. Forty fanatics had taken a vow to fast until they had killed Paul. When he hears of this plan, and foresees more trouble ahead, the commandant makes the decision to get Paul out of the city as soon as possible and to send him to Caesarea. With a guard of two hundred infantry and seventy cavalrymen, they marched Paul out of the city by night. It was the last time he would see the city where he had been educated, the city where Jesus had died on the cross, a city where many of Paul's most intense and self-contradictory visions and changes of heart had been experienced. As he was led out by the troops, he must have known that the apocalypse was going wrong. Whether or not, like the mad Egyptian three years previously, he had predicted that the walls of the temple would collapse as a beginning of the End, Paul must have realised as he left Jerusalem that life was continuing much as before. The signs which had been so clear to him personally in his journeys around the Mediterranean were stubbornly refusing to appear in the very place where you would have expected them most: Jerusalem.

The next morning, the party reached Antipatris. The infantry returned to barracks in Jerusalem and the cavalry took Paul the remaining twenty-seven miles to Caesarea. The commandant Claudius Lysias was handing Paul over to the Roman governor, Felix.

[24] Acts 23:11.
[25] Acts 21:20.

XIII

CAESAREA

CAESAREA IS THE creation of Herod the Great. As an engineering feat, the harbour that he created there, which took twelve years to build, is one of the wonders of the world. Larger than the Athenian sea-haven of Piraeus, it had been regarded as an impossibility by most of the architects and engineers whom Herod had consulted. Huge blocks of limestone fifty feet by ten by nine had been lowered twenty fathoms into the sea, rising into a vast sea-wall 200 feet wide furnished with towers, the largest of which was named Drusus, after Augustus's son. The port itself was named, of course, after Augustus Caesar, and the whole place is a demonstration by Herod that he could out-Roman the Romans in grandiosity and ingenuity. Above the all-weather harbour, he laid out a magnificent town according to a grid plan based on that of Alexandria. The port was dominated by a colossal temple of Caesar, inside which were two huge statues, one of Augustus, copied from the Zeus at Olympia, and another of Roma, modelled on the Hera of Argos. There were a theatre, an amphitheatre and a hippodrome. Running water was pumped in from the surrounding hills. There were annual games in honour of the emperor.[1]

No wonder the Roman procurators, in the years after Herod the Great's death, had chosen to make Caesarea their base, deciding to visit Jerusalem only when strictly necessary at festival times.

The procurator in 57, Marcus Antonius Felix, had an unusual background, which explains Tacitus's snobbish dismissal of the man that he exercised the power of a king with the mind of a slave. Unlike most Roman governors of Judaea who had belonged to the equestrian order, Felix was a freedman (*libertus*) who had once been a slave in the household of Antonia, Mark Antony's daughter, and of the mother of the emperor Claudius, Octavia – widow of Tiberius's brother Drusus. Felix's brother, named Drusus after their royal master, had

[1] Stewart Perowne, *The Life and Times of Herod the Great*, pp. 125–7.

risen high under the emperor Claudius (to chief accountant of the public treasury) and Felix had presumably got his present position in Caesarea in consequence. He had a particular talent for marrying well, which must have served him well in his career. Each of his three successive wives was of royal birth. The first was the granddaughter of Antony and Cleopatra. By the time he met Paul, Felix was married to his third, Drusilla, who was the youngest daughter of Herod Agrippa the elder and Bernice.

Felix had arrived in Judaea when a fresh wave of disturbances had broken out among the so-called terrorists, or sicarii. One of their first victims after he arrived was a former high priest, Jonathan. So successful had Felix been in crushing revolt that he had survived the change of emperors (Nero acceded in 54) and remained in office for over four more years – until 59.

When Paul and his guard reached Caesarea, Felix was presented with a letter from the commandant of the Antonia fortress explaining that Paul had been seized in Jerusalem, that the Jews accused him of various offences against their law but that as far as Claudius Lysias was concerned there seemed to have been no breach of Roman law on the prisoner's part. Hearing that Paul was a Roman citizen, Felix immediately asked to which province Paul belonged. When he heard it was Cilicia he said, 'I will give you a hearing when your accusers arrive.'[2]

In the matter of Paul's court hearings and indictments at Caesarea, the historians have inclined to be generous to Luke, largely because so little is known about provincial courts in the first century. Knowledge of such courts in the previous century can be reconstructed from the abundant correspondence of Cicero and the utterances of the illustrious jurists of the late Empire. But for the reigns of Claudius and Nero there is scanty evidence, and most of it is in fact contained in these very chapters from Acts. Arguments about the authenticity of Luke's accounts have therefore tended to be circular.[3] The scholars seem agreed that the application of law by local governors such as Felix would tend to have been ad hoc and casual. The nonexistence of comparable cases should not, therefore, make us dismiss Luke's account of Paul's hearing before Felix, or his later trials in Caesarea.

[2] Acts 23:35.
[3] See A. H. M. Jones, *Studies in Roman Government and Law*, and A. N. Sherwin White, *Roman Society and Roman Law in the New Testament*.

While remembering that Luke was not infallible and that he wrote with the specific agenda of presenting Christians in a good light to Romans, there is no reason why we should not follow, in broad outline, his picture of what happened to Paul over the next couple of years. That it was obviously important to Luke's purpose is shown by the amount of space he devotes to the hearings – the next three chapters of Acts, 24–6.

Felix behaved towards Paul with extreme caution. Josephus reminds us that these were days when 'the affairs of the Jews grew worse and worse continually'. The country was full of riotous bands, robbers, imposters inflaming the multitude. It was a time of extreme tension[4] and, as had been shown by the riot over Paul's behaviour in Jerusalem, any incident could provoke anarchy. Initially, Felix played a waiting game: having heard that Paul belonged to Cilicia, he saw a chance of washing his hands of the whole affair, since at this date Cilicia lay not in Felix's province but in that of neighbouring Syria. Presumably, how-ever, the comparatively minor nature of the case prevented Felix from persuading the governor of Syria to arrange transfer of the prisoner to a different court.[5]

So, Felix holds Paul in tight security in Herod's praetorium. After five days, the high priest came down to Caesarea with his own hired advocate, one Tertullus. In his speech, we are told by the great historian of Roman law, 'the charge is precisely the one to bring against a Jew during the Principate of Claudius or during the early years of Nero'.[6] The parallels between Tertullus's charge against Paul and the emperor Claudius's letter to the people of Alexandria are certainly close. 'We have found this man', says Tertullus, 'a pestilent fellow, an agitator among all the Jews throughout the world'; just as Claudius describes the Jews as producing, 'a universal plague all over the world'.[7] Tertullus accuses Paul of causing agitation as the ringleader of a sect. Paul, in his reply, deftly avoids the use of this word ('party' would be another translation for the word *hairesis*) and says, 'I admit to you, that according to the Way, which they call a sect, I worship the God of our ancestors, believing everything laid down according to the law or written in the prophets. I have a hope in God – a hope that they themselves also

---

[4] *Ant*, XX, v.
[5] A. N. Sherwin White, *op. cit.*, pp. 55–6.
[6] *ibid.*, p. 51.
[7] F. P. C. Hanson, *The Acts*, (Oxford, 1967), p. 10.

accept – that there will be a resurrection of both the righteous and the unrighteous.'[8]

The case as it stands could very well be historically accurate; and we note that the Paul who makes this speech is much closer to the Paul of the epistles than the 'late Christian' Paul of other parts of Acts. He is here recognisably the Paul of Romans, not starting a new sect, but arguing within the very bosom of Judaism. In all likelihood, Luke is using an early piece of reportage of the actual court hearing. At the same time, he is providing the Christian community of his own generation with an archetypical response before Roman governors when adherents of the Way are accused either of anarchy, disruption or lawbreaking.

Felix, Luke tells us, 'was rather well informed about the Way', and he immediately prorogued the hearing. Luke says he did so hoping for a bribe, and this would fit what we read of Felix in Tacitus and Josephus, both of whom speak of the procurator's readiness to accept bribes.

There follows an ambiguous sentence: 'After two years had passed, Felix was succeeded by Porcius Festus; and since he wanted to grant the Jews a favour, Felix left Paul in prison.'[9] This could mean that Paul spent the next two years in prison in Caesarea; or it could mean that 'when his next tenure of office of two years' duration had elapsed, Felix was succeeded by Porcius Festus'. The truth is, we do not know. Felix was probably recalled to Rome and replaced by Festus as procurator in 59 or 60, so that, in any event, Luke has made a muddle. Of Festus we know almost nothing except the cursory references to him in Josephus.[10] But the natural interpretation of the sentence is to suppose that Paul spent two years incarcerated in Caesarea. In one version of Acts[11] we read that Paul was kept in prison 'because of Drusilla', Felix's Jewish wife. It is claimed that since Paul argued, before Felix and Drusilla, 'about justice and self-control and the coming judgement', the lady was offended. (She had eloped from her first husband King Aziz of Emesa in order to marry Felix.)

In three of Paul's letters, he describes himself as being 'in bonds'. Usually referred to by the scholars as the prison epistles, it was

[8] Acts 24:14–16.
[9] Acts 24:27.
[10] *Ant*, XX, viii, 10–11.
[11] The so-called 'Western' tradition, represented by the Harclean Syriac version alone (Syh), of c. 616 AD.

traditionally imagined that they were written in Rome shortly before the Apostle's death. But there is no reason to suppose that they were all in fact written by Paul, still less to believe that they were all written from the same place. One of these letters, however, to the Philippians, contains phrases which would 'fit' his period of incarceration at Caesarea and there are those who believe that it was at this low ebb in Paul's fortunes that he wrote this particular letter.

One reason for thinking this is that, while the letter is clearly written from a Roman prison,[12] Paul feels himself in conflict most especially with those strict old-fashioned adherents of the Torah, and in particular with his fellow Jews over the question of circumcision. This, according to Luke, was what provoked the quarrel in Jerusalem which led eventually to Paul's arrest – the hope expressed by James that Paul had not been telling Jews of the Diaspora that circumcision was of no importance. Unlike the diplomatic Acts, Philippians gives us the authentic voice of our man. Writing of his dear brethren who believe in the necessity of circumcision, he says, 'Beware of the dogs, beware of the evil workers, beware of those who mutilate the flesh! For it is we who are the circumcision, who worship in the Spirit of God and boast in Christ Jesus and have no confidence in the flesh – even though I, too, have reason for confidence in the flesh.'[13]

This leads in to one of those passages of autobiography when Paul claims to be more Jewish than the ultra-Jews. The spiritual Mr Toad gets out his big drum and beats and bangs it for all he is worth: 'If anyone else has reason to be confident in the flesh, I have more: circumcised on the eighth day, a member of the people of Israel, of the tribe of Benjamin, a Hebrew born of Hebrews; as to the law, a Pharisee; as to zeal, a persecutor of the church; as to righteousness under the law, blameless.'[14]

Paul, however, is the most extraordinary mixture of mysticism and rancour, furious scorn and humility. In case anyone thinks he is trying to start a new religion, or a breakaway movement from Judaism, he here underlines his position with almost comic forcefulness. What the Jews of Paul's day seem so slow to recognise is that Paul alone understands the inner, spiritual implications of the Jewish Scriptures. This spiritual autobiography is the preface to one of the most moving

[12] Philippians 1:13.
[13] Philippians 3:2–4.
[14] Philippians 3:4–6.

passages in his entire *oeuvre*, a testimony which we may believe to be the very heart and essence of this extraordinary genius. This if anything is the voice of Paul, and this explains why he continues to exercise not merely a religious influence two thousand years after he wrote, but also a perennial psychological fascination.

All such assets, he writes, all the spiritual privileges of having been born as a strict and observant Jew, 'whatever gains I had, these I have come to regard as loss because of Christ. More than that, I regard everything as loss because of the surpassing value of knowing Christ Jesus my Lord. For his sake I have suffered the loss of all things, and I regard them as rubbish, in order that I may gain Christ and be found in him, not having a righteousness of my own that comes from the law, but one that comes through faith in Christ, the righteousness from God based on faith. I want to know Christ, and the power of his resurrection and the sharing of his sufferings by becoming like him in his death, if somehow I may attain the resurrection from the dead.'[15]

Compared with the tame speeches put into his mouth by Luke, these words are a burning fire of mystical love. If we believe that they were written in the period of the Caesarea captivity, it is not perhaps too fanciful to suppose that the memory of Christ's death had been stirred up for Paul by his recent visit to Jerusalem. As he walked in the temple and saw the furious crowds coming towards him across the court of the Gentiles, would he have retained a memory of another riot, and the money-changers' tables upturned? As the crowds bayed for his blood, did he remember 'Crucify! Crucify!'? As he was taken off to the Antonia fortress, the very prison where Jesus spent the last night of his life, did he not feel the peculiar fusion of their destinies, his own and that of the young man who had taken hold of his imagination and changed his life? 'All I care for is to know Christ . . . to share his sufferings, in growing conformity with his death' (NEB).

And now he was in prison, and facing the greatest test to his faith; for the Parousia had not occurred while he was in Jerusalem, and he writes back to the friends he has left behind in Macedonia, yearning for the Day of Jesus Christ.

During the last two decades, the scholars have done their best to disentangle Paul from his historical admirers — above all from Augustine, who made Paul the archetype of the penitent sinner turning to Christ as an act of individual salvation, and from Luther, who

[15] Philippians 3:7–11.

believed Paul to be the exponent of the doctrine of justification by faith only. Paul, it has been emphasised, was a first-century Jew, writing from a first-century Jewish perspective about first-century Jewish concerns. He was concerned, it has been hinted, not with individual salvation so much as with God's concerns for the whole of humanity. No one can doubt that there was room for this correction of emphasis by the scholars. Equally, however, it would be an insensitive reader of Philippians who did not see it as a document which reflects a profound personal piety, albeit a personal piety nurtured by the collective love for the primitive church – Paul's friends in Philippi.

> I am confident of this, that the one who began a good work among you will bring it to completion by the day of Jesus Christ. It is right for me to think this way about all of you, because you hold me in your heart, for all of you share in God's grace with me, both in my imprisonment and in the defence and confirmation of the gospel. For God is my witness, how I long for all of you with the compassion of Christ Jesus.[16]

Paul is in no doubt that as he lies imprisoned, his life is in danger. He feels no fear of death.

> For to me, living is Christ and dying is gain. If I am to live in the flesh, that means fruitful labour for me; and I do not know which I prefer. I am hard pressed between the two: my desire is to depart and be with Christ, for that is far better; but to remain in the flesh is more necessary for you.[17]

Extraordinary sentiments! The theories and suppositions which he had expounded in Romans have been exploded by events. With one part of himself, he already fears that he is not going to reach Spain, he is not going to be able to preach the Gospel to all the Gentile races of the known world; in other words, that his mission is a failure. With another part of himself he simply yearns to see his friends again. 'I am torn two ways' (*Sunechomai de ek ton duo*). This is not a sentence about the generalised fate of the people of God; it is not a generalisation about God's purposes in history. It is the aspect of Paul which Augustine and Luther were right to find in his writings, and which was to guarantee his immortality even after the Old Moore's Almanac side

---

[16] Philippians 1:6–8.
[17] Philippians 1:21–4.

to his genius – predictions about the end of the world and so forth – had been shown to be so fallacious. Philippians is a deeply personal document by a man confronting his own destiny, his own death, his own faith; and he is torn two ways. Warm, glowing with the mystical love of Christ, he also feels profound love and kinship with those who share his faith. And the letter contains two glorious hymns which Christendom has understandably made its own. First, the extraordinary hymn to the exalted Jesus in which Paul now sees the Lord as divine. (Perhaps older than Paul and remembered from his early days with the Hellenists in Antioch.) Even though Paul's own mission to bring about the state in which 'every tongue will confess' the truth of the Gospel may fail, Paul believes that God will somehow bring his purposes to pass, and that 'at the name of Jesus, every knee shall bow.'

In his other great hymn a divine sense of urgency, the knowledge that the Coming is just about to happen, and a strangely holy calm blend together with love of his brothers and sisters in Christ.

> Rejoice in the Lord always; again I will say, Rejoice. Let your gentleness be known to everyone. The Lord is near. Do not worry about anything, but in everything by prayer and supplication with thanksgiving let your requests be made known to God. And the peace of God, which surpasses all understanding, will guard your hearts and your minds in Christ Jesus.[18]

Paul is perhaps the greatest poet of personal religion. In all his rages with his supposed or actual enemies – 'Beware of the dogs' (Philippians 3:2); 'You foolish Galatians!' (Galatians 3:1); 'Do not be mismatched with unbelievers' (2 Corinthians 6:14) – the essence of his 'gospel' and the secret of his immortality as a religious writer and teacher is his belief that the believer has access to God. This access comes not through a system of beliefs or rituals but through the operation of the heart and the thoughts. To this extent, it is not surprising that Paul, revered as he is as one of the great twin Apostles of Rome, should be held especially dear by the traditions of Protestantism.

> I have not yet reached perfection, but I press on, hoping to take hold of that for which Christ once took hold of me.[19]

It is not surprising that academics should have tried to make sense of

[18] Philippians 4:4–7.
[19] Philippians 3:13 (NEB).

Paul's writings. That, after all, is their job. It is not surprising that they should have tried to form systems out of his letter-poems, erecting theories and explaining where he 'stands' in relation to the rabbinic traditions of Jewry or in relation to other Christians, contemporary or near-contemporary. Philippians reminds us that though this is a useful exercise and even, in its place, a necessary one, it is not the only way to read Paul. Those to whom he has meant the most are those who have taken these words as their own. 'Christ' is enthroned not as a shared Jewish political ideal, as the word might once have denoted, but as the highest aspiration of which the human heart is or feels capable.

> Finally, brethren, whatsoever things are true, whatsoever things are honest, whatsoever things are just, whatsoever things are pure, whatsoever things are lovely, whatsoever things are of good report; if there be any virtue and if there be any praise, think on these things.[20]

These are not the words of a philosopher. They are the testimony of the first romantic poet in history.

[20] Philippians 4:8 (AV).

XIV

I APPEAL UNTO CAESAR

PORCIUS FESTUS, HAVING succeeded to the procuratorship, reopened Paul's case. Acts suggest that the motive for doing so came from the chief priests in Jerusalem, who wanted Paul brought to the capital and charged with blasphemy before the Sanhedrin. The penalty for this, were the defendant found guilty, would be stoning. A few years later, in the interregnum following the death of Festus, stoning was to be the fate of Jesus's brother James, a killing which was carried out on the authority of the high priest Ananus.[1] The point is not whether any blasphemy was perpetrated by James or by any of the other followers of Jesus but whether the Jesus-movement was deemed by the temple authorities to be seditious and dangerous. Paul knew that it would be impossible to get a fair trial before such people. When Paul started his career working for the high priests, they were still Roman nominees. After 41, however, Agrippa I negotiated from Rome the right to select the high priests himself. From the year 50, six out of the last seven high priests had been appointed by Agrippa II. Far from settling things down, this created greater tensions in the land than there were before. 'Judaea experienced the concurrent, and conflicting, exercise of the governor and a king's power at the same time.'[2] Paul had become caught up in the highly localised Palestinian troubles with the Romans. The high priests would have been particularly anxious at this date to insist on severe punishment for anyone who appeared to be undermining Jewish hegemony, Jewish independence, the sanctity of Jewish traditions and laws. There is also the possibility that Paul felt that the guard and staff employed by the high priest would be vindictive towards one whom they deemed a turncoat. Paul was lucky to persuade the new governor to hear the case himself, in Caesarea. In due course, the delegation came down again from

[1] *Ant*, XX, 197, ix.
[2] Fergus Millar, *The Roman Near East 31 BC–AD 337*, p. 63

Jerusalem, 'bringing against him many serious charges which they could not prove'.

When asked by the governor if he wished to go and be tried in Jerusalem, Paul made his famous utterance:'I appeal unto Caesar.'[3]

There are all sorts of problems about this for those who wish to treat the trials of Paul in Acts as neutral historical narratives.[4]

Basically, the scholars worry about why or how a defendant in a criminal process can lodge an appeal before his case has even been heard. Under the Republic, all Roman citizens had a right of *provocatio*. This entitled the citizen to appeal to any holder of the *imperium*, or power, against torture, flogging or execution. Under the Empire, the right of *provocatio*, the right to be heard in a voting assembly, was changed to the right of *appellatio*, an appeal to Caesar. However, although there seems something very irregular about a defendant putting in an appeal before a trial, we do not have enough case histories to know whether such a thing was possible, or whether Luke has confused the issue.

The rhetorical effect of Luke's narrative, however, has very little to do with points of Roman law. It is all of a piece with the rest of Luke's message to his patron Theophilus – namely, that the great Apostle of Christianity turns away from Judaism and its provincial, petty laws towards those of Rome. He does so in total confidence that Caesar will look kindly on Christianity since, 'Neither against the law of the Jews, nor against the temple, nor against Caesar have I offended at all.'[5]

But before the matter was resolved, Paul was to be confronted with two of the more farcical characters of ancient history, Agrippa II and his sister Bernice, who came down to Caesarea to meet the new governor and who stayed to hear Paul's self-defence at what we in Britain should call the committal proceedings. As Luke represents the

[3] Acts 25:11 (AV).
[4] See Fergus Millar, *The Emperor in the Roman World*, p. 511: 'No adequate criterion exists for checking the historicity of the narrative of Acts; as it stands, it will tell us nothing about any precise rules of Roman law which may have been applicable in this area, but a lot about the power of the name of Caesar in the minds both of his subjects and of his appointees.'
    The key books are A. H. M. Jones, *Studies in Roman Government and Law*; A. N. Sherwin White, *Roman Society and Roman Law in the New Testament*; and P. Garnsey, *Social Status and Legal Privilege in the Roman Empire*, pp. 71–9. A good summary of the arguments is to be found in Richard Wallace and Wynne Williams, *The Acts of the Apostles*, pp. 122–3.
[5] Acts 25:8.

incident, it becomes Paul's opportunity to witness before the highest in the land, and – who knows? – there might be some element of accurately-remembered speech in their exchange. They are certainly vivid and memorable, the more so when we have read about Agrippa and Bernice (more properly, Berenice) in the other writings of the period.

Berenice was to be most famous to posterity as the ostentatious mistress of the emperor Titus, ten years her junior. Juvenal wrote satires about the flashy way this libidinous Jewess in her forties showed off her enormous diamonds and bewitched the young soldier-emperor who would destroy the city of her ancestors. Racine was to write an affecting tragedy about her. At the time that Paul encountered her, she was aged about thirty. She had been married twice, first to a commoner called Marcus, son of Alexander, and *en secondes noces* to her uncle Herod, King of Chalcis. She was then persuaded, for diplomatic motives, to marry the King of Cilicia, Polemo, who was sufficiently infatuated by her, or her prodigious and famous riches, to offer to submit to the Mosaic Law. After his painful conversion, however, Polemo found that marriage to Berenice did not last long. She abandoned him, and, with him, the pretence that she was a practising Jewess. She was now a flamboyantly incestuous adornment to the court of her brother, King Agrippa II.

They had come, Agrippa and Berenice, to meet the representative of Rome. The last procurator, Felix, had been married to their sister Drusilla, whom they hated. Now that he had gone, the pair could present themselves before the new Roman governor. Agrippa, though of the Herodian line,[6] had been born in Rome in the household of the emperor Claudius. Only seventeen when he inherited his kingdom, he was considered too young for the office by the emperor, but he was not out of his teens before he had been given not merely his father's kingdom of Chalcis, but also 'care of the temple'. After the death of Claudius in 54, Agrippa's kingdom grew to take in an area larger than that of Herod the Great's domains. Roman-born Agrippa, brother-in-law of a Roman procurator and all-but-brother-in-law (eventually) to the emperor Titus, was destined to be the king during the Roman war, and long beyond it. He it was who made one of the most famous speeches in Josephus, imploring the Jewish people to make peace with the unconquerable might of Rome. This is the

[6] He was the son of Herod Agrippa I, himself son of Aristobulus, son of Herod the Great.

PAUL

Agrippa, now in his mid-twenties, and this the Berenice, with whom Paul (perhaps now in his late forties?) comes face to face. The scene is stylised for us by Luke, who puts into his hero's mouth a Greek speech in 'high style', fully padded out with appropriate quotations from the Scriptures. It has been called Paul's *Apologia Pro Vita Sua*. If it contains the smallest particle of historical accuracy then one of its most striking aspects is Paul's ready assumption that, in his own circle at least, he is extremely well known. 'All the Jews know my way of life from my youth, a life spent from the beginning among my own people and in Jerusalem.'[7] Quite a claim. Luke's Paul is not an obscure, small-town figure of no reputation; he is famous, a somebody. And Luke emphasises that he has no anti-Roman political agenda.

'I stand here on trial on account of my hope in the promise made by God to our ancestors, a promise that our twelve tribes hope to attain, as they earnestly worship day and night. It is for this hope, your Excellency, that I am accused by the Jews! Why is it thought incredible by any of you that God raises the dead?'[8] There is no denying that to the real Paul – if we assume that he wrote Philippians near this date –the resurrection was absolutely vital: 'I want to know Christ and the power of his resurrection . . . if somehow I may attain the resurrection from the dead.'[9] But whereas for Paul the resurrection is part of a whole experience – the coming of Christ into his life, and the common expectation of God's people for the Day of Christ – for Luke's generation, for whom religion has become 'spiritual' only, the resurrection has become 'life after death', the longed-for gift of immortality beyond the grave: something rather different from the all-embracing, and disturbing, and politically potentially dangerous meaning that the word *anastasis* has for Paul. It is not true that the Jews believed it to be impossible for God to raise the dead.

When Paul has delivered himself of his *apologia*, the Roman procurator replies, 'You are out of your mind, Paul! Too much learning is driving you insane!' Agrippa, famously, but bafflingly, replies in a different vein. When Paul says, 'King Agrippa, do you believe in the prophets? I know that you believe', the young king replies: 'Are you so quickly persuading me to become a Christian?' There might be satire in the king's reply.[10]

[7] Acts 26:4.
[8] Acts 26:6–8.
[9] Philippians 3:11.

– 226 –

Agrippa's most baffling comment is reserved for the last. When the king, the governor and Berenice have withdrawn from Paul's hearing, Luke's novelist's licence allows Agrippa to say, 'This man could have been set free if he had not appealed to Caesar.' We can not begin to guess what this means in law. Rhetorically, fairly obviously, Luke wishes to emphasise to Theophilus that Paul had in fact vindicated himself, and had been taken a prisoner to answer a charge in Rome only as a result of a legal quibble, although he had done nothing wrong.

The nonentity Roman governor Festus accused Paul of being mad. Most of us, to our shame, would probably be inclined to agree with him. A man who sees visions and who claims to know the mind of God, must by some definitions be mad. Perhaps by some definitions, like so many religious geniuses, Paul was as mad as Blake, as mad as Dostoevsky, as mad as Simone Weil. He had an answer to such a view. 'Has not God made foolish the wisdom of the world? For since, in the wisdom of God, the world did not know God through wisdom, God decided, through the foolishness of our proclamation, to save those who believe.'[11]

---

[10] Acts 26:28. 'You make short work of turning me into a missionary' is the rendering by F. J. Foakes Jackson and K. Lake in *The Beginnings of Christianity*. The phrase in Greek is an idiom found in LXX. F. F. Bruce, *The Acts of the Apostles*, cites I Kings xxi. 7 and would render it, 'In short you are trying to persuade me to act the Christian.'

[11] I Corinthians 1:20–1.

XV

THE SCHOOL OF PAUL

ON ONE OF the occasions that Paul was in prison, he encountered a runaway slave with the name or nickname of 'Useful' – Onesimus. The friendship between Paul and this slave led to Onesimus embracing Paul's faith. It would seem as if Onesimus had come to Paul from another friend, Philemon a believer from Colossae. Had he been sent to Paul by Philemon and then 'deserted'? Or had he run away from Paul's friend Philemon, and been imprisoned with Paul by pure chance? We cannot tell. The letter to Philemon concludes with a reference to the fact that Paul is with Luke, Aristarchus and Demas; also one Epaphras, the evangelist who converted the Lycus valley (Colossians 1:7), so we could speculate that Onesimus was brought to Paul by Epaphras.

Whatever the case, the letter reveals that Paul was devoted to the slave 'Useful' and that he found it heartbreaking to part from him ('it is like tearing out my heart to do so')[1] and send him back to his master. This is what the letter to Philemon is all about, asking Philemon to be generous to the runaway when he returns: 'So if you consider me your partner, welcome him as you would welcome me. If he has wronged you in any way, or owes you anything, charge that to my account. I, Paul, am writing this with my own hand: I will repay it.'

Some modern readers of Paul's letters have asked themselves whether the Apostle was 'gay'. It might account, they think, for the passionate devotion he expresses in his writings, first to the young Greek boy Timothy and again for the slave lad who helped him in his prison cell. Wrestling with his true nature, Paul hated the carnal aspects of his homosexuality and denounced homosexual practices in passages (notably Romans I) which have caused anguish to gays and lesbians ever since. Would not some such dichotomy explain what lies at the heart of his message to the world (in Romans 7 and 8) that human

[1] Philemon: 12 – F. F. Bruce's translation in *Paul*, p. 393.

nature is at war with itself, 'that nothing good dwells within me, that is, in my flesh. I can will what is right, but I cannot do it. For I do not do the good I want, but the evil I do not want is what I do.'[2]

But the point about this statement is that it is a description not of human sexuality but of human nature in general. He is not so much speaking of our inability to control lust as about the natural discrepancy between human desire and achievement, the inevitable tendency of human schemes to rebound upon themselves and human beings to undermine their own best interests. Sex inevitably might come into this. Sexual behaviour might demonstrate vividly, even comically, the general truth of Paul's proposition that intention and achievement are very different things. But he is speaking of something more than simply sex. So, was he gay?

Perhaps, if it pleases you to think so. The fact is, we do not know enough about Paul to be able to psychoanalyse him in this way. In any event, no ancient would have understood what we mean by 'gay'. Homosexuality or bisexuality were accepted facts of life and forms of behaviour, and, even if a man of Paul's time had been what we call gay, he might not have recognised it as such. Paul the tormented closet queen does not ring true to this writer, who mentions it only because others have, and because it has even been uttered as an accepted 'fact' that Paul was attracted sexually to his own gender. Not proven, and, surely, supremely unimportant?

In the year 110, when Ignatius, the bishop of Syrian Antioch, was on his way to Rome to be thrown to the wild beasts, he wrote a letter to the Christians of Ephesus in which he echoes Paul's letter to Philemon. He tells the people of Ephesus to 'obey the bishop and the presbytery with an undisturbed mind', and he mentions the bishop of Ephesus no fewer than fourteen times. The bishop's name was Onesimus, and Ignatius incorporates the same puns on his name in which Paul had indulged. 'Let me have this profit from you [onaimen sou]', Paul says; and Ignatius – 'May I always have profit from you [onaiemen hymon] if I am worthy'.

The bishop's name was Useful or Profitable or Onesimus. It is not too far-fetched, surely, to suppose that the slave-boy convert of the Apostle Paul should, in his venerable old age, have become the Father in Christ of the Ephesian Church? And, more than that, scholars have concluded that it was likely that this Onesimus was

[2] Romans 7:18–19.

largely responsible for preserving and editing the body of Paul's letters.

If this were the case, it would certainly explain why the letter to Philemon has been preserved to us. It is unlike any of the other indisputably authentic letters of Paul in that it is seemingly uninterested in a great theological or religious question. It is concerned with the practicality of returning a slave; and it is entirely personal.

This is not the sort of book in which the reader will want a line by line explanation of why it is extremely unlikely that Paul wrote some of the letters which are attributed to him in the New Testament. That there was some kind of 'school of Paul', even in his lifetime, seems overwhelmingly likely, and, after he had departed from any church of his own foundation, the school which he had founded (he borrowed a lecture hall in Ephesus and was at work in it for two years, we remember) could propagate and develop his ideas. It was not considered dishonest in the ancient world to write something and then attribute it to the pen of someone you greatly admired. A modern might think it was 'forgery' to write, say, the letter we know as Ephesians and then claim that its author was Paul. The modern concept of authorship, and the jealousy a modern author would feel of her or his own words being written down unaltered is really entirely post-medieval; in many cases a post-Enlightenment phenomenon. (Samuel Johnson saw nothing wrong with 'ghosting' lectures and sermons and even whole books on behalf of other people.) One scholar has gone so far as to say, 'we do not have to explain or justify the phenomenon of anonymity or pseudonymity in early Christian literature. It is the other way round. We need an explanation when the real author gives his name.'[3] The writer is simply a tool of the Holy Spirit. Since he is possessed by the Spirit he modestly attributes his words to the Apostle.

It is necessary to remember that we do not possess any manuscripts of Paul's letters which are even remotely contemporaneous. The oldest we possess is the Chester-Beatty Papyrus, usually called $\mathfrak{P}^{46}$,[4] a codex measuring eleven by six and a half inches, containing 104 leaves and ten epistles – Romans, Hebrews, 1 and 2 Corinthians, Ephesians and Galatians, Philippians, Colossians, 1 and 2 Thessalonians. Outside the Orthodox Church, no one any longer thinks that Paul wrote Hebrews. Few could believe that he wrote 2 Thessalonians. And the doughty believers in his authorship of Ephesians are a dwindling band. But by

[3] K. Aland, 'The Problem of Anonymity and Pseudonymity in Christian Literature of the First Two Centuries', pp. 39ff.
[4] Bruce Metzger, *The Text of the New Testament*, p. 37.

the year 200, someone had gathered all these letters up and attributed them to Paul.

Much earlier than that the school of Paul had been at work. Someone, call him Onesimus for the sake of argument (it is a good name for an editor), had put in hand the copying and collecting and collating of many writings, some of them Paul's, some probably written by others in his circle. In the process of writing and copying, as the years wore by, and the Day of Christ seemed indefinitely delayed, we find the thing we call the Church developing.

Someone claiming to be Paul, who does not seem much like our man, sits down to write the so-called Pastoral Epistles – the letters to Timothy and Titus. In the course of editing or copying these letters, perhaps some scraps of papyrus containing genuine writings of Paul might have been preserved. (We think here of those very personal sentences such as, 'When you come, bring the cloak that I left with Carpus at Troas, also the books, and above all the parchments.')[5] But in general, when we read these letters, with their worthy concern for tradition and church order, we feel either that they belong to a later generation or that Paul survived into a very ripe old age and somehow changed character, abandoning the wilder flights of the letters he wrote in his forties and settling down into being a slightly boring old codger. Would our man be interested in spelling out the necessary qualifications for a 'bishop'? We seem only a step away here from the writings of the Apostolic Fathers and the establishment of a definite church order, based on a panel of bishops/presbyters (the same thing in this period) and deacons. 'Timothy, guard what has been entrusted to you'[6] (*ten paratheken fulaxon*) – one of the favourite texts of the Tractarian movement – seems a strange message if we imagine it coming from the same urgent pen which reminded us that the night was far spent and the day at hand. Yet without such guardianship, such institutionalism, no one would have preserved the letters of Paul, and we should know nothing about him.

In any case, not all the development of Paul's doctrine was in this sense dull. So original and forceful a thinker would be bound to win over many imitators, who would wish to follow through strands of thinking which the master had merely hinted at in a throwaway phrase. Romans is implicitly determinist. Ephesians is out and out predes-

[5] 2 Timothy 4:13.
[6] 1 Timothy 6:20.

tinarian ('he chose us in Christ before the foundation of the world').
Moreover, in Ephesians and Colossians, those two cognate works which
would seem to come from the same stable, we find Paul's Christ-
mysticism developed, in sentences which are wholly unlike his in style,
to a point where Jesus has been all but forgotten and Christ, a purely
spiritual being, seems synonymous with our most spiritual selves. 'So
if you have been raised with Christ, seek the things that are above,
where Christ is, seated at the right hand of God. Set your minds on
things that are above, not on things that are on earth, for you have
died, and your life is hidden with Christ in God.'[7]

Strangers to Christianity, who suppose that it is a religion which
claims some kinship with, or connection to, the historical Jesus, must
find such passages in the New Testament hard to understand, and
such a seeker after truth might equally be baffled to discover that of
the twenty-seven books of the New Testament only four are about
Jesus. The rest are letters, and the overwhelming personality to
dominate the whole collection is Paul.

There are still those who will echo the nineteenth-century cry
that Paul changed the simple message of the Gospel into one of
'theology'; well, on one level we see what they mean, but on another,
they have surely got everything the wrong way round? How could
'we' – a slave in Corinth, a Roman noblewoman, a Jewess of
the Diaspora selling cloth, an Athenian student – identify with the
highly localised concerns of Jesus and his disciples? As far as the
Palestinians were concerned, Jesus was the fulfilment of Jewish
prophecy and the 'king' who failed to overthrow the Romans; or he
was the king who, in the presence of so much political tension,
tried to promote a simple kingdom of peace and love. Paul was the
one who turned all this on its head. He barely alluded either to the
teaching or to the virtue of Jesus of Nazareth, or to his famous
healing power. In Romans he made the astonishing claim, which
would certainly have shocked later Christian eras, that 'we' are sharing
in the suffering of Christ. We share in his suffering and we share in
his glory.[8] The drama has been generalised (to include non-Jews)
and interiorised.

The most inspired and brilliant product of 'the school of Paul' was
Marcion, who 'endeavoured to push Paulinism to its logical conclusion,

[7] Colossians 3:1–3.
[8] Romans 8:17.

and of course it has none'.[9] Marcion believed that Christ was all spirit. Folk-tales about his human birth revolted him. 'Away with that poor inn, those mean swaddling clothes and that rough stable!' he exclaimed.[10] Christ, who was a manifestation, not an incarnation, of the goodness of God, arrived on the scene at Capernaum, fully formed, rather as the Gods in Homer make emanations of themselves in human guise. The death of Christ on the Cross rescues those who believe from dominion of the old law. Marcion considered that the old dispensation had passed away. He therefore discarded the Jewish Scriptures entire, and his followers even went so far as to fast on Saturday, since this was the Jewish Shabbat.

Marcionism and the Marcionites was the first major 'heresy' to assail Orthodox Christianity. In the course of vilifying the heretics and anathematising the chief heretic – not a line of Marcion's writings survives except in the voluminous assaults on his name by Tertullian and Justin Martyr – the Orthodox picked up several of his tunes. It is largely owing to his influence that later Christianity, in spite of holding fast to the Jewish tradition so despised of Marcion, adopted his belief that Jesus was divine, which he had drawn out of Paul's writings. Perhaps it was the most supreme example of taking Paulinism to a logical conclusion of which there was none. To appease Marcion's numerous followers – perhaps there were as many Marcionites as Orthodox in the middle of the second century – the Orthodox also made sure, when the canon of the New Testament finally came to be drawn up, that Paul would be given pride of place. The idea of a canon had come not from the Judaising Orthodox but from Marcion himself. Without him, we should probably not have a book called the New Testament at all.[11]

While some believers, even in Paul's lifetime, must have been drawn to the life in Christ as an interior, mystical experience, in which they

---

[9] Robert Smith Wilson, *Marcion: A Study of a Second-century Heretic*, p. 180.
[10] Quoted by Tertullian, *De Carne Christi*.
[11] Andrew B. du Toit, 'Canon: New Testament', in *The Oxford Companion to the Bible*, ed. Bruce M. Metzger and Michael D. Coogan (1993), p. 103: 'Marcion was the first person, as far as we know, who actually visualized the idea of a New Testament canon.' The paradoxes multiply. Without the fervent Christ-mysticism of Marcion, his opponents would never have established the NT canon; but nor would they have taken quite such trouble to make sure that the Gentile world knew of the Jewish Scriptures. Thus it is the great spiritual anti-semite Marcion whom we have to thank for our knowledge of Adam and Eve, Moses, Noah's Ark, the Psalms and the Prophets, which would probably otherwise have been unknown in the West.

died to the world and the world to them, there must always have been others – in the Church of Rome, say – who said, 'Yes, but you know Rufus? Well, his father is old Simon and he actually *remembers* what the Lord Jesus was like. He was there when he died. He was there when he preached, and when he healed the sick.'

From the earliest days, perhaps before Jesus died, his disciples would have memorised stories about him, and repeated his sayings. In the second generation, the need to preserve this oral tradition, and to make sense of it in terms of the theological understandings of each individual church, led to the evolution of the written Gospel traditions. The Gospel grew out of the clash between the mission of Paul and that of Peter. It grew out of 'Yes, but . . .' To the purely spiritual worshippers of the exalted Christ, Petrines would say, 'Yes, but you know he was a real person. He lived in a village called Nazareth. I heard that he chose Peter while he and his friends were mending their nets by the Sea of Galilee.' We have got all these stories from someone who knew Peter, and Jesus's family; we have heard them speak about the Lord. And in turn, the Paulites would have said, 'Yes but . . .' And there would follow – perhaps true – stories designed to diminish the mother of Jesus and his brothers, stories of Jesus rebuking them, or of their calling him mad; stories of Peter's faithlessness in the very extremity of the Lord's death.

Papias, a second-century bishop of Hierapolis, is reported to have said, 'on the authority of an elder', that Mark, 'who became the interpreter of Peter, wrote accurately as far as he remembered them, the things said or done by the Lord, but not however, in order. For he had neither heard nor seen the Lord or been his personal follower, but at a later stage . . . he followed Peter, who used to adapt his teachings to the needs of the moment but not as though he were drawing up a connected account of the oracles of the Lord.'

Mark's Gospel as it now stands 'bears all the signs of having been community tradition' and 'cannot therefore be derived directly from St Peter or any other eye witness'.[12] But this is not to say that the traditions handed down to Papias were wholly false. We have no idea who Marcus was (it was perhaps the commonest Latin name of the Roman Empire – one thinks of Marcus Tullius Cicero, Marcus Brutus, Mark Antony to name only the three most famous). Mark's Gospel, probably written down in Rome at about the time when the first

---

[12] D. E. Nineham, *Saint Mark*, pp. 26–7.

generation who had known the Lord were dying off, reflects both strands, the Jewish and the Hellenist, the Peter and the Paul, of the Christian movement and tradition. It is not the work of one man. It is the culmination of a whole series of visions and revisions. It is not, perhaps, in the modern sense, a book at all – if by a book we mean a single coherent composition by one individual. It seems appropriate that the author's name should be the commonest, as if it is the Gospel of John Smith. The 'author' is really the Church of Rome shortly before (probably) the Fall of Jerusalem in 70. And its great achievement is its composite portrait of the historical Jesus, a picture on which at least two subsequent revisions and drafts and Gospels would all seem to be based. In this spare, short book, Jesus appears, fully grown-up, from Nazareth. As soon as he has arrived in Capernaum, 'they were astounded at his teaching, for he taught them as one having authority, and not as the scribes'. The strange tale is all of newness; new wine in fresh wineskins – it is obvious what that meant to the generation which had fought through and witnessed the disagreements between Peter and Paul about circumcision and the status of the old law; a new twelve – no more the tribes of Israel, but twelve apostles; a small seed planted – a huge bush growing. To the generality of Jews, the secret of Jesus's Messiahship, and what it might mean, is concealed; for this was a generation that hearing, did not understand. The kingdom is at hand; it is very near. Those who enter it will be as little children. Holy poverty is enjoined. One third of the short narrative is concerned with the Cross, and the passion and death of the Lord, which already has become a thing to be perceived through liturgy, through ritualised uses of the Scriptures.

Like the letters of Paul, the Gospel of Mark contains no physical resurrection of Jesus, though the Church of Rome probably believed in it. Coming to the tomb at daybreak, the women find a young man (he has become an angel by the time Matthew retells the story) who tells them, 'Do not be alarmed; you are looking for Jesus of Nazareth, who was crucified. He has been raised; he is not here.' And the women run away, 'for they were afraid'.

That is how Mark's Gospel ends. Without it, Paulism and its 'logical conclusion', Marcionism, would have been, well, incomplete.

The quarrel between Paul and Peter, the apparently irreconcilable tension, becomes the seedbed of the new faith for the next generation. We imagine the scattered congregations, particularly after the Fall of Jerusalem in 70, meeting in house-church and synagogue and, yes, some are undoubtedly those who 'belong to Paul' and others to Apollos and others to Cephas. But they remember Paul's words: 'all things are yours, whether Paul or Apollos or Cephas or the world or life or death or the present or the future – all belong to you, and you belong to Christ, and Christ belongs to God.'[13] So one of them says, 'We are Gentiles – and we belong to Christ, as Paul taught. Fed by his Body and Blood in the Eucharistic meal, the Lord's Supper, we look for his coming in glory. We have no need of the synagogue and its regulations.' And another says, 'But remember what Peter taught concerning the Master himself, the stories he told about the kingdom being no bigger than a grain of mustard, which, when it is planted in the ground, will grow to be the greatest of all shrubs. Remember the stories of the Master healing the sick, walking on the water, stilling the waves and the winds . . .' 'But', says another, 'all these things were emblems, tokens, stories with a meaning. The miracles were not magic tricks, they were signs, signs of God's purpose. Peter could remember the Lord, but he is less anxious to remember the night the Lord was arrested, when he denied . . .' 'Oh really? But isn't that just a story put about by the followers of Paul to discredit Peter and his followers?'

And so the oral traditions and the theology build up. On the one hand, the authentic memories of Jesus's words – the stories and analogies drawn from rural Galilean life. On the other, stories which seem at variance with the Galilean scene in the 20s but seem to have much to do with the story of Paul and his friends in the Gentile world of the 50s and 60s – quarrels in the synagogue about diet, about those who do not keep the Torah in all its smallest particulars. Above all, casting its shadow over the whole story, is the Cross. If Luke is right, the early teaching of Jesus's friends saw the Crucifixion as a betrayal of Jesus by quislings. 'This man . . . you crucified and killed by the hands of those outside the law'[14] – i.e. the Romans. God has vindicated Jesus by raising him up, he has undone the terrible sin of the crucifixion which had come, like so many of the other sins against the prophets in the history of Israel, as a result of not heeding God's word.

Not so for Paul, for whom the Crucifixion is not a calamity redeemed by the happy ending of resurrection. For Paul, the Cross contains the mystery of life, the mystery of God's purposes for the

[13] 1 Corinthians 3:21–2.
[14] Acts 2:23.

world. 'For Jews demand signs and Greeks desire wisdom, but we proclaim Christ crucified, a stumbling-block to Jews and foolishness to Gentiles, but to those who are the called, both Jews and Greeks, Christ the power of God and the wisdom of God.'[15] So, the stories and the memories and the teachings come to be written down, with this underlying conviction lying at the heart of the compilation. Already, when the stories come to be written down, the separation between 'church' and 'synagogue' has begun, and perhaps it is already irrevocable. So, Jesus the Jew appears as someone at war with his own people, despising his own family, quarrelling with his friends the Pharisees. And Jesus the rebel against the authority of Rome becomes the friend of centurions, the man who says that he finds in the centurion a faith which he has not discovered in the whole of Israel. The high priests and the Sanhedrin discover Jesus to be not a Galilean exorcist who caused a threat to public order one Passover and had to be killed, but a mysterious Saviour who moves among his people, keeping the secret of his true nature and identity from all but the inner circle. He dies not as a result of his claim to be a King of the Jews, not for speaking against Caesar, but because he has blasphemed against the Jewish Torah, and made himself divine. He dies, in fact, because he thinks of himself not as a Galilean peasant teacher who lived 4 BC[16]–AD 30 might plausibly have thought of himself, but because he has absorbed the wisdom contained in Philippians – that 'though he was in the form of God, did not regard equality with God as something to be exploited, but emptied himself, taking the form of a slave, being born in human likeness. And being found in human form, he humbled himself and became obedient to the point of death – even death on a cross. Therefore God also highly exalted him and gave him the name that is above every name, so that at the name of Jesus every knee should bend, in heaven and on earth and under the earth, and every tongue should confess that Jesus Christ is Lord, to the glory of God the Father.'[17] Jesus, who, as some Jewish friend of his tactlessly remembered, even rebuked someone for applying to him the epithet 'good',[18] would not have understood how such a hymn could possibly been composed. But then, the religion of Jesus, whether the actual religion of Jesus

[15] 1 Corinthians 1:22–4.
[16] Herod died in 4 BC, so if you accept the Gospel story that Jesus was born in the reign of Herod, he must have been born four years before the Christian era began.
[17] Philippians 2:6–11.
[18] Mark 10:17.

the Jew or the religion of Jesus reconstructed by sentimentalists, could only have the most limited appeal to the human heart. The actual religion was localised in the time and situation of first-century Galilee, and was not intended to have a universal application, still less to become the framework for a new world religion. The repro-versions of, say, Francis of Assisi or Tolstoy or Gandhi attempt to make systematic what can at the time only have been meant as axiomatic – for instance, the calls to poverty attributed to Jesus in the Gospels, startling and even thrilling as they may be do not sit easily besides the injunctions to pay tax. The sayings of Jesus can shock us but they scarcely represent a cohesive oral framework on which we can base our lives.

The religion of Paul, by contrast, wild, ecstatic and confused as it must often appear as we turn the pages of his few surviving writings, contains all the makings of a religion with universal appeal even though he himself, just like Jesus, would perhaps have been astonished by the turns and developments which the Christian religion was to take after his death. The orderliness of the Pastoral Epistles and the writings of the School of Paul would have enraged him – it is the replacement of one religious enslavement for another, the idolatry toward Torah replaced by idolatry towards Church. But all that lies ahead. The essential things – the certainty of human unworthiness before the perfection of God, the atoning sacrifice of Christ on the Cross, the glorious promise of the Resurrection and everlasting life – these are the core of Paul's religion. And above all, the knowledge that Christ, the drama of his passion, death and resurrection, but also the continuing presence in the world are *in us*. That is the winning formula which determines that a rival to the old gods has entered the world, a rival stronger than Caesar because it can touch and transform every human heart. The fact that Paul died in obscurity, and perhaps with a sense of total failure, does not blind us to the magnitude of that achievement. While the Petrines, the Palestinians, clung to the memory of Jesus, Paul was able to apply as a universalised creed the perceptions of heaven which were perhaps Jesus's own: the confidence that each individual could turn to God as to a Father and meet a response of love.

XVI
=

THE VOYAGE TO ROME

BUT WE LEFT Paul having appealed to Caesar and begun his journey from Caesarea to Rome. If Jesus and his companions travelled across the Sea of Galilee in the Gospel accounts, they would do so in something called a *ploion*. This is the Greek word for a ship, and this is the word generally used in Acts for the various vessels in which Paul and his friends take their sea journeys. It is also the word generally used in LXX. For example, it is the word used for the ship in the Book of Jonah, the ship in which the man of God is travelling, trying to escape his destiny, and from which he is thrown, in order to save the lives of the other passengers, into the bosom of the deep, there to be swallowed by a fish for three days and three nights.

There are some deliberate echoes of the Book of Jonah in the account of Paul's voyage to Rome, not least in the passage when the ship gets into difficulties and the sailors begin to throw their cargo overboard. The difference between the two stories, very pointedly, is that whereas the sailors travelling with Jonah believed themselves accursed until they could throw the prophet into the sea, the sailors who travel with Paul are saved from certain death precisely because they are the Apostle's companions.

At the moment of shipwreck, however, the regular *ploion*, the cargo-ship on which Paul and the others are being transported, becomes the much grander and more ancient *naus*. This is Homeric Greek, the word that Homer would have used to describe the boat in which Odysseus and his companions took their voyage. Indeed the phrase to describe the ship running aground is Homeric – *epekeilan ten naun* – a direct echo of the Odyssey, book 9, line 148: *prin neas eusselmous epikelsai*, the same epic, nautical expression. 'Must we not accept it for a certainty', asks the old scholar, 'that Luke, the physician of Antioch, had gone through his Homer?'[1]

---

[1] F. Blass, *Philology of the Gospels*, quoted by F. F. Bruce, *Paul: Apostle of the Free Spirit*, p. 467.

If it is a matter of certainty that Luke wants to make Paul into a many-wiled Odysseus, we can certainly take note of the way in which the narrative is going to work. In his letter to the Roman Christians, Paul hopes that he might be able to reach the capital of the Empire as a mere staging post, on a journey from the eastern end of the Mediterranean to its western limits in Spain. In his vocabulary, the journey to Rome would be that of a stranger and sojourner, completely alienated from the paganism and false wisdom and sexual immorality of the capital, which he denounced with all the violence of which his language was capable. But in Luke, the voyager has become, by implication at least, an Odysseus, that is, a tired, wily old sailor going home. Though the winds will blow him off course, and he has to outwit monsters on his journey, he will eventually reach the place where the narrative has its natural conclusion. Rome is not a frightening or a threatening place, as Jerusalem had been. Rome is home, and all that is required is for the hero with his few companions to turn out the wicked suitors before peace and prosperity are restored. That is the implication of making Paul's last sea voyage into an Odyssey.

Most readers of the final journey in Acts, however, will recognise that, though all language carries its own codes, this is as lively a narrative of a sea voyage as we are ever likely to read, and 'one of the most instructive documents for the knowledge of ancient seamanship'.[2] This must be true, though it is by no means obvious that the voyage which it describes is originally that of Paul himself. It seems likely that the passage relating to the voyage, undoubtedly describing a real voyage, has been spatchcocked into Acts by the editor/author whom we have been calling Luke, in order to give it vividness. We might assume that Luke has used an account of Paul's last voyage. But is there any reason, asks the sceptical German,[3] for supposing that Paul was the subject of the original narrative? Might not Luke, searching around for some narrative means to get his hero from Caesarea to Rome, have stuck in a crudely edited version of some other person's sea voyage? The extent to which we believe that Acts 27 originally describes a voyage of Paul's will to some degree depend on the extent to which we believe that Paul ended up in Rome at all. It might be intellectually (but not emotionally) satisfying to say that we do not know and can not exactly say what happened to Paul after he was

[2] H. J. Holtzmann, *Handcomentar zum Neuen Testament*, quoted by F. F. Bruce, *op. cit.*, p. 369.
[3] H. Conzelmann.

arrested and taken to Caesarea. The rest is folklore and we do not have the means of checking the historical accuracy of any of Luke's narrative. But if it is all fiction, we have to ask ourselves what possible motive Luke can have had for making Paul a prisoner in Rome. For Luke's purposes, it would have been better had Paul never appeared before a Roman magistrate, let alone been had up on a serious charge which had culminated in an appeal to Caesar and a journey to Rome. Much better, if he were simply writing a piece of fiction about Paul, to say that the Apostle had died, in good odour with the Roman authorities, in some provincial capital with which he was always associated, such as Ephesus. Much easier to say this than to connect Paul with the two tinder-boxes, Jerusalem and Rome, at precisely the era of history when those two capitals were not just at war but deeply and spiritually at odds. For, apart perhaps from Boadicea, the British warrior-queen who massacred the legions in East Anglia, was there any nation during the turbulent 60s, who made more trouble than the Jews in the war of 66–70, who did not merely defy the Romans – Scythians, Huns and Goths of many tribes were always likely to do that – but who questioned the very idea of the Empire, questioned its legitimacy? No, much easier, had Luke been no more than a propagandist, without any pretensions to historical accuracy, to keep Paul well away from Rome.

So it is on the whole reasonable to suppose that Paul did reach Rome. And if he did not do so in the lively way that Luke describes, then we must assume that some other person, in very similar circumstances, did so. The puzzles, of course, will always remain: if Luke knew that Paul went to Rome, stood trial for some offence, and was acquitted; or if he was successful in his appeal to Caesar, why does not Acts tell us? An abundance of internal evidence suggests that Acts was written after Paul's supposed martyrdom, or disappearance, from the scene.

The *naus* or *ploion* on which Paul embarked at Caesarea, with his friends Luke and Aristarchus, was one of the huge grain ships which plied their trade between Egypt and the other parts of the Roman Empire. Given the vast slave population of Rome itself, and given the politically catastrophic consequences of hunger, it is interesting that the emperors did not themselves take the responsibility for transporting grain. Egypt exported 133,000 tonnes of wheat during the reign of Augustus. A substantial fleet was needed to move grain on this scale but it was all in the hands of private entrepreneurs who would command high sums and personal advantage. Claudius is known to have offered privileges to shipowners who would undertake to transport grain to Rome on six-year contracts.

Just as Paul's missionary activities happened on trade routes and were in all likelihood trade journeys or business trips with a religious slant rather than being 'missionary journeys' per se, so his last voyage is not completely a passion narrative, not completely a military or legal affair. Even the military depend on the trade vessels, not the other way about.

Paul and his party were in the charge of a centurion called Julius, of the Augustan cohort. The honorary title *Sebastes* is quite often found in inscriptions and refers to his auxiliary status. The *frumentarii*, the auxiliary officers responsible for transporting grain, also acted as special police in the reign of Hadrian (117–38) and it is possible that Julius was acting in just such a capacity now with Paul.

The Egyptian grain harvest was over in May, but there was normally not time to thresh it, dry it and load it on to the ships before the sailing season ended in November. So, it would usually be garnered and stored during the winter and transported from Alexandria during April, May and June. With any luck, the boats could do two round trips within the season, and it was up to the captain to calculate whether there was time to make the second run before the weather broke. In the case of the boat which took Paul, the captain had miscalculated.[4]

They set out in late September.[5] The ship, which had obviously come from Alexandria to bring grain to Caesarea, but was now intending to go on, still with a considerable cargo, towards Puteoli in Italy, hugged the coast for forty-seven miles and put in at Sidon. Julius, another of Luke's highly civilised centurions, allowed Paul ashore to see his friends. By the time they had put out to sea again, however, the winds were against them. They sailed under the lee of Cyprus, then across to the south coast of Asia Minor with the wind against

[4] Richard Wallace and Wynne Williams, *The Acts of the Apostles*, p. 128.
[5] Perhaps the most delightful book ever written on a New Testament subject is *The Voyage and Shipwreck of St Paul* by James Smith Esq. of Jordanhill. (Due for a reprint?) Smith establishes that, whoever wrote Acts 27, it is a completely authoritative and accurate account of a voyage in these waters. The weather, the sailing conditions and the geography are all absolutely accurate. For instance, Smith describes contemporary sailors trying to make their way westwards from Rhodes, coming into a nor' nor' wester and being blown southward of Crete in exactly the way that Luke describes.

them. When they reached Myra in Lycia it was obvious that the ship was not capable of going on, so the passengers were transferred to another grain ship, one which had sailed direct from Alexandria. It was by now that crucial week in the year when the weather was turning. Yom Kippur, the Jewish Day of Atonement, had passed (5 October that year, tenth of the Jewish month of Tishri) by the time they had, with great difficulty, sailed under the lee of Crete and docked at a place called Fair Havens (*Kaloi Limenai*), the modern name of which is Limeonas Kalous.

The narrative represents Paul, at this juncture, making a speech to the centurion, the captain, and the owner of the ship, all of whom are aboard, imploring them not to continue with the voyage. The owner, obviously anxious to squeeze as much profit out of the season as he can, disregards the advice. Do we believe that Paul, a prisoner, would have had the temerity to give his advice to these authoritative figures? Certainly, the author of the letters is very widely travelled and he has known what it is like to be in a shipwreck. It is quite possible that the centurion already knew Paul and that they had met on previous voyages. Certainly, he would have been known as an experienced traveller and there seems no reason why they should not have been advised by him. We can safely infer that he was not slow to come forward with an opinion when he had one, in any circumstance of life. The vignette, if a true one, of Paul advising the shipowner, reminds us of our earlier idea that the tentmaker of Tarsus was a man of some substance and quite likely from a family who did not feel shy about approaching ships' captains and offering them the benefit of advice.

The centurion was persuaded by the merchant seamen and the shipowner that it was worth risking a continuation of the voyage. The easy part of the journey was over. Now that they had to launch out into the open sea, there was no chance of hugging the coast should a storm blow up. With the first moderate southerly wind, they set sail. No sooner had they sailed past Crete, however, than the wind changed. A violent north-easter blew up. The ship could not be turned head-on into the gale, so the captain gave way, and for fourteen days, they were driven before the storm. They did everything they could to lessen its impact. They tried to undergird the hull of the ship with ropes. They lessened its weight by throwing overboard all the tackle and all the provisions, which insured that, after two weeks, everyone was very hungry. For many days, the clouds were so thick that they could not see the sun or the stars, so that navigation became impossible.

In the middle of this storm, Luke has Paul get up and announce to the sailors: 'Men, you should have listened to me and not have set sail from Crete . . .' Interestingly, in spite of this message of 'I told you so', none of the crew yielded to a temptation to throw the Apostle overboard. He continued, 'I urge you now to keep up your courage, for there will be no loss of life among you, but only of the ship. For last night there stood by me an angel of the God to whom I belong and whom I worship, and he said, "Do not be afraid, Paul; you must stand before the emperor; and indeed, God has granted safety to all those who are sailing with you." '[6]

The interesting thing about this speech, from the narrative point of view, is that, in Luke's terms, it is clearly true, or meant to be taken as true. Angels often appear in Luke's works – to announce the incarnation of Christ to the Virgin, to proclaim his birth to the shepherds of Bethlehem, to proclaim his resurrection, to release Peter from prison. They do not lie, for they are the messengers of Almighty God. So, we can assume that the author of Acts believes, and wants us to believe, that Paul is indeed destined, not merely to reach Rome and be tried, but that he will come face to face with Nero himself.

Even if we suppose that Acts is very much a compilation, drawn, like the Gospel of Luke, from several sources, the joint two-volume work does show signs of having been put together with carefulness, even if not with the editorial skills of a modern historian. The end is promised but does not come. We must assume, though, that in Luke's eyes Paul and Nero are destined to meet. Is it a meeting which Luke planned for a further instalment of his history? Or is the ending of Acts, which leaves Paul still awaiting his encounter with the emperor, a deliberate rhetorical device designed to make us believe that the trial would take place and that Paul would, as Christian tradition held, be acquitted? Or is it all an accident? Is the ending of Acts actually lost? Like Oscar Wilde, we shall never know, but it does make a difference to our understanding of the story.

After a fortnight, the storm died down and the sailors began to take soundings: twenty fathoms, and the next time they did so, fifteen fathoms. Fearing that they might be about to run aground on rocks, they let down four anchors and lowered the boat into the sea. Paul took it that they were trying to abandon ship and urged them not to do so. Then Paul urged everyone on board to eat in order to give

[6] Acts 27:22–4.

themselves strength. There were 276 people. Presumably some of the remaining wheat cargo was made into flour and baked. When everyone had satisfied their hunger they threw the remaining wheat into the sea to lighten the ship. As the light of the next morning dawned, they struck a reef and ran the ship aground. We read that it was the soldiers' plan to kill the prisoners but that the centurion, 'wishing to save Paul',[7] prevented them from doing so. Presumably, therefore, there were quite a number of prisoners who had been picked up between the journeys from Caesarea and Sidon, all bound for Italy. And so, on Paul's advice, everyone jumped ashore, and, by clinging to driftwood, everyone was saved, and they all landed up on Malta.

The experience had been enough to persuade the captain and the ship's owner that they should not venture to sea again until the spring. So, Paul was three months on the island of Malta, which reveres his name to this day. Luke describes two miraculous happenings that occurred on Malta. The first occurred when they were lighting a fire on the beach and Paul gathered a bundle of brushwood, out of which a viper sprang on to his hand. In their terror, the Maltese assumed that this was a sign that Paul was a murderer, but, when he shook the creature off into the fire, they changed their minds and decided that he was a god.

The second miracle occurred when the 'leading man' of the island, Publius, invited them to his house. Publius's father was sick with dysentery and fever and Paul cured him. 'After this happened, the rest of the people on the island who had diseases also came and were cured.'[8] This sounds like a genuine piece of Maltese tradition, since, as so often, Luke has got hold of an authentic local title. Inscriptions remaining on the island reveal that the 'leading man' was indeed called the *protos*, as Luke tells us.

When the spring came, another grain ship arrived from Alexandria, and they boarded it, putting in first on the east coast of Sicily, at the Greek city of Syracuse, and then to Rhegium. Finally, after a gusty voyage they arrived at the port of Puteoli, modern Pozzuoli. It is the place where Virgil is buried. (Cumae, the shrine from which Aeneas makes his descent into the underworld is just outside the town.) There was a group of Christians there, who welcomed Paul, Luke and

[7] Acts 27:43.
[8] Acts 28:9.

Aristarchus. When they had stayed with them for a week, they began the final part of their journey – to Rome.

What happened next? We might belong to the school of thought which supposes that Luke only takes the story up to Paul under house arrest in Rome because Acts was written in *circa* AD 62. If this is our belief, then we think that Acts really is the story so far. There are a number of objections to this theory. One is the whole 'synoptic problem', the difficulty of dating Luke/Acts as early as this, since it plainly draws on the traditions of Mark/Matthew, and they are, in all likelihood, written down later than Paul's arrival in Rome.

But if that were the whole reason, it would have a circularity and indeed a lack of generosity about it. Why not, if that were the only reason, accept that most scholars of the last hundred years have got the dating of the New Testament wrong, and revert to the assumption that Luke is writing an up-to-the-minute account of what happened to Paul in his Roman confinement?

There are a number of reasons for not going down this path, attractive and neat as it may seem. First, are the indications within the later chapters of Acts that the story is going to end with some sort of confrontation between Paul and the emperor Nero; the strong suggestion that Paul will go on trial in Rome. If you believe Acts is written down before Paul's trial (the idea proposed is that it is in a sense a brief being offered to some senior Roman official before the trial to make him think the best of the defendant) then you have to accept the strange fact that no one – after the trial was over – ever thought to append a note to the end of Acts saying, 'and by the way, he got off'; or, 'in spite of all our best endeavours, the case went against brother Paul and he had his head chopped off.' The point is, if anyone had known, definitely, what had happened to Paul, we should certainly have been told, and the fact that several different stories circulated about him in the early church is surely an indication that no one did really know. His end is a mystery just as the end of Acts is a mystery; and the most intelligent guess one can make is that the author of Acts had no more idea than we do how Paul ended his days.

Both these notions – that Paul was acquitted, and that he died a martyr's death in Rome – enjoyed currency in the early church. Of course, they could be true. Equally possible is the other story which did the rounds of early Christendom, that Paul achieved his ambition to go to Spain.

My book ends, therefore, rather like a work of experimental fiction, whose conclusion the readers can pick as they choose. If you are a Roman Catholic reading these pages, you will probably want to end it thus: just as you will believe that Peter became the first Bishop of Rome and suffered a martyr's death (crucifixion) in the Imperial Capital, so you will give credence to the extremely old tradition that Paul, as befitted a Roman citizen, was beheaded with a sword. The head is supposed to have bounced three times when severed from the saint's body, and at each spot where the head struck the ground, it caused a fountain to spring up. At Tre Fontane. In the basilica of San Paolo fuori le mura, which is nineteenth-century (the old church burnt down in a disastrous fire of 1823), the pilgrim can see the traditional site of Paul's martyrdom. It is here that a tomb may be found with its inscription, of great antiquity, 'PAOLO APOSTOLO MART'.[9] Certainly, as you tread the sites of the celestial city, it is hard not to feel stirred by the thought of those deaths. And the name of Paul was undoubtedly contained in the early martyrologies.

If, however, you were being a strictly dispassionate historian you would have to recognise that while these stories might be pleasing to Christians of a certain persuasion, there is no copper-bottomed evidence that Peter ever so much as visited Rome; and there is certainly no hard evidence that Paul died the death of a martyr.

Another version of the story is that Paul went to Spain. This particular ending appeals to me the best. He arrived in Rome, where there were Christians already, with Good News. The Day of Christ was at hand, etc. He left it, in fact, a legacy of total mayhem. Whether it was true before his visit to Rome, it was certainly true after, that it was now possible to single out 'Christians' as a particular group – a troublesome one if Suetonius is believed, and one (if Tacitus is right) whom it was easy to isolate and blame for the fire of 64.

While the human torches screeched with agony in the Vatican

---

[9] A good general archaeological survey written from the point of view of faith is to be found in *The Tombs of St Peter and St Paul* by Engelbert Kirschbaum SJ. S. G. A. Luff's *The Christian's Guide to Rome* is an excellent guide to the sites, written with wit and charm. Commenting on Augustus Hare's dismayed view of San Paolo's resemblance to a railway station, Canon Luff adds, 'This would not be inappropriate for so tireless a traveller as Paul.' Other books which might interest the Roman traveller in search of Paul would include H.V. Morton's classic *In the Steps of St Paul*, which I found to be the most helpful and wonderful companion in Turkey, Italy and Palestine. Pierre Grimal's *In Search of Ancient Italy* is a good, learned general introduction to the archaeology of the region. Margherita Guarducci's *The Tomb of St Peter* has a fascinating final chapter on 'The Cult of the Apostles Peter and Paul on the Appian Way' in the third and fourth centuries.

Gardens of a sadistic emperor, some will have imagined Paul already dead; others perhaps have supposed he died with them. But I prefer to think of him, far away in the west, wholly oblivious to what he had started, eagerly gazing towards the heaving sea on which he had so often been tossed and awaiting the coming of Christ.

APPENDIX

THE EVOLUTION
OF THE NEW TESTAMENT

ANY STUDY OF Christianity in the first decades of its development must be based on an implicit set of assumptions about the evolution of the New Testament. It was not until the second century that there existed anything approaching a canon, a list of normative texts which the Christian community regarded as 'scriptural'. In the early part of the second century, however, such writers as Clement of Rome (*circa* 96) or Justin Martyr (*circa* 150) were quoting from written sources which we can recognise as 'books' of the 'New Testament' – for instance, the Gospel of Matthew and the letters of Paul. By the middle of the second century AD, therefore, we can be reasonably certain that the twenty-seven documents which comprise the 'New Testament' had reached something approaching the form in which they are known to us.

(The manuscript tradition is more recent. The oldest fragment of New Testament manuscript which we possess is tiny, measuring 2½ by 3½ inches of papyrus, on which a few verses of the Fourth Gospel (John 17:31–3; 37–8) can be descried. This fragment, which is in the John Rylands Library at Manchester, England, perhaps dates from the second century. It remains the case, however, in spite of claims by journalists and non-papyrologists in recent times, that it is difficult if not impossible to date papyrus within a fifty-year margin.)

So, here we have twenty-seven documents – known as the New Testament, since, years after they were written, Christianity grew and developed not merely as a religion distinct from Judaism, but as a force which had to battle against its own 'heresies', and define itself by the creation of its own sacred texts.

From the point of view of the historian, how can the New Testament writings be used, and how do we know when they were written?

The simplest way of answering this apparently simple question is to plunge *in medias res* into the question of Gospel origins. Then it will be appreciated that it is not, as a matter of fact, a simple question at all, but one of considerable delicacy and complexity which is unlikely to yield very clear results.

Consider the so-called 'synoptic problem', which is the natural place to start.

If you read the first three Gospels, Matthew, Mark and Luke, it becomes obvious, even without a close examination of the texts, that these three books are all reworkings of the same material. Looking at them side by side (Greek *'synopsis'*, hence 'synoptic') it seems fairly clear that Mark, Matthew and Luke all have a measure of material in common; not just in common, but almost word for word transcriptions. (See for instance the story of the healing of a paralytic man in Mark 2:1–9; Matthew 9:1–8 or Luke 5:17–26.) Such overlap is repeated and multiplied throughout the texts. There is material which all three Gospels have in common. There is material unique to Luke, and material unique to Matthew, though very little unique to Mark. This is one of the reasons, though not by any means the only reason, why textual scholars have concluded that Mark is the oldest Gospel and has been 'used' by Matthew and Luke as a source.

When we look for internal evidence within these texts for a *terminus ad quem* which would determine the latest point at which they could have been composed, there is no definitive material to help us. The natural place to look is in the apocalyptic prophecy placed into the mouth of Jesus in Mark 13:14–23; Matthew 24:15–22 and Luke 21:20–4. This is the part of the Gospel when Jesus speaks of the Abomination of Desolation (or sacrilege) being set up in the temple; of those living in Judaea being compelled to flee into the hills; of a calamity befalling the holy city and the people of God. Many scholars (perhaps most) believe that this text derives from an older Jewish piece of apocalyptic writing relating to the profanation of the temple by Antiochus Epiphanes in 168 BC. But in the Christian reworking of the text, there would seem to be some allusion to events of the first century AD. A recent commentary on St Matthew's Gospel, wishing to argue that this is the first of the Gospels, assumes that this passage is a clear reference to the sack of Jerusalem by the Roman armies in AD 70.[1] Where Mark has, 'Pray that it may not happen in winter', Matthew

---

[1] J. Enoch Powell, *The Evolution of the Gospel* (Yale, 1994), p. 185.

has, 'Pray that it may not happen in winter or on the Sabbath', which
Mr Powell interprets as 'a joke . . . at the expense of the judaizers by
way of a snide allusion to strict observance of the Sabbath, always a
problem in wartime or emergency'.

Apart from the difficulty of seeing this 'joke' as particularly funny,
there remains the problem – if this is taken as a reference to the siege of
70 – of wondering why those who are in Judaea should take to the hills.
This sentence is kept in all three Gospels. Anyone who had read Josephus
would know that during the terrible siege of Jerusalem in 70 the Judaean
hills were full of Roman troops, and there was no chance of anyone
successfully fleeing from the city into the surrounding countryside.

Luke has the telling detail – omitted by the others – 'when you see
Jerusalem encircled by armies'. But when we say that the reference is
'telling', what does it tell us?

One explanation could be that the historical event which lies behind
this 'prophecy' of Jesus is not the siege of 70, but the threat to Jerusalem
by Caligula in 40, when Roman armies, carrying the statue of the
emperor which they intended to set up in the holy precincts of the
temple, marched on the city and then withdrew. Another explanation
is that Mark's original does refer to the siege of 70, but that Luke,
who knew nothing of the details of the siege, left intact the injunction
to flee to the hills, but added what he considered a plausible note on
the encircling legions.

The tradition preserved in Matthew and Mark (omitted in Luke)
carries the parenthesis, 'let the reader understand' ('*ho anaginoskon
noeito*'). This would seem to suggest that in the communities where
the Mark Gospel and the Matthew Gospel developed (Rome?) these
mysterious prophecies could be expounded orally, without the political
risk involved of writing down any specific topical interpretation. So,
'When you see the Abomination of Desolation usurping a place which
is not his . . .' And at this point, the scribe leaves the preacher to explain
to the congregation what is meant. It leaves the reader of a later
century in the dark.

How convenient it would be for the historian if, instead of this 'let
the reader understand', Mark had written, 'let the reader understand
that this is a reference to the tragic events of 70 in which our faithful
brethren in the Jerusalem church were all put to the sword'. But no
such specific reference exists. Any attempt to date the Gospels will
have to depend on evidence more substantial than this vague
'apocalyptic'.

So, how about a different approach? The Acts of the Apostles and Luke's Gospel are clearly written by the same pen. Both are addressed to 'Theophilus', both share the same literary style and the same theological outlook; both claim to be written by one person, 'following traditions handed down to us by the original eye-witnesses' and from written sources. Acts ends, as we have observed in this study of Paul, in a very baffling way, with Paul in Rome under some form of house arrest, living at his own expense for two years and (we assume) waiting for his appeal to Caesar to be heard in the appropriate Imperial court.

Why not take this as a historical and accurate statement? Why not assume that Acts genuinely peters out because it is finished in Paul's own lifetime, i.e. in *circa* 62?

There are very strong arguments against the belief that Luke's is the first Gospel.[2] So, if we believe that Luke/Acts were written before 60, we must logically suppose that Mark (and almost certainly Matthew) was written before this. There is a great attractiveness about this notion of an early dating for the entire New Testament, not least its neatness. After all, there is no concrete and inescapable reference, in any of the New Testament books, to the destruction of Jerusalem, and is this in itself not a pretty surprising fact? Would we not expect one of these writers, particularly those of a triumphalist turn of mind (such as Mr Powell's anti-Judaisers), to make it clear that the very core and centre of Jewish worship had been obliterated?

Such a radical view inspired J. A. T. Robinson's *Redating the New Testament*, which made a spirited case for supposing that all the books of the canon were completed before 70. The majority of New Testament scholars, however, were resistant to Robinson's ideas, not merely because he was shaking a scholarly orthodoxy to which they had grown comfortably attached, but because he took so little heed of the very obvious 'development' of Christian theology from its origins in the Galilean preacher to the exalted flights of Christ-worship to be found in the Gospel of John.

The truth is that the questions of New Testament dating will never be solved: there is no fool-proof apparatus which will establish irrefutable evidence, and such evidence as would be required is (to put it mildly) unlikely to materialise after 1900 years. Far more depends on hunch, in this area, than any tidy-minded or exact analyst would want. The dates of Acts or of Mark will never be established by textual

---

[2] See H. Conzelmann, *The Theology of St Luke*, p. 125.

criticism alone, nor by external historical references, nor by a judicious or fanciful juxtaposition of the two. Of course, as the discovery of the Dead Sea Scrolls has shown us, archaeology can provide marvellous surprises. Future generations might be treated to the discovery of a jar containing the papyrus diaries of Peter or the Virgin Mary, but until that day dawns, we remain in the dark.

So much was established, in the early days of modern biblical scholarship, by textual criticism, that we have developed a tendency, over the last hundred years, to treat textual scholars as if they were wizards. The old German method of Form Criticism, for instance, was an invaluable tool, since it enabled readers of the Gospels – really for the first time since their composition – to go behind the texts and recapture the original 'forms' in which the material of the Gospel writers came to hand. Here is an individual saying, perhaps attributable to the historical Jesus. Here is the story of a healing miracle. But – and here the school known as Redaction Criticism came to the Form Critic's aid – look what the writer has done with his 'forms'. The Gospels are not neutral narratives, such as Hansard's Parliamentary Reports. They are documents which reflect the 'situation in life' (*sitz im leben*) of the particular communities for which they were written. For example, we have seen in this book about Paul that it was highly unlikely that the historical Jesus ever broke with Judaism, or disputed with his fellow-Jews about, let us say, the dietary laws. Acts makes plain that, well after the death of Jesus, his followers in Jerusalem observed the dietary laws, and the requirement that Jews should circumcise their males. Paul's letter to the Galatians (*circa* 50, i.e. twenty years after the Crucifixion) makes it clear that the quarrel between Gentile Christians, converts of Paul, and the original followers of Jesus (Peter, James and the rest) about this matter occurred a whole generation after Jesus.

So when, in Mark's Gospel, we read of Jesus (Mark 7:20) that he declared all foods clean, we know that this can not be historically true. Similarly, in stories of Jesus denouncing his own family and friends and proclaiming that those who do the will of God are his true family (Mark 4:31–5) we are reading a story made up to fortify a later Christian community in its quarrel with the Jews. Jesus's statements that his followers will be thrown out of synagogues make sense only as afterthoughts to explain the quarrels which Paul and his followers had with the synagogues, not of Palestine, but of the Diaspora.

Once we have seen the overpowering force of this argument, we will become clear in our minds that the Gospels belong to a period which post-dates Paul's missionary activities in Asia Minor and, in all likelihood, his visit to Rome. This does not mean, however, that all the material in the Gospels is unhistorical, or that none of the sayings of Jesus, for instance, or the miracle stories, have a Galilean origin. Probably what happened is that a body of oral tradition was carried round, learnt by heart, passed from Christian group to Christian group before any of it was written down by Mark, Matthew or Luke. Similarly, the Fourth Gospel – usually known as the Gospel of John (whoever he may have been) – contains many specific historical memories of the events of Jesus's last days, and many accurate topographical references which could easily date from a period twenty, thirty, forty years before the final redaction of the Gospel as we now read it.

Because there are no first-century manuscripts of the Gospel tradition, we do not know precisely how that tradition evolved. Probably, the majority of scholars who have worked on this problem so patiently and collectively for more than a hundred years are right – i.e. that Mark achieved something like its present format some date in the very late 60s; and that Matthew belongs perhaps a decade later, and Luke some time in the 80s. (There are few better presentations of the argument than those to be found in D. E. Nineham's masterly introduction to Mark, *The Gospel of Mark*.)

There is always room, however, for puzzlement, or even scepticism about what has become the scholarly orthodoxy. While it looks likely that Matthew and Luke both used Mark and other sources, it would be a fallacy to suppose that Matthew, Mark and Luke all reached a finished state in, say, 68, 75 and 85, with no one adding to or emending their traditions. A later copier, having read Matthew in some form more or less similar to the Gospel of that name which we can read today, might easily have rewritten this or that passage of Mark with his memory of Matthew in mind, and this could explain those few moments where those arguing for the priority of Matthew might appear to be making a convincing case.

In other words, textual criticism is a more fluid discipline than some of its more rigid adherents might wish. Paul would appear to 'quote' from Matthew's Gospel. In his hymn to Agape in 1 Corinthians he says that it will not profit him, even if he has faith strong enough to move mountains, a clear reference to the saying of Jesus (Matthew 17:20) 'If you have faith no bigger than this mustard seed, you will say to this mountain, "Move from here to there!" and it will move.' The critic who believes that all New Testament problems can be solved by textual criticism and by textual criticism alone will be forced to the conclusion that Matthew's Gospel antedates the letter to the Corinthians. If, like Mr Powell, you believe that Matthew is post 70, and did not reach its final form until *circa* AD 100, then you are forced into the conclusion that 'Paul' is little more than a fictitious figment, and the epistles which bear his name are all pseudonymous.

Such a reading defies common sense. The patiently authentic autobiographical portions of Galatians and the Corinthian epistles contrast so vividly with those Pauline letters which are in all likelihood pseudonymous (such as Ephesians or 2 Thessalonians) that we know Mr Powell must be barking up the wrong tree. Merely because Paul could allude to sayings of Jesus (or in 1 Thessalonians 5:7 to the parable of the wise and foolish maidens) does not mean that we have to posit a finished, edited (in modern terms a *published*) text of Matthew which antedates work which nearly all scholars would place in the 50s. What these allusions show us, more probably, is that the stuff of which the Gospel tradition is made – the oral and written material which will one day be written down as 'the Gospel according to . . .' – was circulating probably decades before the books which we know as Gospels came to be finished.

If we accept this, the common-sense view, then we shall realise that Paul's letters – the body of work which is authentically Paul's: Romans, Galatians, the Corinthian letters, 1 Thessalonians, Philemon and Philippians – are the oldest Christian documents which we possess. 1 Thessalonians, perhaps the oldest, probably antedates the first version of Mark by nearly twenty years.

The Gospels are not the creation of Paul, but they grew up in the controversial milieu which Paul had done more than anyone else to ferment. Paul himself (as we have seen) echoes and quotes from the body of tradition relating to Jesus the Preacher. But two very distinctive features of Paul's Christ – features which we can be reasonably sure are not part of the earliest Jewish traditions of Jesus – help to fashion the Jesus of the Gospels.

Jesus the Jew (for an analysis of what he must have been like and what his teaching could have contained, see the author's *Jesus* or Geza Vermes's *The Religion of Jesus the Jew*) might conceivably have seen his death as the beginning of the messianic age, or the End of Time. There was nothing in the religious vocabulary of his tradition which would have enabled him to see his death as an atoning sacrifice. It is Paul's letters which see Christ as the Herculean *Saviour*, and the Cross as the gateway to salvation. In all the Gospels, this idea is fundamental, which is why they could be seen as Passion Narratives with preliminary matter, rather than stories about a great preacher and exorcist who had the misfortune to be executed by the Romans. The Shadow of the Cross, and its Glory (to use a very Paul-ite word), dominate and animate the pages of all four Gospels, revealing them to belong to the world which Paul has imaginatively transformed.

Secondly, a point already made, but which can not be overstressed, the conflicts of the Gospels – which depict, for instance, Jesus having heated disputes with the Pharisees, and with the very people who will form the corpus of the Jerusalem Church – are really conflicts of Paul.

It could be seen, then, that the essence of the Gospels, the thing which makes them so distinctive, and such powerful spiritual texts, namely the notion of a spiritual saviour, at odds with his own kind and his own people, but whose death on the cross was a sacrifice for sin, is a wholly Pauline creation. The strange contrarieties which make the Jesus of the Gospels such a memorable figure – namely his insistence on peace and kindness in all his more notably plausible or 'authentic' sayings, and his virulent abuse of Pharisees, his Mother, and the temple authorities on the other – could point less to a split personality in the actual historical Jesus, and more to the distinctive nature of Paul's spiritual preoccupations a generation later. Even in this respect, therefore, Paul seems a more dominant figure in the New Testament tradition than Jesus himself. The Jesus of the Gospels, if not the creation of Paul, is in some senses the result of Paul. We can therefore say that if Paul had not existed it is very unlikely that we should have had any of the Gospels in their present form. The very word 'gospel', like the phrase 'the New Testament' itself, are ones which we first read in Paul's writings. And though, as this book has shown, there were many individuals involved in the evolution of Christianity, the aspects which distinguish it from Judaism, and indeed make it incompatible with Judaism, are Paul's unique contribution. It is for this reason that we can say that Paul, and not Jesus, was – if any one was – the 'Founder of Christianity'.

SELECT BIBLIOGRAPHY

The place of publication is London, unless otherwise stated.

Aland, K., 'The Problem of Anonymity and Pseudonymity in Christian Literature of the First Two Centuries', *JTS*, 12 (1961)

Allison, D. C., 'The Pauline Epistles and the Synoptic Gospels: The Pattern of Parallels', *New Testament Studies*, 28 (1982)

Applebaum, S., *Jews and Greeks in Ancient Cyrene* (Brill, 1979)

Arnold, Clinton E., *Ephesians: Power and Magic* (Cambridge, 1989)

Bardon, H., *La Littérature latine inconnue* (Paris, 1956)

Barnes, T. D., 'Legislation against the Christians', *JRS*, 58 (1968)

— 'An Apostle on Trial', *JTS*, 20 (1969)

Baur, F. C., *Paul: His Life and Works* (ET, 1875)

Bayer, J., *Littérature Latine* (Paris, 1965)

Betz, Hans Dieter, *Der Apostel Paulus und die Sokratische Tradition* (Tübingen, 1972)

— (ed.) *The Greek Magical Papyri in Translation* [including the demotic spells] (2nd ed., p. 199, Chicago, 1992)

Blass, F., *Philology of the Gospels* (1898)

Bornkamm, G., *Paul* (ET, 1971)

Bowker, J., *Jesus and the Pharisees* (Cambridge, 1973)

Bruce, F. F., *The Acts of the Apostles* (Carlisle, 1951)

— *Paul: Apostle of the Free Spirit* (Revised ed., Carlisle, 1995)

Bultmann, R., 'The Theology of Paul' in *Theology of the New Testament* (ET, 1952)

Burkett, W., *Homo Necans* (1975)

Casson, L., *Ships and Seamanship in the Ancient World* (Princeton, 1971)

— *The Ancient Mariners* (Princeton, 1991)

Chadwick, Henry, *The Enigma of Paul* (1969)

Charlesworth, James H. (ed.), *The Old Testament Pseudepigrapha* (1983)

Collection of Ancient Greek Inscriptions in the British Museum, British Museum Department of Greek and Roman Antiquities (Oxford, 1874–1916)

Conzelmann, H., *The Theology of St Luke* (ET, 1967)

Cross, F. L. (ed.), *The Oxford Dictionary of the Christian Church* (1974)

Cumont, Franz, *The Mysteries of Mithras* (ET, 1903)

Cupitt, Don, *After All* (1994)

Davies, W. D., *Paul and Rabbinic Judaism* (1965)

— *Jewish and Pauline Studies* (1984)

De Ste Croix, G. E. M., *The Class Struggle in the Ancient Greek World* (1981)

Deissmann, A., *Paul, A Study in Social and Religious History* (ET, 1926)

Dessau, H., 'Der Name des Apostel Paulus', *Hermes*, 45 (1910)

Dibelius, Martin, *Studies in the Acts of the Apostles* (1956)

Dodds, E. R., *Pagan and Christian in the Age of Anxiety* (Cambridge, 1965)

Dunn, James, *The Parting of the Ways Between Christianity and Judaism and Their Significance for the Character of Christianity* (1991)

— 'The Justice of God', *JTS*, 43 (1992)

— 'Prolegomena to a Theology of Paul', *NTS*, 40 (1994)

Edmundson, George, *The Church of Rome in the First Century* (The Bampton Lectures, 1913)

Ellis, E. E., *Paul's Use of the Old Testament* (Edinburgh, 1957)

—*Paul and His Recent Interpreters* (Grand Rapids, 1961)

Ellis, E. E. and Grasser, E. (ed.), *Jesus und Paulus: Festschrift für W. G. Kummel* (Gottingen, 1975)

Elsner, Jaś and Masters, Jamie (eds), *Reflections of Nero* (1994)

Encyclopaedia Judaica (Jerusalem, 1972)

Eycyclopaedia of Religion, The (1987)

Finley, M. I., *The World of Odysseus* (1956)

Foakes Jackson, F. J. and Lake, K., *The Beginnings of Christianity* (1920)

Foerster, Werner, *Palestinian Judaism in New Testament Times* (ET by Gordon Harris, Edinburgh, 1969)

Fraser, J. W., *Jesus and Paul* (Appleford, 1974)

Fredriksen, Paula, *From Jesus to Christ: The Origins of the New Testament Images of Jesus* (Yale, 1988)

French, D. H., *The Roman Road System of Asia Minor* (1961)

Garland, Robert, *Religion and the Greeks* (1994)

Garnsey, P., *Social Status and Legal Privilege in the Roman Empire* (Oxford, 1970)

Glover, T. R., *Paul of Tarsus* (1925)

— *The Influence of Christ in the Ancient World* (Cambridge, 1932)

Goodman, M., *The Ruling Class of Judaea* (Cambridge, 1987)

Goulder, Michael, *A Tale of Two Missions* (1994)

Grant, Michael, *The World of Rome* (1974)

— *Saint Paul* (1976)

— *Saint Peter* (1994)

Grant, Robert, *Gods and the One God: Christian Theology in the Graeco-Roman World* (1986)

Gray, W. D., 'The Founding of the Aelia Capitolina and the Chronology of the Jewish War under Hadrian', *American Journal of Semitic Language and Literature*, XXXIX (July, 1923)

Green, Peter, *Alexander to Actium: The Hellenistic Age* (1990)

Griffin, Miriam T., *Nero: The End of a Dynasty* (Yale, 1984)

Grimal, Pierre, *In Search of Ancient Italy* (ET, 1964)

Guarducci, Margherita, *The Tomb of St Peter* (ET, 1960)

Gunther, J. J., *Paul, Messenger and Exile* (Valley Forge, 1972)

— *St Paul's Opponents and their Background* (Leiden, 1973)

Halperin, D. J., 'Crucifixion, the Nahum Pesher and the Rabbinic Penalty of Strangulation', *Journal of Jewish Studies*, 32 (1981)

Harnack, Adolf von, *Marcion: Das Evangeliusm von fremden Gott* (Leipzig, 1913)

SELECT BIBLIOGRAPHY

Harrison, Jane Ellen, *Prolegomena to the Study of Greek Religion* (Cambridge, 1903)
Harvey, A. E., *Companion to the New Testament* (1970)
Hastings, James (ed.), *Encyclopaedia of Religion and Ethics* (Edinburgh, 1911)
— *Dictionary of the Bible* (1898–1904)
Henderson, Bernard W., *The Life and Principate of the Emperor Nero* (1903)
Hengel, Martin, *Crucifixion* (ET, 1962)
— *The Pre-Christian Paul* (ET, 1991)
Henneke, E. and Schneemelcher, W. (ed.), *Neutestamentliche Apokryphen* (ET Lutterworth 1965), vol. II, p. 133ff. for the apocryphal correspondence between Paul and Seneca.
Herford, R. Travers, *The Pharisees* (1924)
— *Judaism in the New Testament Period* (1928)
Hicks, E. L., *Ancient Greek Inscriptions in the British Museum* (Oxford, 1874–1916)
Holtzmann, H. J., *Handcomentar zum Neuen Testament* (Freuberg-im-Breisgau, 1899)
Hooker, M. D. and Wilson, S. G. (eds), *Paul and Paulinism* (1982)
Hopkins, K., 'Taxes and Trade in the Roman Empire (200 BC–AD 400)', *JRS*, 70 (1980)
Hugede, N., *La Métaphore du Miroir dans les Epîtres de Saint Paul aux Corinthiens* (Geneva, 1957)
— *Saint Paul et la Culture Grecque* (Geneva, 1966)
Inge, W. R., *Outspoken Essays* (First series, 1927)
Jackson, Ralph, *Doctors and Diseases in the Roman Empire* (1988)
James, E. O., *Sacrifice and Sacrament* (1962)
Jeremias, Joachim, *Jerusalem in the Time of Jesus* (ET, 1969)
— *Jewish Encyclopaedia, The* (New York, 1901)
Jones, A. H. M., *The Herods of Judaea* (Oxford, 1938)
— *The Greek City from Alexander to Justinian* (Oxford, 1940)
— *Studies in Roman Government and Law* (Oxford, 1960)
— *The Cities of the Eastern Roman Provinces* (2nd ed., Oxford, 1971)
Judge, E. A., 'Paul and Classical Society', *Jahrbuch für Antike und Christentum*, 15 (1972)
Kee, Howard Clark, *Medicine, Miracle and Magic in New Testament Times* (Cambridge, 1986)
Kenyon, Kathleen, *Jerusalem* (1967)
Kiefer, Otto, *Sexual Life in Ancient Rome* (1994)
Kirschbaum, Engelbert, SJ, *The Tombs of St Peter and St Paul* (ET, 1959)
Klausner, J., *From Jesus to Paul* (ET, 1944)
Knox, John, *Marcion and the New Testament* (1957)
— *Chapters in a Life of Paul* (1950)
Knox, Wilfrid, *St Paul and the Church of the Gentiles* (Cambridge, 1939)
Levick, Barbara, *Roman Colonies in Southern Asia Minor* (Oxford, 1967)
Liebeschuetz, J. H. W. G., *Continuity and Change in Roman Religion* (Oxford, 1979)
Ludemann, Gerd, *Paul Apostle to the Gentiles: Studies in Chronology* (ET, 1984)
Luff, S. G. A., *The Christian's Guide to Rome* (1967, revised 1990)
Maccoby, Hyam, *The Mythmaker* (1986)
— *Paul and Hellenism* (1991)
Machen, J. G., *The Origin of Paul's Religion* (New York, 1921)
Mackinnon, Albert G., *The Rome of Saint Paul* (Manchester, 1930)
Malinowski, Bronislaw, *Magic, Science and Religion* (New York, 1954)
Marx, Karl, 'On the Jewish Question', in Karl Marx and Frederick Engels, *Collected Works*, vol. 3 (1975)

PAUL

Meeks, Wayne A., *The First Urban Christians: The Social World of the Apostle Paul* (Yale, 1983)
— *The Moral World of the First Christians* (Yale, 1986)
Meijer, Fik, *A History of Seafaring in the Classical World* (1973)
Mellor, Ronald, *Thea Rome: The Worship of the Goddess Roma in the Greek World* (1975)
Metzger, Bruce M., *The Text of the New Testament: Its Transmission, Corruption and Restoration* (Oxford, 1964)
Michel, O., *Paulus und seine Bibel* (Gutersloh, 1929)
Millar, Fergus, *The Emperor in the Roman World* (1977)
— *The Roman Near East 31 BC–AD 337* (Harvard, 1993)
Misch, G., *A History of Autobiography in Antiquity* (ET, 1950)
Mitton, C. L., *The Formation of the Pauline Corpus of Letters* (1955)
Momigliano, Arnaldo, *Claudius: The Emperor and His Achievement* (Oxford, 1934)
— *Alien Wisdom: The Limits of Hellenization* (1975)
Montefiore, C. G., *Judaism and Saint Paul* (1936)
Morgenstern, Julian, *Rites of Birth, Marriage and Death and Kindred Occasions among the Semites* (Cincinatti, 1966)
Morton, H. V., *In the Steps of St Paul* (1936)
Morton Smith, J., *Jesus the Magician* (1978)
Moule, C. F. D., 'The Problem of the Pastoral Epistles', *BJRL*, 47 (1965)
Newman, J. H., *Historical Sketches* (1896)
Nickelsburg, George W. E., *Jewish Literature Between the Bible and the Mishnah* (1981)
Nilsson, Martin Persson, *Greek Piety* (ET, Oxford, 1948)
Nineham, D. E., *Saint Mark* (Harmondsworth, 1963)
Ogg, G., *The Chronology of the Life of Paul* (1968)
Parkes, James, *The Conflict of the Church and the Synagogue* (Sancino, 1934)
Patai, Raphael, *Man and Temple in Ancient Jewish Myth and Ritual* (1947)
Perowne, Stewart, *The Life and Times of Herod the Great* (1956)
— *The Later Herods* (1958)
— *The Journeys of Saint Paul* (1973)
Pope, R. Martin, *On Roman Roads with St Paul* (1939)
Powys, John Cowper, *The Pleasures of Literature* (1946)
Rajak, T., *Josephus* (1983)
Ramsay, W. M., *St Paul the Traveller and the Roman Citizen* (1895)
— *The Church in the Roman Empire* (1900)
— *The Bearing of Recent Discovery on the Trustworthiness of the New Testament* (1915)
Rawson, Beryl (ed.), *Marriage, Divorce and Children in Ancient Rome* (Oxford, 1996)
Reinach, J. (ed.), *Textes des Auteurs Grecs et Latins relatives au Judaisme* (Paris, 1895)
Robinson, J. A. T., *Jesus and His Coming: The Emergence of a Doctrine* (1957)
— *Redating the New Testament* (1976)
Sanders, E. P., *Paul, the Law and the Jewish People* (1973)
— *Paul and Palestinian Judaism* (1977)
— *Jesus, Paul and Judaism* (1981)
— *Paul* (1991)
Sandmel, S., *The Genius of Paul: A Study in History* (New York, 1970)
Sandys, John Edwin (ed.), *A Companion to Latin Studies* (Cambridge, 1929)
Schoeps, H. J., *Paul: The Theology of the Apostle in the Light of Jewish Religious History* (ET, 1961)

SELECT BIBLIOGRAPHY

— *The Jewish Christian Argument* (ET, 1965)

Schürer, Emil (revised ed., G. Vermes, Martin Goodman and Fergus Millar) *History of the Jewish People in the Age of Jesus Christ* (Edinburgh, 1973–87)

Schwartz, R., 'A propos du status personnel de l'apotre Paul', *Revue d'Histoire et de Philosophie Religieuse* (1957)

Schweitzer, Albert, *The Mysticism of Paul the Apostle* (ET, 1931)

Segal, A. F., *Paul the Convert* (1990)

Seltman, Charles, *Women in Antiquity* (1956)

Sherwin White, A. N., *Roman Society and Roman Law in the New Testament* (1963)

Smallwood, E. Mary, *The Jews Under Roman Rule* (Leiden, 1976)

Smith, George Adam, *Jerusalem* (1907–8)

Smith, James, *The Voyage and Shipwreck of Saint Paul* (1848)

Syme, Ronald, *The Roman Revolution* (revised ed. Oxford, 1952)

Thackeray, H. St J., *The Relation of St Paul to Contemporary Jewish Thought* (1900)

Theissen, G., *The Social Setting of Pauline Christianity* (ET, Edinburgh, 1982)

Tucker, T. G., *Life in the Roman World of Nero and St Paul* (1910)

Turchi, N., *La Religione di Roma Antica* (Bologna, 1939)

Vermes, Geza, *The Religion of Jesus the Jew* (1993)

Wallace, Richard and Williams, Wynne, *The Acts of the Apostles: A Companion* (1993)

Walter, Gerard, *Nero* (Paris, 1955)

Webster, G., *The Roman Imperial Army of the First and Second Centuries AD* (1969)

Whiteley, D. E. H., *The Theology of St Paul* (Oxford, 1964)

Wiles, M. F., *The Divine Apostle: The Interpretation of St Paul's Epistles in the Early Church* (Cambridge, 1967)

Wilson, Robert Smith, *Marcion: A Study of a Second-century Heretic* (1933)

Witherington, Ben, *Women in the Earliest Churches* (Cambridge, 1988)

Wright, Dudley, *The Talmud* (1932)

Wycherley, R. E., 'St. Paul at Athens', *JTS*, 19 (1968)

Yamauchi, Edwin, *The World of the First Christians* (1981)

Yerkes, Royden Keith, *Sacrifice in Greek and Roman Religions and Early Judaism* (1953)

INDEX

INDEX

RV *see* Synagogue of the Libertines
Sabbath, 168n, 253
sacrifice (religious), 44, 51, 170–1
Sadducees, 8n, 44–6, 50–1, 211
Salamis, 119–20
Samaria, 107, 113
Samaritans, 56
Samuel, 189
Sanhedrin, 44–5, 54, 64, 211
Saul, King of Israel, 189
Saul of Tarsus *see* Paul
Saviour: in Paul's teaching, 33, 121–2,
 155, 258
Sceva, high priest, 185
Schliemann, Heinrich, 73
Sebaste (now Sebastiyeh), 40–1
Secundus (Thessalonian), 202
Seleucids, 5
Seneca, 2–3, 123, 149, 153–4, 161, 162 &
 n, 199
Sepphoris (city), 28, 82
Septuagint (LXX), 31 & n, 241
Sergia Palla, 120n
Sergius Paulus, 120
sex: attitudes to, 140, 161–3, 230
Shakespeare, William: on Antony and
 Cleopatra, 24
sicarii, 99, 210, 214
Silas (or Silvanus), 135, 138, 145, 147–8,
 150
Simeon Niger, 117
Simmias, 77
Simon Magus, 106–7, 109–10
Simon Peter *see* Peter, St
Simon, son of Gamaliel, 48
Simon the Zealot, 59, 190
Simonides, 47
Smith, James: *The Voyage and Shipwreck of
 St Paul*, 244n
Smyrna, 181, 188
Socrates, 77, 80, 153–4
Sopater, son of Pyrrhus, 151, 202
sorcery *see* magic
Sosthenes, 175
Soviet Union, 190
Spain, 193, 207, 209, 249
'speaking in tongues', 62, 168–9
Spiritual Ones (*Pneumatikoi*), 168–9
Stalin, Joseph V., 41, 104
state-worship, 96, 189–90
Stephanas, 164, 167
Stephen, deacon (the martyr), St, 15, 51,

 55, 64–6, 70, 113, 120
stigmata, 78–9, 184
Stoics and Stoicism, 105, 122–4, 156–7
Strabo, 161
Strauss, G.F., 194
Suetonius, 13, 103–4, 106, 123, 129,
 151–2, 174, 249
Sulla, Lucius Cornelius, 153
superstitions: in Rome, 146–7; and
 medicine, 185
Syme, Ronald, 23–4
Synagogue of the Freedmen (NEB), 65
Synagogue of the Libertines (RV), 65
synoptic gospels *see* Gospels
Syria: Paul in, 81–3, 93; Agrippa rules,
 98

Tacitus: exonerates Christians from
 burning Rome, 4, 12; on Poppaea, 5,
 7; on Jesus, 7, 18; on Nero, 10, 13,
 152; on crucifixion of Jesus, 56; on
 Rome's border troubles, 151; Jewish
 expulsion unmentioned by, 174; on
 Ephesian Artemis, 190; on Agrippina's
 murder of Claudius, 199; on Felix,
 213, 216
Talmud, 46
Tarsus: character, 23–7, 29, 88, 122; Paul
 revisits, 88, 92
Temple (Jerusalem): Herod builds, 40–1,
 43; Gentiles barred from, 42–4, 113,
 209; rituals in, 43–5; Paul employed at,
 51, 53, 55; Caligula orders
 blasphemous statue installed, 89–90;
 profaned, 209
Teresa, Mother, 116
Tertullian, 133, 140, 167n, 234
Tertullus, 215
Theodotus, son of Vettenius, 47
Theophilus, 62, 66–8, 209, 224, 227, 254
Therapeutae (Alexandria), 185
Thessalonians, Paul's Epistles to, 148–9,
 156, 176–7, 231, 257
Thessalonica (now Salonica), 147–50
Theudas, 50
Thrasymachus, 153–4
Thyatira, Macedonia, 138
Tiberias, 28, 82
Tiberius, Roman emperor, 2, 7, 11, 82–
 3, 93, 97
Timothy: Paul meets, 128–9, 135;
 circumcision, 129, 131; travels with